Ethics and Integrity in British Politics

Public perceptions of political ethics are at the heart of current political debate. Drawing on original data, this book is the first general account of popular understandings of political ethics in contemporary British politics. It offers new insights into how citizens understand political ethics and integrity, and how they form judgements of their leaders. By locating these insights against the backdrop of contemporary British political ethics, the book shows how current institutional preoccupations with standards of conduct all too often miss the mark. While the use of official resources is the primary focus of much regulation, politicians' consistency, frankness and sincerity, which citizens tend to see in terms of right and wrong, are treated as 'normal politics'. The authors suggest that new approaches may need to be adopted if public confidence in politicians' integrity is to be restored.

NICHOLAS ALLEN is Senior Lecturer in Politics in the Department of Politics and International Relations at Royal Holloway, University of London. He is the co-editor of *Britain at the Polls 2010* (2011).

SARAH BIRCH is Professor of Comparative Politics at the University of Glasgow. Her most recent monograph is *Electoral Malpractice* (2011).

Ethics and Integrity in British Politics

How Citizens Judge their Politicians' Conduct and Why it Matters

NICHOLAS ALLEN
Royal Holloway, University of London

SARAH BIRCH
University of Glasgow

CAMBRIDGE
UNIVERSITY PRESS

CAMBRIDGE
UNIVERSITY PRESS

University Printing House, Cambridge CB2 8BS, United Kingdom

Cambridge University Press is part of the University of Cambridge.

It furthers the University's mission by disseminating knowledge in the pursuit of education, learning and research at the highest international levels of excellence.

www.cambridge.org
Information on this title: www.cambridge.org/9781107642348

© Nicholas Allen and Sarah Birch 2015

First published 2015

Printed in the United Kingdom by Clays, St Ives plc

A catalogue record for this publication is available from the British Library

Library of Congress Cataloging in Publication data
Allen, Nicholas.
Ethics and integrity in British politics : how citizens judge their politicians' conduct and why it matters / Nicholas Allen, Sarah Birch.
  pages cm
ISBN 978-1-107-05050-1 (Hardback) – ISBN 978-1-107-64234-8 (Paperback)
1. Political corruption–Great Britain. 2. Political ethics–Great Britain.
3. Politicians–Great Britain. 4. Great Britain–Politics and government. I. Birch, Sarah. II. Title.
JN1361b.A55 2015
172.0941–dc23 2014031652

ISBN 978-1-107-05050-1 Hardback
ISBN 978-1-107-64234-8 Paperback

For our parents

Contents

Figures

Tables

Preface and acknowledgements

It is always tempting at the end of a project to reflect back on its origins and progress. The origins of this book can be pinpointed to a chance conversation on a stairwell in the Department of Government at the University of Essex. One of us was an established member of staff there, undertaking comparative research into electoral corruption. The other had recently completed a PhD thesis on standards of conduct in the British House of Commons. Both of us were thinking about political ethics, albeit from different perspectives, and both of us expressed the view that academic researchers had so far paid insufficient attention to public attitudes on the topic. Some months later an opportunity presented itself to participate in the British Cooperative Campaign Analysis Project (B/CCAP), a collaborative multi-wave survey led by Ray Duch, Simon Jackman and Lynn Vavreck, and to explore, in a small way, some of the issues we felt ought to be addressed. A chance conversation thus became a small self-contained project, which became a slightly larger project as we secured funding to participate in additional B/CCAP waves and to conduct several focus groups.

Little did we know when we began planning the project in the autumn of 2008 that Britain was about to be rocked by one of the largest and most unsettling political scandals of recent times. Scandal is, of course, no stranger to British politics. But rarely does a single scandal embrace virtually the whole political class, as it did in the late spring of 2009. Back in the 1990s, a number of 'sleaze' allegations, some serious, some not so serious, had besmirched and embroiled the Conservative Party and, in turn, prompted the creation of a new ethics infrastructure across the public sector. In 2009, allegations about MPs' use and systematic abuse of their allowances and expenses besmirched and embroiled the whole of national political life. Like many others, we were taken aback by the force and power of the media frenzy that followed the publication of leaked details of MPs' expenses by the

Daily Telegraph. Like the pounding of an artillery barrage, each day brought new information about apparent abuses, which only served to fuel the fires of popular outrage and shock. Many colleagues were quick to tell us that our project was now 'very topical' when we told them what we were up to. We could not disagree. Yet, as we were equally quick to point out, our project could have been described as very topical at almost any point over the last two decades.

The book we have written is very much an academic work, but we have not written it just for academics. The subject matter is important for everyone, for citizens and politicians, for the represented and representatives alike, and we have sought to make our findings as accessible as possible for a wider audience. Those interested mainly in the book's practical implications can even skip straight to Chapter 8, though a brief perusal of Chapter 1 will help such readers to understand how we reached these findings.

What did we find out over the course of the project? Our research confirmed, if any confirmation was needed, that politicians' motives and conduct are distrusted. It also shattered our prior, and perhaps naive, belief that individuals' ethical judgements were more balanced and measured than survey responses suggested them to be. Most importantly, our research also revealed that current elite institutional preoccupations with ethics, if not individual elites' understandings, often miss the mark. In line with most contemporary political codes of conduct, citizens think that politicians should not advance private interests or be motivated by personal gain, and most citizens think that sexual transgressions and other traditional personal vices should not be a matter of public concern. At the same time, however, citizens see politicians' consistency, frankness and sincerity in terms of right and wrong, no less so than the reconciliation of public and private interests. While financial integrity is the focus of much ethics regulation, what might be termed verbal or 'discursive integrity' is not. What many citizens see in ethical terms, politicians tend to see as 'normal politics', and as political leaders go about their daily business, they earn the public's opprobrium. There are no easy solutions, to be sure, but politicians do have some scope for responding to this state of affairs. And they should do so. Politics demands a certain amount of verbal dexterity, but democracy is the greatest loser if politicians' conduct in the pursuit of power creates a desert of public engagement, goodwill and trust.

We have incurred many debts over the course of the project on which this volume is based. Our biggest gratitude goes to the British Academy (grant No. SG-52322), and the Economic and Social Research Council (grant No. RES-000-22-3459), for the funding that enabled us to collect the original survey and focus group data that form the core of our empirical evidence. We are grateful to Ray Duch, Iñaki Sagarzazu, Akitaka Matsuo and the rest of the B/CCAP team for guidance and support. We also owe a special debt to YouGov, and in particular to Joe Twyman and Ellen Vandenbogaerde, for their help with the survey data.

Our thanks are also due to those who provided advice and encouragement at various stages in our research, including Clare Ettinghausen, Robert Hazell, Blendi Kajsiu, Graham Keilloh, Anthony King, Paul Whiteley and Andrew Wroe. We particularly wish to thank Surya Monro, Max Paiano and Ruth Yeoman, who all helped in different ways with the planning, organising and transcribing of our focus groups. We also wish to thank Sarah Green and Elizabeth Davey of Cambridge University Press for their support as the book neared completion.

Although the research on which this book is based grew out of a chance conversation in the Department of Government at the University of Essex, changing professional circumstances have meant that it has been housed in a variety of institutions. In addition to Essex, we owe debts to the supportive intellectual environments provided by the Constitution Unit at University College London, the Department of Politics and International Relations at Royal Holloway, University of London, and the School of Social and Political Sciences at the University of Glasgow.

We also wish to thank a number of friends and colleagues for comments on earlier versions of our work, including Gavin Drewry, Oliver Heath, Donald Searing, Gerry Stoker and Paul Whiteley. In time-honoured tradition, it is only fair to absolve them from any errors of fact or interpretation. These remain ours alone.

Finally, we wish to thank Isabelle and Keith for their patience these past few years. Isabelle has been a constant reminder that there is more to life than researching, teaching and administration. The same goes for Keith, who has shown forbearance in enduring yet another book.

Nicholas Allen
Sarah Birch

1 | *Why study perceptions of politicians' conduct?*

W E ALL have standards we agree to. We agree you should not lie, hide anything, use public money for yourself ... that goes all the way through politics, it's just a matter of enforcing it.

(Female focus group participant, Hackney)

The May 2009 parliamentary expenses scandal was a remarkable episode in British politics. Day after day, the newspapers, led by the *Daily Telegraph*, were filled with lurid details of MPs' past expenses claims, many of which had been made in contravention of the spirit, if not the letter, of the rules (Winnett and Raynor 2009). The remorseless media coverage suggested widespread impropriety at the heart of democratic life and triggered an explosion of apparent outrage at politicians' conduct. One seasoned commentator compared the goings-on with the condition of British politics in the late eighteenth century and described them as 'the new corruption' (King 2009). For another, the expenses scandal was 'the biggest crisis of legitimacy for a century' to hit the country (Kenny 2009: 504).

Perhaps inevitably, the expenses scandal reinvigorated a long-standing debate about standards in British public life and what people could expect of their politicians. It also led to the creation of yet another ethical regulator, in this case the Independent Parliamentary Standards Authority (IPSA), whose grand title masked a narrower remit of paying and overseeing MPs' salaries and expenses. The scandal was, in both respects, merely the latest in a series of similar events that have occurred recently in Britain. In keeping with an established pattern, the shock and outrage that greeted the allegations of misconduct were soon followed by introspection and then institutional reforms intended to restore public confidence in politics. But if previous reforms were anything to go by, the latest changes were unlikely to transform levels of trust. Britons did not suddenly come to see their elected representatives as dishonest in May 2009; they had long regarded them in this way (Newell 2008).

This book is about improving our understanding of the prevailing mood of disaffection with British politicians. More specifically, it is about how citizens evaluate the integrity and propriety of politicians' conduct and elite political practice, and what consequences those evaluations have for the health of the political system. It is also about why a large proportion of existing institutional attempts to promote high ethical standards of conduct often miss the point. The book focuses primarily on the ethics and conduct of Westminster-based politicians, especially Members of Parliament, who, collectively, constitute the population of Britain's only directly elected national representative institution. Politicians in general are one of the least trusted groups in British society, as shown in Figure 1.1. In regular honesty contests, they lag far behind other groups, such as doctors, teachers, judges and even the ordinary man or woman in the street, and compete with journalists for the reputational wooden spoon. Yet politicians are absolutely essential to the smooth working of British representative democracy and perform crucial governmental functions. Ministers direct the government of the day. MPs represent us,

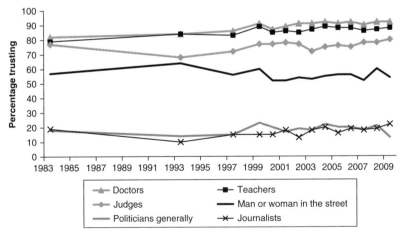

Figure 1.1 Percentage willing to trust members of different groups to tell the truth

Source: Ipsos MORI, 'Trust in Professions', available at: www.ipsos-mori.com/researchpublications/researcharchive/poll.aspx?oItemId=15&view=wide.

intervening with government on our behalf, scrutinising government actions and conferring popular assent on binding measures of public policy. Their conduct and their collective reputation matter.

While popular perceptions of elected representatives' conduct are much lamented, they are ill-understood. Anyone seeking to address this puzzle could follow several lines of inquiry. They could focus on citizens' expectations and the ethical standards they demand from their politicians. They could examine politicians' actual behaviour, including changing patterns of misconduct. They could investigate the role of the media and citizens' exposure to mediated accounts of politicians' misconduct. They could assess citizens' personal experience of dealing with politicians and their first-hand knowledge of misconduct. Last, but not least, they could analyse politicians' own understandings, and possible misunderstandings, of how citizens judge them. After all, when politicians fail to see things from others' points of view, it weakens their ability to act according to the standards that others demand of them and to respond effectively to their own ethical lapses.

The following pages touch upon all these issues. However, the book's primary purpose is to improve our knowledge and understanding of what drives individual citizens' beliefs about the ethics and behaviour of those holding public office. In particular, the book aims to shed light on what citizens actually think is proper conduct for politicians, and what they think is morally dubious, but perhaps unavoidable. It aims to investigate how much weight citizens attach to misconduct in public office compared with other considerations when they make judgements about actors and institutions, and how citizens respond to allegations of impropriety. Perhaps most importantly, the book aims to explore how citizens' evaluations affect the way they act in and engage with – or fail to engage with – social and political life.

The importance of perceptions

There is an obvious challenge to any research that focuses on perceptions of politicians' conduct: that a study of actual conduct is more important and pressing than a study of mere perceptions. After all, the integrity of office holders and the way they perform their duties can directly affect the quality of governance in a political system. A disregard for accepted standards can lead, among other things, to the misappropriation of public money, to the appointment of incompetent or unqualified people to positions of authority and influence, to decisions being taken for improper reasons, and to the neglect of pressing and important matters of public policy (Herrick 2003: 6–7). Yet citizens' perceptions do matter, as do their conceptions of political ethics, by which we mean the rules of conduct recognised as appropriate to political leaders. Both are an integral part of the fabric of any society. Shared norms and values play a central role in facilitating communication, enabling cooperation towards common goals, and articulating shared identities. They also help to define the content of accepted standards. Moreover, citizens' ethical evaluations of their politicians – often studied in the behavioural literature under the rubric of regime support, political support or public trust – are of fundamental importance in structuring public engagement with the political system. In this respect, citizens' perceptions constitute a reality of their own.

There are a number of reasons for wanting to improve our understanding of the present reality. For a start, public concerns about the honesty and integrity of elected office holders are thought to be one aspect – if only one aspect – of a wider malaise surrounding democratic politics in Britain and elsewhere (Stoker 2006, 2011; Hay 2007; Riddell 2011; Flinders 2012). As the literature on comparative regime support has demonstrated, this 'anti-politics' mood has a number of attitudinal and behavioural symptoms, notably declining levels of turnout and expressed support for democratic institutions (Pharr and Putnam 2000; Seligson 2002; Anderson and Tverdova 2003; Bowler and Karp 2004; Dalton 2004; Chang and Chu 2006; Birch 2010; Norris 2011). It is a discomfiting development for advocates of democratic participation. The health of any democracy is in part dependent on citizens having confidence and trust in those who rule them. Though a certain level of popular scepticism is healthy and may well strengthen democracy, democratic politics invariably suffer when there are high levels of cynicism and distrust (Norris 1999, 2011; Warren 1999; Hetherington 2005). Citizens who are very mistrustful of their political leaders are likely to disengage from politics, which has the potential to breed a vicious cycle of mistrust and further disengagement (Wroe *et al.* 2013). In turn, the mechanisms of accountability that are the foundation of any democratic system may be eroded and may potentially stop working altogether.

Political trust is a broad and multifaceted concept. Thus, a recent book on the subject defines it in general terms as 'the degree to which people perceive that government is producing outcomes consistent with their expectations' (Hetherington 2005: 9). Not surprisingly, there are many (potentially legitimate) reasons why citizens mistrust politicians. Politicians may be incompetent or inefficient, or they may have opposing ideological beliefs or belong to parties that represent divergent interests. It is entirely understandable, for instance, if left-wing voters are less inclined to trust right-wing governments. Trust may also reflect citizens' moral beliefs or the inadequacy of existing mechanisms for protecting them from betrayal (Fisher *et al.* 2010). While our work contributes to the wider academic literature on political trust, we are interested in it only insofar as it reflects citizens' ethical evaluations of conduct and the perceived integrity of politicians as trustees. If the literature is to move beyond generalised talk about distrust in politicians, it is important to begin focusing on what citizens actually expect of their elected politicians' conduct, how they judge them, and what shapes their general perceptions of integrity in politics.

A better knowledge of citizens' ideas about political ethics and integrity may also be of practical benefit to politicians. A major backdrop to this book is the comparatively recent enthusiasm in Britain for codified standards in political life, and for more and more ethics regulation. The demand for such measures achieved an institutional breakthrough in the 1990s, prompted by a moral panic about 'sleaze' and standards of conduct in public life (Oliver 1997; Behnke 2002). Codes of conduct and official investigators now extend throughout the British political system, the product of attempts by politicians to bolster public confidence in their integrity, as well as to improve actual standards of conduct. Most ethics reforms have followed high-profile scandals, as exemplified by what happened in the wake of the 2009 expenses scandal. Yet most such reforms have failed to achieve all their objectives insofar as they have not led to a pronounced improvement in perceptions of politicians' conduct. Efforts to 'scandal-proof' British political institutions have thus been no more successful than similar attempts in the United States, where a growing number of rules and regulations have done little to bolster public confidence or prevent the types of scandal that undermine it (Anechiarico and Jacobs 1996; Mackenzie 2002). By improving our knowledge of what political integrity means to ordinary citizens, we may learn more about why, despite the raft of measures introduced in recent decades, public perceptions of politicians' integrity continue to be so critical.

Improving our understanding of citizens' poor evaluations of elected representatives may also point the way towards a clearer view of other political attitudes and behaviours, in particular the importance of leaders' 'moral authority'. From voting in elections, through obeying the law, to participating in socially beneficial activities, such as recycling and undertaking voluntary work, politicians need to persuade individuals to act in ways that they might not otherwise do. On the one hand, politicians lead by example, and their standards of conduct send signals about what is acceptable behaviour throughout society. On the other hand, their ability to provide public leadership relies on some measure of legitimacy and moral authority, which in turn rests on perceptions of their integrity. There has been considerable debate in recent years among policy analysts over how people can be persuaded to modify their behaviour voluntarily (Thaler and Sunstein 2008; John *et al.* 2009). If it is the case that poor ethical evaluations of elected officials impede the ability of political actors to 'nudge' citizens in desired directions – or to accept more noticeable personal sacrifices – this may have significant implications for a number of long-term policy challenges, for example, the need to tackle environmental degradation or the problems posed by an aging population.

The basic argument set out in the following pages is essentially threefold. The first part of our argument is that most members of the British public tend to have a more expansive understanding of political ethics than is reflected in institutional rules, codes and cultures. Citizens tend to construe more broadly the scope for understanding elite behaviour in ethical terms. Or, put another way, what many politicians take for granted as 'normal politics', many citizens will think about in terms of right and wrong, and make their judgements accordingly. In this sense, the present study adds further weight to the claims made by others that stress the disjuncture between official preoccupations and citizens' own conception of ethics (Committee on Standards in Public Life 2004).

There has long been a tendency among political actors and decision makers to limit the potential scope for applying ethical principles to political conduct. In official practice and discourse, as well as everyday politics, the space set aside for ethical consideration is small, and it has usually centred on concerns about conflicts of interest, whether apparent or actual. Usually, the conflict of interest dilemma is framed even more narrowly as a clash between the proper administration or exercise of public office – which is seen as a public trust – and an office holder's private financial interests (Stark 2000). Writing specifically about legislative ethics, Bruce Jennings (1985: 151) describes this tendency to focus narrowly on financial conflicts of interest as 'moral minimalism' in which: 'Financial disclosure and conflict of interest are virtually the only issues given much attention … and the prohibition against the use of office for personal financial gain is the only ethical principle that has been clearly defined.' Needless to say, institutional norms and socialisation processes help to inculcate politicians into this more 'minimalist' mindset.

Yet, while official practice is often to view the scope of ethics in minimalist terms, the public tends to extend ethical judgements to more aspects of elite behaviour. To be sure, the use and misuse of public office for private gain is accommodated within this broader conception of integrity, but so too is the discursive dimension of political conduct. Indeed, in the public's mind, the scope of political ethics also embraces the conduct of politics itself and especially how politicians relate to and engage with them. The boundaries of the ethical in this broader conception thus embrace the words that politicians use, the promises they make and break, and the extent to which elite behaviour accords with the standards that politicians themselves claim.[1]

The second part of our argument, which is related to the first, is that there is a pronounced gap between citizens' aspirations as to how their politicians should behave and their perceptions of how politicians actually behave. The idea of such gaps is not a new one and has been applied recently to public attitudes towards specific institutions and even democracy itself (Flinders and Kelso 2011; Norris 2011; Flinders 2012). It is, however, especially useful for understanding public attitudes towards politicians' conduct. The gap that we identify and flesh out in the following pages can be explained by a number of factors, both systemic and cognitive. One of these factors relates to citizens' somewhat broader conception of political ethics than official and institutional preoccupations, as noted. Because politicians generally see things differently, it is hard for them to be responsive to public preferences or to alter their behaviour. Put simply, politicians often

---

[1] As we will see in Chapter 4, the broader conception of political integrity does not generally extend to such things as politicians' sex lives or drinking habits. Most individuals tend to draw the familiar distinction between purely private behaviour and public behaviour, and to discount the former.

appear unethical, since empty or broken promises and evasive answers tend to be part and parcel of 'normal politics' for them, but are a question of integrity for citizens. Most elected representatives are career politicians and want to get ahead in politics. They have to play a game that the public dislikes and have little incentive not to do so.

Another factor that helps us to account for the perceptions gap relates to the nature of the modern media and contemporary coverage of political conduct. The relationship between politicians and journalists has always been uneasy, even if both sides belong to the same 'political class' (Oborne 2007), but it has arguably become more antagonistic in recent decades. Many journalists take great delight in highlighting failings in politicians' conduct, partly because they think it is their democratic duty, partly because it sells newspapers or increases viewing audiences. Moreover, in the era of 'sound bite' politics, politicians are trained to get across a pre-prepared answer rather than to answer the questions asked: politicians are being trained in a way that makes them appear dishonest to citizens. The fact that they mostly prefer to risk not answering questions rather than appearing unprepared or ineloquent is an obvious problem. But this is what they are often told to do by their parties. The current structure of the media environment is thus geared towards driving a wedge between citizens' preferences and perceptions, which suggests a variation on the older arguments about 'media malaise' – the idea that the media should be responsible for negative attitudes towards politics.[2]

Yet another factor has to do with human psychology: most individuals, when presented with new information, tend to reach a judgement that is consistent with their prior beliefs and values. When it comes to politicians, cynicism and mistrust are deeply ingrained, and every new case of alleged misconduct will affirm most people's pre-existing negative views. At the same time, people also tend to generalise from more salient incidents, such as reported cases of misconduct. Good conduct, which is rarely reported, will almost inevitably be discounted. In other words, citizens are psychologically inclined to project dishonesty and malign intentions onto politicians. They are almost predisposed to mistrust.

The third and final part our argument is perhaps the most straightforward and relates to the consequences of citizens' negative

---

[2] For a review of the literature on this topic, see Kenneth Newton (1999).

evaluations. As we show, these evaluations matter. The views that many citizens hold about standards of conduct in Britain and politicians' integrity lower their enthusiasm for participating in formal democratic processes, their willingness to comply with the law, and their susceptibility to political leadership.

There are precedents in the academic literature for each of our claims, but their combination here represents a major advance in developing a full account of citizens' perceptions of politicians' conduct. The result is the first general account of popular understandings of political ethics in the British context. It offers insights into what is perceived to constitute ethical behaviour among different categories of political actor, the dimensions that structure respondents' values and evaluations, how people go about forming judgements of their leaders' integrity, and the relationship between popular understandings of political conduct and other social and political beliefs, including partisan support.

Methods and data

There are many ways to study popular perceptions of political objects, including politicians' conduct, from laboratory experiments to participant observation. This book has opted for the stock tool of the political scientist, the representative survey, but with a couple of twists. Our surveys were sandwiched between a series of focus groups, which enabled us both to hone our survey questions and to explore the results in greater detail. Our surveys also embedded several experiments that allowed us to simulate a wide range of different practical situations. This combination of qualitative and quantitative, observational and experimental methods enabled us to approach our research questions from several different angles.

The core of the research project on which this study is based is a three-wave representative survey of British citizens. The unique character of the survey was a product of both design and serendipity. The advent of the two-year British Cooperative Campaign Analysis Project (B/CCAP) made it possible to administer an extended range of questions to the same respondents at regular intervals between 2008 and 2010. The project, which was run by a team of researchers at the universities of Oxford and Stanford, included a total of approximately 10,000 respondents, who were all asked to complete a baseline survey in late 2008. B/CCAP was designed so that individual teams of researchers could 'hire' sections of this sample and ask them questions at various points before the 2010 general election. We 'hired' a tranche of approximately 1,000 respondents, who were asked to answer our questions at three points in time: spring 2009 (B/CCAP's wave 2); autumn 2009 (B/CCAP's wave 3, immediately before the party conference season); and spring 2010 (B/CCAP's wave 5, fielded in the run-up to the general election).[3] Finally, all 10,000 respondents who formed part of the B/CCAP panel were invited to take part in a post-election wave, fielded in June 2010.

The project's multi-wave design enabled us to trace the views of individuals over time and to probe their responses to events.[4] For this purpose, a number of key questions were posed in all three bespoke waves of the survey, while other sets of questions, including a number of survey experiments, were designed to be asked only once. The resulting dataset thus includes data from five points in time, with the questions that formed the core of this study included in the spring 2009, autumn 2009 and spring 2010 waves. Details of the questions we employed from the B/CCAP surveys, and how we constructed our variables, can be found in the Appendix.

The element of serendipity in our research involved the timing of the first wave of the survey, which was fielded in late April 2009, only days before the *Daily Telegraph* newspaper began its daily coverage of MPs' past expenses claims in May 2009. The timing of our surveys meant that it was possible to measure the impact of the scandal by comparing respondents' views before it took place with those expressed in the following autumn and then again twelve months later.

The surveys were conducted online by the YouGov polling organisation. Some readers may wonder whether online surveys can achieve the same level of scientific accuracy as the more traditional face-to-face

---

[3] The spring 2009 wave was completed between 21 April and 6 May, the autumn 2009 wave between 23 and 28 September, and the spring 2010 wave between 23 April and 4 May.

[4] While the panel design provides us with rich individual-level data, the limited timeframe inevitably imposes constraints on our study. In particular, we are unable to explore long-term changes in citizens' beliefs about political ethics and their attitudes towards politicians' conduct. We are also unable to explore how such beliefs and attitudes respond to changing elite-level practices, as well as the importance of historical events, such as the Blair government's alleged misuse of secret intelligence to justify Britain's participation in the 2003 invasion of Iraq. See Whiteley *et al.* (2013).

methods often employed in survey research. Yet recent analyses of the two survey modes have established the validity – and in some cases the superiority– of online surveys (Sanders *et al.* 2007; Twyman 2008; Vavreck and Rivers 2008).

The study also makes use of a number of focus groups conducted in 2009 and 2010 with the twin aims of helping us to design survey items and to collect qualitative data on attitudes towards standards in public life. The focus groups were held in different parts of Britain in order to capture different regional subcultures and the attitudes that might potentially be associated with them: Hackney, Colchester, Egham and Bradford.[5] Colchester and Egham are affluent locations in the southeast of England (both are also university towns). By contrast, Hackney and Bradford are ethnically diverse and relatively deprived areas with large numbers of people reliant on state benefits. At least one of the authors was present at each focus group. The resulting transcripts provide a valuable resource that helps in understanding how different individuals formulate and express views of politicians' behaviour, as well as shedding considerable light on the language and symbolism that people employ to convey their evaluations. This qualitative evidence complements the quantitative survey data and puts life on the bare bones of the statistical results that form a large part of this investigation. The use of both qualitative and quantitative data also makes it possible to cross-validate the findings. Quotations from the focus groups have been anonymised when reported in this study in order to protect the confidentiality of our focus group participants.

Overview of the book

The remainder of the book proceeds as follows. Chapter 2 provides a theoretical introduction to the study of political ethics and evaluations of politicians' conduct, outlining the existing approaches to the topic

[5] Altogether we conducted six focus groups in four locations on five different dates. For each group we report the number of men and women who participated, together with the general age characteristic of each group, that is, whether it was structured around younger or older participants: Hackney, 26 January 2009, four men, six women, older participants; Colchester, 28 January 2009, five men, two women, younger participants; Egham, 27 January 2010, seven men, three women, older participants; Egham, 24 February 2010, six men, four women, younger participants; Bradford, 19 August 2010, two men, six women, older participants; and Bradford, 19 August 2010, three men, three women, younger participants.

and carving out the theoretical framework that will guide the remainder of the volume. It surveys some of the general ideas surrounding politicians' standards of conduct in Western liberal democracies, outlines the nature of political conduct as an object of ethical judgement, and explores the various individual-level and systemic factors that might influence citizens' judgements about politicians' integrity.

Chapter 3 offers a survey of political ethics in contemporary British politics, thereby enabling readers to locate our findings about citizens' beliefs against the backdrop of a complex and gradually changing ethical landscape. It outlines the main preoccupations of elite-level concerns and engagement with ethics, the structures that have been put in place to maintain high ethical standards of conduct, and some of the more noteworthy lapses in conduct that have occurred in recent years. Britain has a rich tradition of theorising about ethical political conduct, which is intimately entwined with cultural understandings of politics. This chapter lays the ground for the empirical assessment of citizens' evaluations by highlighting the nature of elite understandings of political ethics and how they accord with other aspects of British political practice. These understandings may or may not correspond with popular expectations; but if they do diverge too much, they may be a source of tension between citizens and their elected representatives.

Following the analytic and conceptual overview provided by the introductory chapters, Chapter 4 turns to an empirical examination of citizens' ethical beliefs and some of the general expectations they have in respect of their politicians. In the process, it also explores some of the individual-level cognitive features of the gap between citizens' aspirations as to how their politicians should behave and their perceptions of how they actually behave. Drawing on focus group and survey data, the chapter makes the case that there is a significant divergence between what the concept of ethical behaviour means in elite circles and what it means to members of the public. Institutional preoccupations tend to frame ethical questions in terms of the husbandry of public resources. Citizens, by contrast, include in their understanding of political ethics a range of concerns related to how politicians use words, how politicians relate to them, and the relationship between politicians' words and deeds. Specifically, the popular understanding of ethical conduct includes *both* abstention from plundering the public purse and the avoidance of conflict of interest, *and* straight talking, carrying out campaign promises and telling the truth. As will become evident in later chapters, this gap between elite and mass understandings of the scope of political ethics has far-reaching consequences for the way in which politicians are evaluated and for the consequences of those evaluations.

Chapter 5 provides a more detailed examination of how ordinary members of the public think about political ethics and how their judgements are affected by the information to which they are exposed. Since political misconduct is largely mediated, it is crucial to understand just how information can shape judgements. The analysis in this chapter draws both on survey questions about media usage and on three survey experiments that enabled us to manipulate precisely the information that respondents received. Experimental techniques are being used increasingly frequently in political science; but they have not yet been used by scholars of British political ethics. The results of these experiments illustrate key features of citizens' normative beliefs and important systematic differences in how different groups of citizens judge political conduct.

Chapter 6 is devoted to an analysis of citizens' integrity perceptions and what they think about the behaviour of their elected representatives. This chapter assesses the extent to which British politicians live up to the standards set for them, and how much of a problem people consider different types of misconduct in public life to be. Changes over time in citizens' integrity perceptions – particularly in the wake of the 2009 expenses scandal – are analysed, together with differences between subgroups of the population. The results of the analysis undertaken in this chapter demonstrate that most people are highly sceptical about the conduct of politicians, and that they believe misconduct in public life to be a serious problem in Britain. There are, however, noteworthy differences between groups in the electorate.

Chapter 7 considers the political consequences of citizens' ethical beliefs and integrity perceptions. It examines the impact of popular perceptions on other attitudes towards the political system, on democratic participation, on citizens' willingness to follow the advice of political leaders, and on the extent to which citizens take their moral cues from politicians. The analysis is designed to address the 'so what' question that has haunted the study of integrity perceptions for years: whether – and how – it really matters if people do not have confidence in the honesty of their elected representatives. It will be shown that lack of faith in the conduct of politicians has significant consequences for the way politics and society work, in that it suppresses political participation and a willingness to follow the law, and it reduces citizens' susceptibility to political leadership.

Chapter 8 considers the key question of what might be done to address the gap between people's expectations of politicians and their evaluations of elite behaviour. Like Chapter 3, it examines some of the systemic features of contemporary British political ethics, and engages with debates about actual standards of conduct in British political life and institutional arrangements for ensuring high standards. It charts the failure of recent official attempts to bolster wider public confidence in the integrity of national-level politics and explores why the momentum for more standards has largely missed the point. Having established weaknesses in existing arrangements, it suggests seven remedies for bringing together the ethical worlds inhabited by politicians and the public.

Finally, Chapter 9, a brief concluding chapter, summarises the principal findings of the study, highlights their implications and suggests a number of directions for future research.

2 | *Thinking about political ethics and conduct*

THAT's why people feel that politicians are more corrupt now than they used to be. It's because people are more educated now. And also the media are more likely to report that sort of behaviour.

(Male focus group participant, Colchester)

The study of political ethics has been a major preoccupation of political thought since ancient times. In recent years, the subject has attracted the attention of more empirically minded scholars, especially those concerned with trying to explain declining levels of support for democratic institutions and actors. As is well known, the liberal democratic form of government spread throughout the late twentieth century, but many liberal democracies, both old and new, found themselves beset by diminishing levels of trust in government during the same period (Flinders 2012). These trends highlight an apparent contradiction in the minds of many electorates. Democracy as a system of government is generally held in high regard, yet elected politicians and the institutions they populate are generally not. Various factors are thought to have contributed to declining trust, ranging from the diminished capacities of governments and diminishing rates of economic growth, through deep-seated generational changes and the rise of 'critical citizens' (Norris 1999; 2011), to the very nature of democratic politics, which require consensus and compromise and thus a willingness to accept disappointment. To some extent, therefore, our elected representatives have become the focus of popular disapprobation and distrust for reasons entirely beyond their control. Yet trust is also partly a function of the honesty and integrity of elected representatives and policy-makers. Some politicians undoubtedly behave dishonestly, and a few almost certainly behave corruptly. Such behaviour almost inevitably undermines trust. Whether all politicians everywhere deserve to be tarred with the same brush, however, is obviously another matter.

This chapter addresses some of the normative and empirical features of political ethics and how they are perceived. It examines the importance of 'appearance' as a distinct ethical principle, and why we ought to be concerned with citizens' perceptions of political conduct; and it sets out the conceptual framework that we use to make sense of these perceptions and the factors that are likely to shape them. The basis of this framework is straightforward. Political conduct can be understood as both an objective and subjective phenomenon, in much the same way that people distinguish between the real economy and the perceived economy. The one refers to objective conditions, the other to subjective understandings of those conditions. Moreover, the integrity of conduct can be conceived of in both an individual and a systemic sense in the way people may talk about the conduct of a given politician or the conduct of a political class. Citizens may have beliefs and understandings about the honesty of individual politicians and particular deeds; they may have beliefs and understandings about the honesty of all politicians and their habitual behaviour. Our chief concern is with the latter. These beliefs or integrity perceptions are ultimately the product of both micro-level factors, including individuals' prior ethical beliefs or ideas about right and wrong, and macro-level factors, such as the tone and tenor of press coverage and the scale of ethics regulation in a given political system.

The remainder of this chapter develops these various themes in four parts. The next section explores ideas about what constitutes ethical behaviour or integrity in political life, with a particular emphasis on the normative importance of how conduct is perceived. The third part begins to flesh out the subjective nature of political conduct by identifying different objects of ethical judgement. The fourth part explores the various micro-level or personal factors that influence individuals' ethical judgements and perceptions of politicians' integrity. The final section then examines the macro-level or systemic factors that are likely to affect citizens' judgements about politicians in advanced liberal democracies.

The ethics and appearance of political conduct

The practice of politics involves the authoritative allocation of who gets what, when and how (Lasswell 1936). It is a process that affects us all. But politics is also a process in which some people play more significant roles than others. No modern democratic political system is a flat hierarchy in which all members of the community have an equal voice in, and exert an equal influence over, decision making. A commitment to political equality is fundamental to any conception of modern liberal democracy, but so too is some, and usually a very considerable, division of political labour (Dahl 1998). Thus, modern liberal democracies tend to be of the representative variety, with individuals – in practice mostly party politicians – acquiring the power to make political decisions on the basis of 'a competitive struggle for the people's vote' (Schumpeter 1954). The amount of power that any group of politicians can wield will vary from system to system. In some places, such as in Britain, power has tended to be concentrated in the hands of a relatively small group (Lijphart 1999). In other places, such as in the United States or in postwar Germany, power has been more widely shared and divided. Yet, whatever the constitutional arrangements, individuals who hold positions of authority clearly have enormous potential to influence the lives of those who do not. How they conduct themselves, and how they appear to behave, matters.

Underpinning most norms about political conduct is the assumption that it takes place in a distinct 'public' sphere (Thompson 1987; Philp 2007). As Stuart Hampshire (1978: ix) observes, there is 'a moral threshold which is crossed by both those who assume power to change the lives of many men through public action and by those who undertake to represent in a public role the will and interests of many other men'. Those who have crossed this threshold are generally expected to conduct themselves according to a set of standards distinct from those that bind other citizens. They may not enjoy certain rights that other citizens enjoy, for instance, a right to privacy. Perhaps most importantly, they are not allowed to use public resources for personal profit. As Mark Philp (2007: 216) notes: 'The crucial element in defining public office is that it is devoted to public rather than private ends; that is, to the public interest rather than to the occupant's private interests.' Holders of public office are expected to act for us, the public, and to be responsive to our preferences. They are certainly not expected to act for themselves. They hold public office as a public trust. From this assertion stems most ideas about what constitute ethical conduct in modern political life.

In performing their duties, exercising their powers and fulfilling their responsibilities, holders of public office are likely to encounter conflicts between various competing principles of action, including those that relate to public action and those that relate to their own personal conduct. They may sometimes need to behave in ways that would be deemed unethical in their private lives. Depending on the circumstances, they may need to manipulate citizens, break promises and lie for the sake of those they represent (Thompson 1987: 4). According to the well-known 'dirty hands' dilemma, decision makers may need to do a little wrong in order to do a greater good (Walzer 1973).

A key point to bear in mind is that merely holding public office does not usually prescribe specific courses of action. Much depends on the institutional and normative environment, as well as the immediate circumstances, in which an office holder operates. These factors will usually determine whether the service of the public has been compromised by the pursuit of personal gain or by some other deviation from accepted principles. This context will also change. Just as ethical standards shape political action, so action can shape ethical standards. Ethical norms and principles evolve, and, as they evolve, they change common understandings of what constitutes appropriate or desirable political conduct.

Amid the wealth of academic writing on the ethics of political conduct, the ideas most relevant for our purposes are arguably those relating to holders of legislative office. Members of legislative institutions constitute the majority of elected politicians in most liberal democracies. How they discharge their institutional duties will have a significant bearing on the health and quality of representative democracy. The insights of 'legislative ethics' thus provide a useful window onto the general principles that commonly structure ideas about political integrity and what is often considered to be unethical conduct, particularly at the elite-level as will be seen in greater detail in Chapter 3. The same insights also highlight the particular importance of appearance – how politicians are perceived to behave, the focus of this book – as a distinct ethical principle.

In his account of contemporary US congressional ethics, the Harvard ethicist Dennis Thompson (1995) identifies three general principles that should underpin elected representatives' work: independence, fairness and accountability. The first of these principles, 'independence', emphasises the importance of politicians' autonomy and holds that members of representative institutions should be able to act free from improper influence. When performing their duties, they should be influenced only 'by reasons relevant to the merits of public policies or reasons relevant to advancing a process that encourages acting on such reasons' (Thompson 1995: 20). The standard of independence does not prescribe total autonomy, of course, since elected representatives have quite proper obligations to their constituents, their parties and their colleagues. Even if it were possible to remain completely independent in the face of such demands, it would be undesirable. 'Instead, what the principle seeks is independence from influences that are clearly irrelevant to any process of deliberation' (Thompson 1995: 20). While there will always be disagreement about what is 'clearly' relevant, following the standard of independence increases the likelihood that decisions will be made that are legitimate, fair and in the public interest.

The second of Thompson's principles, 'fairness', emphasises the importance of politicians' broader responsibilities, and holds that members of parliaments should 'fulfil their obligations to colleagues, staff, challengers [i.e., other candidates for legislative office], other officials, and the institution as a whole' (Thompson 1995: 22). In essence, this standard is predicated on the notion that the overall integrity of a democratic system rests on the integrity of its principal institutions. Politicians should thus ensure that their own conduct does not undermine the integrity of the institution in which they work. They should abide by its rules, perform their share of institutional house-keeping chores and take collective responsibility for its well-being. This last responsibility may require politicians to enforce their own institutional rules vis-à-vis colleagues who act improperly and to correct practices or procedures that undermine the institution's integrity. However, the idea of fairness is, as Thompson himself concedes, difficult to codify in any precise way. It is also possible that different members of the same institution may have different opinions about what is in its interests.

The third of Thompson's principles, 'accountability', speaks directly to citizens' perceptions by emphasising the importance of how others judge politicians' conduct. It holds that members of parliament 'should act so as to create and maintain public confidence in their own actions and in the legislative process' (Thompson 1995: 23). Those whose conduct fails to meet public expectations, or who appear to behave contrary to public expectations, do several kinds of wrong: they erode confidence in the political system; they give citizens reasons to act as if government cannot be trusted; and they undermine democratic accountability. In order to meet the standard of accountability, politicians must not only act for the right reasons, but also appear to act for the right reasons.

The importance of being seen to act for the right reasons is emphasised in other scholars' attempts to flesh out the ethical principles surrounding legislative life. In place of Thompson's principle of accountability, for example, Alan Rosenthal (1996: 65–7) posits two distinct principles: 'publicity' and 'appearance'. The principle of publicity requires that sufficient information about each legislator's actions be made public so that voters may judge their integrity. The principle of appearance is akin to Thompson's formulation of accountability, in that the objective is the maintenance of public confidence. However, Rosenthal concedes that there is an obvious problem with this principle: in an age in which political conduct is largely mediated, who determines the appearance of conduct? Thus, 'it is one thing to ask how a legislator's action would appear to the public as interpreted by the press. It is quite another thing to ask how the same action would appear if the legislator could explain what he or she did and why' (Rosenthal 1996: 69).

The implications of this last point are important. It may be that too much weight is attached to the appearance of politicians' conduct in current debates about political integrity. Mark Philp (2007: 216) makes a similar point in his more general account of political conduct: 'the criteria for whether a public office is exercised well or badly are rooted in the trust that is reposed in the office; not in whether or not people actually trust it, but in on what its claim to authority and public support is based'. What ultimately matters, by this account, is what politicians actually do, and why. All too often, it seems, this point is forgotten in many of the criticisms that are levelled at politicians.

Mark Warren (2006) meanwhile highlights the normative importance of appearance from a slightly different perspective. Ideas about political ethics that stem from the traditional 'public trust' model of public service are 'incomplete and often misplaced' when applied to elected and other political representatives (Warren 2006: 160). This model takes it for granted that there are convergent interests and values between citizens and holders of public office, yet convergent interests are unlikely to be found in a political domain, which is defined by competing interests. Politicians are constantly required to balance the appeals of some constituents or interests against others. Building on this idea, Warren proceeds to distinguish between first-order trust, the notion that public officials are trustworthy because they will attend to someone's interest, and second-order trust, the idea that political actors will provide trustworthy information for citizens to make judgements about whether or not they are attending to someone's interests. From a normative standpoint, first-order trust is not essential for democratic politics, but second-order trust is vital. The appearance of politicians' conduct in the public mind is so important it pertains to the maintenance of second-order trust. When political representatives or institutions act in ways that weaken this form of trust, or fail to heed the importance of protecting it, citizens are potentially deprived of 'their ability to judge when trust is warranted and when it is not' (Warren 2006: 166). If this happens, democratic accountability may begin to break down and citizens may be denied the means of inclusion in public decision making.

It might also be added that the 'electoral connection' between politicians and citizens creates further problems for the 'public trust' model of service as a basis for thinking about the ethics of political conduct and appearance. The manner in which elected representatives obtain their jobs undoubtedly distinguishes them from other public officials, such as civil servants, who enter their chosen field on the basis of demonstrated expertise, skill and adherence to professional standards, and who can expect to remain in post on the condition that they observe these standards. Politicians, by contrast, are elected on the basis of no specific qualifications and typically have no prior training for the job. Their selection and election owes as much to their party loyalty, affability and local popularity as it does to their experience, competence and integrity. Put simply, the ethical demands of power seeking and political life are not always consistent with notions of public service.

Despite attempts by various authors to propose general criteria by which politicians' conduct might be judged, what ultimately constitutes good conduct, in the sense of it being judged as ethical, depends greatly on the context in which it occurs. As Philp (2007: 5) notes, any assessment of political integrity and any distinction between politicians who act well and those who do not must draw 'on the norms and institutional setting in which they act'. Norms and settings differ from system to system and change over time. Consequently, specific ideas about political integrity change with them. Across the spectrum of established liberal democracies, there are unlikely to be huge variations in what constitutes integrity. However, there will almost invariably be some differences, and the threats to the integrity of political conduct are likely to take a range of different forms, reflecting the different characteristics of political systems.

We finish this section by noting that conduct that falls short of accepted ethical standards goes by a variety of names. For our purposes, we use the term 'misconduct'. The *Oxford English Dictionary* defines 'misconduct' as 'improper or unacceptable conduct or behaviour'. It is a term that commentators and politicians use in a general sense to describe behaviour that has fallen short of expected standards. It is also a term that has less baggage than another term used to describe unethical behaviour, 'corruption'. Political corruption has been a feature of social life since ancient times (Alatas 1990). It has also meant different things down the ages. Even in its conventional modern meaning – that corruption reflects an abuse of public office and entrusted power for private gain (Warren 2004) – the term is 'laden with ambiguity' and leaves much room for interpretation (Anechiarico and Jacobs 1996). Context, circumstance and point of view can all influence when an 'abuse' of office or entrusted power is thought to have occurred. As two American scholars note: 'What may be corrupt to one citizen, scholar, or public official is just politics to another, or discretion to a third' (Peters and Welch 1978: 974). Moreover, a charge of corruption is usually much weightier than a charge of misconduct, and carries with it a certain 'moral accusation' (Warren 2006: 806). Misconduct may be very serious, but it may also describe behaviour that is relatively trivial. Corruption is never trivial, and the term deserves to be used sparingly.

Politics and political conduct as objects of ethical judgement

Having examined ideas about what constitutes ethical conduct in modern political life, including the distinct importance of how politicians' actions appear to citizens, it is now time to consider the subjective character of conduct in greater detail. Most of us have ideas about what we want from our politicians. Likewise, most of us have ideas about how we think politics should be conducted, however vague, inchoate and potentially contradictory those ideas may be.

We think politicians should look to deliver certain goals. We think they should act in certain ways. Such ideas help to structure and give meaning to our perceptions of politicians' conduct. They also provide the foundations for our perceptions of integrity in political life.

When talking about citizens' ethical beliefs and judgements, it is important first to recognise that they may pertain to a whole range of political objects.[1] A useful way to approach this point is to consider some of the attempts by political scientists to conceptualise political support more generally. Of these, perhaps the most influential framework is that first proposed by David Easton (1965, 1975). According to Easton, individuals' beliefs about, attachments to and evaluations of different political objects can be located on a continuum with diffuse or general support for the political community at one end, through support for the political regime – the basic framework for governing the country – to specific support for the political authorities – actual office holders and the government of the day – at the other end. This distinction between different levels of political support fed a particularly famous debate between Jack Citrin (1974) and Art Miller (1974) over the importance of Americans' apparent mistrust in politics. Citrin argued that declining levels of trust reflected support for political actors and incumbents, whereas Miller argued that they reflected support for the regime. The former interpretation was reassuring insofar it was consistent with the trials and tribulations of day-to-day party politics. The latter interpretation was more worrying.

Pippa Norris (1999: 9–12) has since refined Easton's threefold categorisation of objects into a fivefold framework that distinguishes between: support for the political community, or the extent of a basic attachment to the nation; support for the regime principles, or the degree of commitment to the ideal of democracy; support for regime performance, or satisfaction with the way the political system functions in practice; support for regime institutions, or attitudes towards

---

[1] When we talk about citizens' beliefs in general, we simply mean that individuals accept that some things exist or are true. When an individual has a belief about the integrity of politicians, he or she accepts as truth some premise about the honesty of politicians. When we talk about a judgement, we mean that moment in which an individual affirms or revises his or her existing beliefs or else acquires new beliefs in response to some external prompt. The difficulty of getting inside people's minds means that it is virtually impossible in practice to distinguish between beliefs and judgements, at least when relying on survey responses and the words articulated in focus group discussions.

parliaments, the police and so on; and support for specific political actors or authorities. Compared with Easton's original conceptualisation, this revised formulation effectively breaks down the second of his objects, the regime, into the ideas that underpin it, its performance and its constituent institutions. This conceptualisation shares with Easton's tripartite distinction the potentially problematic conflation of normative support for political institutions and satisfaction with practical outcomes. Yet thinking about ethical judgements within the context of the Easton–Norris framework helps to highlight the conceptual differences between, for example, citizens' evaluations of institutional ethical standards (norms), their evaluations of politicians' integrity in general and their evaluations of a specific politician's conduct.

In practice, the two most common types of ethical judgement that citizens are likely to make about politics, at least on a day-to-day basis, are those pertaining to the probity or acceptability of specific actions by individual politicians, and those pertaining to general levels of integrity or honesty in political life more broadly. The two types of judgement are likely to be related in practice, but are nonetheless distinct. For example, someone may judge the actions of a prime minister to be dishonest while generally judging all other politicians to be generally honest and trustworthy. Alternatively, someone who generally thinks that politics is conducted in an unethical manner may nonetheless judge a particular deed to be morally correct. As we will see, the relationship between different types of judgement can be further complicated by the fact that general beliefs about political conduct may predispose individuals to judge politicians in certain ways, and specific ethical judgements may prompt individuals to revise their more general beliefs about the integrity of politicians.

In addition to distinguishing between different objects of ethical judgement, it is also important to distinguish between judgements about the means and ends of political conduct. In a fascinating study of American citizens' beliefs about democracy, John Hibbing and Elizabeth Theiss-Morse (2002) distinguished between 'policy space' – the domain of social conditions, policy outcomes and policy outputs – and 'process space' – the domain of how government works. Politicians may be subject to citizens' ethical judgement in both spaces. They may be judged according to their performance in office and the morality of the policies they propose and the decisions they take; they may also be judged on the basis of the manner of their behaviour and the integrity of decision-making processes. In practice, policies and the ends of conduct are more often the preserve of political rather than ethical judgements, at least in media discourse. This is not to say that ethics are absent from policy space; some politicians even use the language of ethics to frame their policies, as the 1997 Labour government did in respect of its 'ethical' foreign policy (Little and Wickham-Jones 2000). Citizens may also judge policies in ethical terms, as many doubtless judged Britain's subsequent involvement in the 2003 invasion of Iraq. But in most liberal democracies, certainly in recent years, concerns about ethics in political life have tended to focus on the processes and context in which decision making takes place rather than on what those decisions should be. In part, this tendency reflects ideas about the scope of politics. There are normative limits to acceptable public policy at any given moment, to be sure, but the scope for legitimate political contestation is normally drawn widely. It is fundamental to modern conceptions of liberal democratic politics that politicians are allowed to pull the levers of political office to move public policy in contested directions.

There is no doubt that ethical judgements about political processes have important consequences. Research has shown how perceptions of misconduct can impact on other political attitudes and behaviour (e.g., Rundquist *et al.* 1977; Peters and Welch 1980; Fackler and Lin 1995; Rose *et al.* 1998; della Porta 2000; Pharr 2000; Seligson 2002; Anderson and Tverdova 2003; Bowler and Karp 2004; Blais *et al.* 2005; Redsawsk and McCann 2005; Rothstein and Uslaner 2005), and how beliefs about appropriate conduct can affect individuals' own behaviour (Beard and Horn 1975; Mancuso 1995; Allen 2008). Perceptions of procedural integrity, for instance, can influence citizens' commitment to that most basic of democratic activities, voting. Sarah Birch's (2010) cross-national study suggests that perceptions of electoral misconduct reduce citizens' propensity to vote. Perceptions of politicians' personal integrity also seem to matter in respect of voting. Philip Jones' and John Hudson's (2000) survey of mature students found that perceptions of British MPs' integrity affected reported turnout in the 1997 general election. Meanwhile, politicians' own perceptions of citizens' judgements may also cause them to change their behaviour. They may seek to use alleged ethics violations as a way of undermining opponents, thereby playing 'politics by other means' (Ginsberg and Shefter 1990). They may also invest considerable amounts of energy into addressing perceived problems by establishing ethics commissions or new laws.

A final general characteristic of citizens' ethical judgements worth highlighting concerns their variability. A number of studies have used survey instruments that require respondents to judge the 'corruptness' of hypothetical actions (Johnston 1986, 1991; Mancuso 1995; Allen 2008). Such surveys reveal considerable variation in how individuals evaluate behaviour, as well as differences between normative definitions of corruption, on the one hand, and the public's understandings of corruption, on the other. In this respect, they have helped to reveal not only how different groups come to hold different views about what constitutes corruption, but also the extent to which academic concerns with ethics may be out of kilter with public understandings.

If ethical judgements about political conduct are characterised by variability, then the obvious question arises: are all judgements to be taken equally seriously? In one sense, it is important for politicians to reflect on the full range of citizens' beliefs and perceptions. However, it is also the case that some judgements will be unreasonable and/or reflect ideas about patterns of behaviour that are far removed from reality. Some citizens may have wholly unrealistic ideas about right and wrong in political life. At the same time, perceived realities may be inaccurate, either because the flow of information to citizens is incomplete, or because citizens are psychologically unable to make good judgements or because citizens' ethical judgements are affected by a general dissatisfaction with politics. People dissatisfied with politics may project malign or dishonest motives onto politicians regardless of the objective reality. Such problems plague attempts to use integrity perceptions as measures of the extent of misconduct or corruption, an issue to which we return in Chapter 8.

Individual-level drivers of integrity perceptions

Public perceptions of politicians and how citizens judge their conduct are an aspect of political life over which elected representatives have relatively little control. When it comes to appearance, politicians are often at the mercy of how others choose to portray and perceive their conduct. Appearance belongs in the eye of the beholder.

A full appreciation of what drives appearance requires an awareness of both the micro- or individual-level factors that affect citizens' ethical judgements and perceptions, as well as the macro-level or systemic factors, especially the behaviour of others, that are likely to do so. In this section and the next, we establish the basics of what we know about how citizens understand and evaluate their politicians' integrity. We begin with the individual-level side of the story.

Existing research into citizens' ethical judgements about political conduct can be located along one of two cross-cutting dimensions. The first relates to the object of judgements. Some studies focus on respondents' perceptions of the prevalence of misconduct (or corruption) in a given institution or society. For instance, Transparency International's annual Global Corruption Barometer explores perceptions of corruption in different domestic sectors, including political parties, parliaments, the police and the judiciary. Other studies focus on respondents' beliefs about the propriety or corruptness of a specific act or type of behaviour. Usually, respondents are presented with an actual or hypothetical account of conduct and asked to judge its propriety.

The second dimension relates to the identity of those who are making the judgements. The distinction here is usually between political elites and members of the public (Heidenheimer 1970). At the elite level, a number of existing studies have examined political actors' own understandings of the ethical norms that structure their behaviour and have shed light on the ethical 'world' of political institutions (Mancuso 1995; Allen 2008). At the mass level, there have been a number of studies into both perceptions of misconduct and normative attitudes towards the behaviour of elected officials, although interest in the former has tended to predominate.

Perhaps the most important general point in respect of citizens' ethical judgements to emerge from this literature – and one that is potentially dispiriting for democrats – is that politicians are for the most part poorly understood by those they represent. The typical citizen pays only limited attention to the conduct of politics, as their daily lives are crowded with more immediate concerns and interests. Formal politics is a peripheral affair. Unfortunately, many people who are preoccupied with politics, including politicians and political scientists, often lose sight of this fact. Citizens may be grabbed by the occasional alluring headline or a particularly salacious scandal, but the detail of politics is something to which they devote little cognitive effort. Such is the reality of modern representative democracy.

The job of a politician is thus largely alien to most people. Citizens are unlikely to have first-hand knowledge of, or appreciate the day-to-day demands placed on, elected representatives. The reality of a politician's job is that it requires a diverse range of skills, long and frequently anti-social hours, and immense devotion. When people are asked to evaluate their political leaders, they are engaging in what might at first appear to be a rather taxing exercise: they are being asked to judge the probity of actions of which they have little understanding, not to mention direct experience. Yet these barriers do not stop citizens acquiring beliefs about politicians' integrity, nor do they impede their willingness to offer judgements about politicians' conduct. In our surveys, for example, there were relatively few 'don't knows'. Most citizens it seems are generally quite willing to express judgements about the actions of their leaders. Ignorance is no handicap.

In order to understand more fully how individuals make judgements about political conduct, a brief foray into the philosophical and social-psychological literatures on ethics is useful. When it comes to the nature of individuals' ethical judgements, there is a long-standing debate in the modern philosophical literature between followers of David Hume and those of Immanuel Kant. According to the Humean view, 'desires', which political scientists refer to as emotions or 'affect', are the original source of ethical judgements. According to the Kantean view, ethics is a matter of 'reason'. This 'desire' versus 'reason' debate framed the philosophical study of ethics during the course of the twentieth century (Singer 1994: 113–17).

The same debate also has parallels in modern psychological approaches to the subject. Some psychologists treat ethical judgements as a matter of conscious rational analysis or cognition; others regard such judgements as being fundamentally driven by individuals' intuition or emotion. The cognitive approach dominated research in the early postwar period. According to this approach and the work of developmental psychologists, ethical evaluations are motivated primarily by conscious deliberative activity, which changes as an individual grows. Affect may play an important role, but ethics are chiefly a matter of reason (Kohlberg 1984; Gibbs and Schnell 1985; Krebs and Denton 2005; Wallace 2007). More recent neuro-psychological research has demonstrated that ethical judgements rely on a combination of emotion and reasoning, with the type of judgement affecting the relative importance of the two factors. Experiments suggest that portions of the brain associated with emotion are engaged to different degrees according to the mental task being undertaken (Greene *et al.* 2001; Greene and Haidt 2002; Haidt 2012). Emotion, however, generally plays the larger role.

Meanwhile, social scientists have also been paying increased attention to the affective and intuitive influences on individuals' reasoning. Another strand of psychological research has demonstrated that cognitive processes do not always generate accurate evaluations (Tversky and Kahnemann 2000). Human reason is subject to several distinct forms of bias, and individuals frequently make bad (inaccurate) judgements about factual reality, especially when they rely on 'peripheral processing' or 'fast' types of thinking that employ cognitive shortcuts (see, e.g., Kuklinski and Quirk 2000; Lodge and Taber 2000, 2013; Sears 2001; Lieberman *et al.* 2003; Kahneman 2011). Work in behavioural economics has emphasised the role of intuition in individual decision making, and it is precisely those 'flaws' in individuals' cognitive capacities that make citizens' behaviour conducive to being 'nudged' (Thaler and Sunstein 2008).

Psychological research can also help us to understand the individual-level relationship between citizens' ethical judgements about specific actions and conduct and more general beliefs about the integrity of politicians. Most individuals seem to process political information on a continuous basis. They maintain a 'running tally' of all prior evaluations, ideas and beliefs, and their response to new information is to update this 'running tally' (Lodge and Taber 2000, 2013). Of course, this process requires individuals to actually be aware of new information. Crucially, this way of processing information is also likely to condition responses to future stimuli. In practice, most individuals will find it virtually impossible to evaluate any new piece of information in an unbiased way. They have pre-existing feelings and beliefs about objects in the world – including politicians and other political objects – and these feelings will almost inevitably shape their response to new information. Individuals will tend to arrive at judgements that they want to arrive at (Kunda 1990). For example, when presented with new information about politicians' conduct, individuals will often respond in line with a subconscious desire to reach a judgement that is consistent with prior beliefs about elected leaders. If an individual believes that most politicians are 'just in it for themselves', they are likely to project dishonesty and malign intentions onto a specific politician. Cases of misconduct will confirm their negative views. Cases of dubious propriety and ambiguous conduct are likely to be judged unfavourably. Cases of good conduct will be discounted and overlooked.

All these features of human psychology have several implications for the research presented in this volume. First, we can anticipate that most people's ethical judgements about politicians' conduct, both general and specific, will deviate from the precepts of cool, rational deliberation and will be influenced to a large extent by emotional feelings towards politics. Our surveys were conducted at a time when the country was in the throes of a severe economic downturn and reacting to a major political scandal, the 2009 parliamentary expenses fiasco. We should thus not be surprised if politicians bore the brunt of popular disquiet at this juncture, and that people's evaluations of their behaviour should reflect both standards that are 'too high' and judgements that are 'too severe' from the perspective of cool, 'rational' political commentators. We should also not be surprised to see that assessments of the economy should creep over into evaluations of politicians' ethics.

Secondly, we can anticipate that individuals will use a combination of different strategies to form ethical judgements, and that different individuals will approach the task of judgement in different ways, depending on their knowledge and experience of politics as well as other personal characteristics. Moreover, we can expect that there will be systematic distortions of perceptions of relatively unfamiliar roles, such as those of politicians, depending on the frames of reference that people have to hand when forming judgements.

Over and above these general expectations, we can also advance several conjectures as to how different groups in the population will form their views. Comparative studies have identified a number of individual-level factors that are likely to influence citizens' normative standards for political conduct as well as their perceptions of political integrity. These include basic demographic factors such as gender, age and socioeconomic status indicators (including income and education) (Grødeland *et al.* 2000; Davis *et al.* 2004; McManus-Czubińska *et al.* 2004; Blais *et al.* 2005; McCann and Redlawsk 2006). Most studies have found that women and older people are more ethically deman-ding of politicians and more critical of their actual conduct than are men and younger citizens, phenomena that are typically traced to the tendency of women and older people to be more censorious in general. At the same time, the same studies also point to a common tendency of those at higher socioeconomic levels to take a somewhat more relaxed attitude towards the ethical conduct of their leaders and to be less critical of them.

These demographic attributes can also be expected to shape citizens' personal moral values in the private sphere, another general factor that may influence ethical judgements about political conduct. If people are morally demanding when it comes to their own behaviour and that of their peers, they can be expected to also hold those who represent them to higher standards.

Other political values and preferences may also influence individual-level judgements about political conduct. At this point, we again wish to make clear that we are talking about judgements in an ethical sense rather than a political sense. This distinction means that we are interested primarily in citizens' judgements about whether actors are behaving according to acceptable principles of action rather than whether an individual supports the objective of such action, or is supportive of its outcomes. Previous studies into political ethics have demonstrated that partisanship and other political beliefs, such as satisfaction with policy outputs, government performance and the state of the economy, affect judgements about the ethical conduct of political leaders (Davis *et al.* 2004; McManus-Czubińska *et al.* 2004; Blais *et al.* 2005; McCann and Redlawsk 2006). However, the comparative evidence obliges us to remain agnostic for the time being as to the anticipated effects of political or partisan considerations on British integrity evaluations, as these vary considerably from political context to context.

Finally, individuals' personal experience of politicians' conduct is likely to affect their judgements. We have already seen that politics is peripheral for most people, and that the majority of citizens lack direct experience of what politicians do, not to mention the ethical challenges that confront them and the institutional norms that structure their actions. It is highly likely that those who have a better knowledge and understanding of these features of political life will judge politicians differently from those who do not. And, of course, citizens who have had direct experience of politicians acting unethically or illegally may well judge things differently still. Studies in other countries have shown that personal experience of corruption affects perceptions (Grødeland *et al.* 2000; Miller *et al.* 2001; McManus-Czubińska *et al.* 2004). Very few Britons are likely to have seen or experienced an MP or some other politician breaking the law or misconducting themselves, but it is a factor that must be considered.

Macro-level drivers of integrity perceptions

While micro- or individual-level factors can help account for variations in how people judge specific actions and in their general beliefs about politicians' integrity, systemic factors – in particular, features of the political system that affect the quality and quantity of information about politicians' conduct to which citizens are exposed – can also be expected to play a major role in driving popular perceptions.

Across the world, people are generally sceptical about the virtue of their leaders and elected representatives. However, there are pronounced national differences in how politicians are perceived. Data from Module 2 of the Comparative Study of Electoral Systems illustrate this point well. This study, which was based on surveys conducted in a large number of countries in the mid-2000s, asked a question designed to tap the extent of perceived corruption: 'How widespread do you think corruption such as bribe taking is amongst politicians in [country]: very widespread, quite widespread, not very widespread, it hardly happens at all?' Answers to the question can be coded on a 1–4 scale, where a higher score means that more corruption is perceived to be taking place. Figure 2.1 reports the resulting mean scores for nineteen established liberal democracies, including Britain. We exclude respondents from more recently democratised countries, since perceived corruption levels in these places tend to be somewhat higher. The resulting data demonstrate both variations in subjective political conduct in the nineteen countries as well as some familiar patterns. Denmark, which is the only country where the mean score fell below 2 on the 1–4 scale, heads a table of high perceived standards in the Nordic countries, whereas Italy, which has the worst score, trails behind Japan, Portugal and France. Britain ranks ninth out of nineteen; with a mean score of 2.4, it is also within the lower half of the scale (2.5 being the midpoint).

A number of systemic factors might explain this variation. Before we turn to them, it would help to make clear that we are primarily

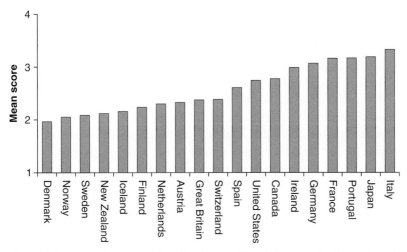

Figure 2.1 Corruption perceptions in nineteen liberal democracies (mean score)
Source: Module 2 of the Comparative Study of Electoral Systems.

interested in elite-level features of the political system and the importance of formal political structures. In the broadest sense, relevant factors might also include citizens' beliefs about and orientations towards politics. The idea that there are distinct national political cultures has long been proposed as way of explaining variation in the way politics is conducted (Almond and Verba 1963). Representation is a dynamic practice, and the way politicians behave is likely to reflect, at least in part, the beliefs and preferences of citizens (Erikson *et al.* 2002; Bartle *et al.* 2011). Related to all this is Colin Hay's (2007) distinction between demand- and supply-side explanations of why citizens have become so critical in their attitudes towards political leaders. He argues that analysts have heretofore looked mainly to demand-side reasons for lack of public confidence in the political classes and have neglected supply-side factors. While some might contest Hay's explanation of declining public support, his basic point is compelling. Different political communities may well place different demands on their politicians, and their citizens may well have different expectations of their representatives and come to judge them differently.

In terms of elite-level political practice and the supply-side drivers of citizens' ethical judgements, key systemic features that are likely to drive perceptions include the wider norms and institutions of representative democracy, governmental performance, the character of political competition and contestation, the ethical rules and regulatory structures surrounding political life, the actual prevalence of misconduct and rule-breaking, and the tenor and nature of media coverage. These features can all be expected to affect the manner in which politicians behave and the way in which it is portrayed to, and experienced by, the public.

At a fundamental level, institutional features such as the electoral system and parliament, as well as democratic 'rules of the game' – ideas about representation and the proper role of elected representatives – are likely to be hugely significant in how politicians interact with citizens (Searing 1982, 1994). Needless to say, such features vary considerably from country to country. British MPs, for example, tend to do more constituency work than German MPs, and they tend to follow the party line to a greater extent than members of the US Congress. Moreover, some systemic features may have a more direct influence on the perceived propriety or otherwise of politicians' conduct. How political parties are funded will affect politicians' interactions with potential donors and the opportunities for relationships that stand up well to external scrutiny. How well entrenched norms of public-sector transparency are will affect how much knowledge citizens can potentially have of their political leaders' actions.

Governmental performance may also matter in terms of how politicians are judged in any place at any given time. While ethical judgements can be distinguished in theory from other kinds of judgement, in practice, citizens' judgements are likely to be bundled up with political and other judgements. In its crudest sense, how politicians in general perform may predispose citizens to judge them more or less harshly. To invoke the distinction between position and valence issues (Stokes 1963), if there is a high degree of correspondence in a political system between policy-makers' positions and those of voters, or if policy-makers have delivered high levels of growth and other commonly desired ends, such as low levels of crime, then politicians may come to be judged favourably. Alternatively, if there is a low degree of correspondence between positions, or if policy-makers have failed to deliver on the economy and law and order, then politicians may come to be judged unfavourably. Different democratic systems perform differently in terms of policy outputs and social and economic outcomes. A system's performance also changes over time.

Another systemic factor that might affect citizens' beliefs about politicians relates to the character of political competition. In most liberal democracies, there is a tendency for politicians to use ethics as a part of their party political arsenal. It pays for them to 'dig dirt' on each other in the hope that some of it, when thrown, will stick. The extent to which such muck-raking occurs varies from polity to polity. In places such as the United States, where parties are comparatively weak, muck-raking is a feature not only of inter-party competition, but also of intra-party competition as rival candidates seek to secure their nomination. More generally, a country's basic constitutional structure and the organisation of democratic life can affect the extent to which consensus or adversarialism characterises politics (Lijphart 1999). In Britain, extreme partisanship plus the existence of a small number of tightly organised parties have encouraged a distinctive adversarial culture in which short-term tribal interests often come first. Such partisanship can encourage politicians to make accusations against their rivals. It can also open politicians up to criticisms of being mindless party supporters, who vote against their conscience in Parliament and whose language stretches the bounds of honesty in their bid to adhere to the party line.

Both the actual and perceived behaviour of politicians are also likely to be influenced by the ethics rules and laws that exist in a given political system. Such rules are likely to address a variety of issues, including, for example, whether elected representatives can retain second jobs or whether they are able to accept gifts from constituents. Every state has its own ethics infrastructure (Behnke 2002), and every political institution will have its own ethics regime. The rules may be more or less restrictive and onerous; there may or may not be specialist bodies created to oversee and police these rules. Moreover, and in addition to these rules, there will also be distinct institutional cultures of what is considered to be acceptable and proper behaviour. The combination of ethics rules and laws and norms is likely to have a pronounced effect on national integrity perceptions. Clear ethics laws that are rigorously enforced may reduce misconduct and bolster general levels of integrity; but the existence of ethics investigators may serve to increase the apparent prevalence of misconduct. If every transgression by a very small number of politicians is prosecuted, levels of misconduct may appear to be greater than if no transgressions by a large number of politicians are investigated. While the precise content of laws and rules varies across the liberal democratic world, the global trend in recent years has probably been for increasingly formal ethics regulation (Saint-Martin 2006: 24). As we will see in Chapters 3 and 8, this trend is very much true of Britain.

Another systemic feature that is likely to have a huge impact on perceptions of politicians' conduct is the structure and conduct of media reporting. Most information reaching the public about misconduct and rule-breaking in political life is likely to be mediated. Few citizens have direct, first-hand experience of political misconduct. Instead, the vast majority of citizens get their information about politicians' behaviour and misbehaviour through the news media. The accuracy of this information is open to question. What misconduct comes to light may or may not be the tip of the iceberg. In practice, it is virtually impossible to measure objective levels of misconduct, in much the same way that it is virtually impossible to measure objective levels of corruption. Such behaviour is all too often concealed.

In addition to carrying information about politicians' conduct, the media have a large role in shaping citizens' expectations of politicians, and they are in a position to set the ethical agenda for politicians. The media also play an obviously huge role in shaping the general image of elected representatives and other office holders. After all, one of the drawbacks of having a free press, at least from a politicians' point of view, is that it greatly weakens elites' control over their collective image. As with the other systemic factors discussed so far, there is likely to be considerable national variation in the role of the media vis-à-vis politicians and politics. How media carry news about politicians, and how journalists and editors interpret their function of holding politicians to account, can vary considerably from place to place and from time to time. The well-documented shift from 'lap-dog' journalism to 'attack-dog' journalism in the United States (Sabato 1991) has been echoed in many other places, including Britain (Barnett 2002).

A final factor, which brings together both politicians' actual behaviour and the role of the media in reporting it, is the prevalence of scandal. Virtually every reported allegation of misconduct is a scandal of sorts, insofar as it involves a violation of widely held ethical norms and prompts a public expression of disapproval (Thompson 2000). Of course, some allegations are clearly more scandalous than others, either because of their individual significance or because they are seen to be part of a broader pattern of misconduct. Occasionally, the scope and scale of ethical norm-breaking, the extent of public disapproval, and the volume with which that disapproval is expressed, may result in what might be termed a 'mega scandal' (Koutsoukis 2006: 232). Such events embrace a very large number of politicians and may bring virtually the whole of the political class into disrepute. Thus, one word, 'Watergate', came to symbolise the perceived moral decline of American political life in the 1970s, just as 'expenses' would come to symbolise an apparent moral decline in British political life in the early 2000s. It is not always clear what makes some allegations more scandalous than others, why some societies seem more prone to scandals than others at given moments in time, and why some scandals are bigger than others. What is clear, however, is that the causes are often systemic, in that they involve the interaction of various public, elite and media actors. The impact on subjective conduct may also be great, even if constant exposure to allegations of wrong-doing desensitises citizens as part of a process of 'scandal fatigue' (Kumlin and Esaiasson 2012).

Conclusion

A consideration of systemic factors goes a long way towards teasing out those structural features of liberal democratic systems that encourage citizens to become critical of elected representatives. These factors also highlight factors that may explain why citizens' beliefs about political ethics and politicians' integrity vary from polity to polity. What such approaches are less successful at is helping us to understand how individuals engage with and judge politicians. For this, an individual-level focus is required. Such an approach helps us to understand how individuals come to form their evaluations of politicians' conduct and how this affects the way they engage with politics and society at large. We return to these individual-level factors in later chapters. But in order to understand more specific expectations of how the British public might approach the task of evaluating its elected leaders, we need to stay with the systemic or macro-level focus and assess the nature of Britain's ethical terrain. By exploring the changing normative, behavioural and institutional features of British political ethics, we can establish the context in which citizens' judgements are formed. It is to this task that we now turn.

3 | Ethics and misconduct in British politics

HAT's the level of corruption in this country? Probably lower than any other society in the world. That's not a bad standard, is it?

(Male focus group participant, Egham)

For most citizens, political ethics are usually an issue of low salience. Thinking about what standards of conduct should guide politicians' behaviour is not a daily preoccupation. Yet citizens potentially form ethical judgements or update their beliefs about politicians' integrity every time they read or hear about political activity. Moreover, reports of alleged misconduct appear in the news nearly every week. They are virtually impossible to avoid. In Britain, from the mid-1990s, when media coverage of various misdeeds and indiscretions fuelled concerns about Conservative 'sleaze', through Tony Blair's decade in power, which included the spectacle of a sitting prime minister being interviewed by police about his knowledge of possible party funding irregularities, to the parliamentary expenses scandal of 2009, a succession of scandals have afflicted almost every part of the political system. The prominence of politicians' misconduct waxes and wanes, but is rarely off the agenda for long.

This chapter provides an overview of political ethics and misconduct in Britain up to the 2010 general election, when the last of our surveys was fielded. Although our study is concerned with improving our understanding of citizens' perceptions of politicians' integrity, it is important to locate these attitudes against the backdrop of the complex and gradually changing ethical landscape inhabited by politicians. This landscape has normative, behavioural and institutional features. It includes those commonly held ideas, beliefs and values that structure and give meaning to what politicians regard as ethical. It includes politicians' actual conduct, including behaviour that may well constitute misconduct. And it includes those rules and procedures that are put in place to maintain high ethical standards of conduct. Together, these features can be expected to shape citizens' understandings of political ethics and perceptions of the nature and extent of misconduct in political life. More importantly, they also constitute a set of ideas, practices and behaviours that may or may not correspond to the public's expectations, but which, if they do diverge too much from expectations, may be a source of dissatisfaction with political institutions and even democratic politics.

From the outset, it is important to stress that the landscape surveyed is construed in narrow terms. It is narrow in the sense that we focus on those parts of the political system that are inhabited by office-seeking politicians, in particular the Westminster Parliament, since it is citizens' perceptions of their integrity that preoccupy our empirical research. It is also narrow in the sense that we focus primarily on political ethics as they pertain to individual politicians. Certain types of corporate actor, most obviously political parties, but also media organisations, trade unions, business, lobbyists and other pressure groups, are important features of the wider ethical landscape, but their activities have tended to be talked about and treated differently from the conduct of politicians. Until comparatively recently, official attempts to define ethical standards and regulate political conduct have focused almost exclusively on individual holders of public office. Finally, our construal is narrow in the sense that the landscape surveyed is one that is largely defined by what politicians themselves tend to experience as being a matter of political ethics, that is, misconduct and, above all, official attempts to prevent its occurrence.

The remainder of the chapter is divided into three parts. The first part sets out the principal preoccupations of British political ethics, including the focus on individual conduct and the historic emphasis on financial conflicts of interest. The second part describes the relatively recent explosion in the scope and scale of institutional arrangements for regulating politicians' conduct, as well as the intended and unintended consequences of these changes. The third part charts the heightened concern with ethics and conduct in recent years and the varieties of political misconduct that have occurred.

Standards in British public life

As we saw in Chapter 2, ideas associated with modern liberal democracy provide a normative structure that defines both what is considered ethical conduct and the general criteria by which others may judge politicians. While these ideas resonate across the liberal democratic world, in every political system more specific and detailed ideas about appropriate political conduct can be found. Some of these ideas are written down and codified, either in laws or institutional rules and regulations, while others remain unwritten and take the form of common understandings. The extent of consensus around particular ideas varies over space and time, likewise the extent of their codification. Even the discourse surrounding such ideas varies. In some jurisdictions, notably the United States, the language of 'ethics' is often explicitly invoked by anyone attempting to define, encourage or enforce high standards of integrity in political life. The British approach to political ethics, however, has been to use the more practical language of 'standards in public life'. Thus, whereas the US Congress created an Office of Government Ethics in 1978 as part of a range of measures 'to preserve and promote the integrity of public officials and institutions', the British government in 1974 appointed a Royal Commission on Standards of Conduct in Public Life to 'inquire into standards of conduct in central and local government', and in 1994 it created a Committee on Standards of Public Life with a remarkably similar remit.

The obvious starting point for understanding elite and institutional preoccupations with political ethics in Britain is the premise that politics is a public rather than a private activity. This premise is a fairly standard feature of modern liberal democracy, as we saw in the last chapter, and is reflected in the notion that political corruption is an abuse of public office for private gain. In British politics, as elsewhere, any behaviour that involves such an abuse has long been considered unacceptable. Yet, as we also saw in Chapter 2, opinions about what constitutes corruption and the abuse of public office can vary. Perhaps for this reason, British law, in the form of the Public Bodies Corrupt Practices Act 1889, the Prevention of Corruption Act 1906 and the Prevention of Corruption Act 1916, historically defined corruption somewhat more narrowly.[1] Under these laws, as Alan Doig (1996: 36) notes, corruption was 'a criminal offence involving the transaction of soliciting or receiving inducements or rewards to local government

---

[1] More recent legislation, in the form of the Bribery Act 2010, which replaced the older Acts, eschews the loaded language of corruption altogether.

politicians (but not to MPs) and all public officials for decisions or actions – or, conversely, the failure to act or to make a decision – that favours the donor or their organization.' Corruption, in other words, was synonymous with bribery.

Bribery is usually easier to demonstrate than corruption. It is certainly something that has long been regarded as contrary to the standards expected in British public and political life. Thus, a House of Commons resolution, first passed in 1695, asserted that:

> The Offer of any Money, or other advantage, to any Member of Parliament, for the promoting of any Matter whatsoever, depending, or to be transacted, in Parliament, is a high Crime and Misdemeanour, and tends to the Subversion of the Constitution.

The resolution may have been disregarded from time to time, sometimes quite brazenly, but it nonetheless reflected a fundamental ethical principle underpinning political practice.

If corruption in British law has tended to be synonymous with bribery, the whole field of standards in public life has often tended to be synonymous with strategies for addressing or regulating conflicts of interest, in particular financial conflicts of interest. A conflict of interest arises whenever an office holder's private interests clash with his or her public duties (Stark 2000). More specifically, it occurs whenever someone's capacity for judgement in relation to a primary consideration – usually the exercise of their public role – is impaired by consideration of a secondary interest – usually a private gain (Thompson 1995: 55). Conflicts of interest may coincide with fairly flagrant forms of misconduct, including bribery and self-dealing, but they can also take more subtle forms, such as when public officials are mindful of gaining future employment with firms and other organisations dealing with the government, a problem known as 'revolving doors', or when incumbent office holders have access to privileged insider knowledge that could enable them to obtain some financial benefit gain (Perkins 1963). Yet, while the 'conflict' in any conflict of interest exists first and foremost in the mind of a decision maker, the appearance of conflict can be as important as the substance. As Sandra Williams, who has written about the topic in the context of Westminster politics, observes: 'A charge of conflict of interest may arise not only when public duty clashes with private interest, but also when they appear to converge' (Williams 1985: 6).

As we saw in Chapter 1, an institutional preoccupation with conflicts of interest and preventing the use of political office for personal financial gain has been described as 'moral minimalism' (Jennings 1985: 151). The British approach to political ethics has largely accorded with this description, especially at Westminster (Allen 2011). For example, a tendency to moral minimalism was quite apparent in the first authoritative statement of ethical principles in contemporary British politics, the 1995 'Seven Principles of Public Life':

Selflessness: holders of public office should take decisions solely in terms of the public interest. They should not do so in order to gain financial or other material benefit for themselves, their family or their friends.

Integrity: holders of public office should not place themselves under any financial or other obligation to outside individuals or organisations that might influence them in the performance of their official duties.

Objectivity: in carrying out public business, including making public appointments, awarding contracts or recommending individuals for rewards and benefits, holders of public office should make choices on merit.

Accountability: holders of public office are accountable for their decisions and actions to the public and must submit themselves to whatever scrutiny is appropriate to their office.

Openness: holders of public office should be as open as possible about all the decisions and actions that they take. They should give reasons for their decisions and restrict information only when the wider public interest clearly demands.

Honesty: holders of public office have a duty to declare any private interests relating to their public duties and to take steps to resolve any conflicts arising in a way that protects the public interest.

Leadership: holders of public office should promote and support these principles by leadership and example.

The Seven Principles were drawn up by the original Committee on Standards in Public Life and were intended to apply across the public sector. Some members of the Committee had hoped to echo Moses with a list of ten principles. In the end, the Committee could only match the number of deadly sins. At any rate, the Seven Principles soon acquired an almost hallowed status. (They have since been revised, as we discuss in Chapter 8.) Yet, as some commentators have pointed out, the original principles contain 'a great deal of uncertainty and ambiguity' when subject to close scrutiny (Peele and Kaye 2008: 169). They are also primarily concerned with protecting the integrity of individual public office holders from the threats posed by private interests.

A useful window onto the normative and practical origins of Westminster's particular preoccupation with financial conflicts of interest, as well as the changing institutional manifestations of this preoccupation, is provided by Samuel Beer's (1965) seminal analysis of British political development. For Beer, Britain's history has been shaped by a series of 'types of politics', or traditions – Old Tory, Old Whig, Liberal, Radical and Collectivist – each of which comprises characteristic sets of ideas about representation and distinct institutional practices. Of these traditions, Whig practices and theories of representation have been especially influential in shaping the scope and focus of political ethics at Westminster.

The Whig tradition has deep roots in British history and can be traced back to the eighteenth century and before. This was an era when full democracy was still some way off and when elections to Parliament were based on a minute, male franchise. A core tenet of this tradition was that Members of Parliament were trustees of the public interest rather than their electors' delegates; they were elected to Westminster to represent wider social interests as well as their constituents, to be sure, but they were not to be in any group's pocket. Edmund Burke formulated the classic defence of this doctrine. To paraphrase his speech to the electors of Bristol, MPs were expected to preserve their industry and judgement for the public good (see Stanlis 1963: 186–7). In keeping with more recent writing about legislative ethics (see Chapter 2), obvious constraints on their independence, such as bribery, were entirely unacceptable. So, too, were any constituents' opinions that were 'evidently opposite to the real good of the rest of the community'. The interests of the nation as a whole came first.

Needless to say, the advent of mass democracy during the nineteenth century and the gradual ascent of Beer's Liberal tradition, with its emphasis on the representation of individuals by individuals, began to alter the weight that MPs attached to constituents' opinions. Growing demands from citizens to be represented placed new ethical obligations on MPs. Yet, Burkean values still held sway at Westminster, just as they continue to influence representative practice to this day.

In addition to emphasising the importance of representatives' independence and autonomy, the Whig tradition simultaneously promoted practices and beliefs that challenged these very values. While MPs were expected to employ their industry and judgement in advancing the wider national interest, they were also free, if not encouraged, to combine their parliamentary duties with extra-parliamentary work. Sandra Williams (1985: 19–34) has called this practice 'the tradition of Members' financial independence'. Only MPs who were financially independent would be able to exercise independent judgement on matters of public policy, or so the theory went. It was even suggested that extra-parliamentary employment would make them better representatives of professional, commercial, business and other interests.

In today's world, which is inhabited by full-time career politicians, it is easy to forget that arrangements were once different. As recently as the early twentieth century, politics was not considered a full-time profession. Only politicians who exercised ministerial office received a salary. Membership of Parliament may have been a public service of sorts, but it was akin to membership of a private members' club. Thus, a Harvard professor of government observed in 1908: 'a seat in the House of Commons is a luxury enjoyed mainly by the only class in the community that can afford it … it is a very pleasant place and the gateway to much that is agreeable' (Lowell 1908: 511). Many MPs, if not directly pursuing an extra-parliamentary career, had financial portfolios and ties to businesses from their time before they entered Parliament. Many MPs also acquired interests during the course of their parliamentary career. Meanwhile, especially as the twentieth century progressed, other MPs, mainly Labour politicians, acquired personal sponsorship agreements with trade unions.

Throughout Parliament's history, conflicts of interest were an inevitable problem for an institution simultaneously committed to its members acting and exercising judgement in the public interest, on the one hand, and their freedom to enjoy private incomes and interests, on the other. To address this problem, the House of Commons passed numerous rulings and resolutions down the years to prevent MPs' financial interests from improperly affecting their decisions. MPs' historic freedom to maintain extensive outside interests was thus tempered by the principle that the public interest should take precedence over their private, extra-parliamentary interests. To reconcile these two sometimes inconsistent aspects of parliamentary life, some restrictions were placed on MPs, but only when their interests threatened to affect their parliamentary activities (Doig 1984). Yet these restrictions, where they existed, did not address, probably because they could not address, the underlying problem, that of conflicts between MPs' outside interests and their official responsibilities. These conflicts would occasionally give rise to widespread public concern about their conduct, as we shall see.

One of the curious features of British political ethics, given the enduring power of Whig ideas about the importance of MPs' independence, is the rarely contested constraint on politicians imposed by party politics.[2] Burke famously said that a representative's 'unbiased opinion, his mature judgement, his enlightened conscience, he ought not to sacrifice to you, to any man, or to any set of men living' (cited in Stanlis 1963); yet MPs have long sacrificed their opinions, judgements and consciences to the party whips. The notion that governments have a mandate, based on voters' support for a manifesto, is a key idea underpinning the most recent of Beer's types of politics, the Collectivist tradition, which has dominated British politics since 1945. Mass political parties, not individual MPs, are at the heart of this type of politics, and it is mass political parties that are the principal agents of representation. Within this context, politicians elected on a specific programme are under an obvious obligation to support its introduction. It might even be considered virtuous for MPs to vote in line with their party's mandated position and against their own personal feelings. Yet such behaviour clearly sits uneasily with Burkean principles, and Collectivist politics may easily lead to an adversarial political culture in which short-term party interests often come first.

---

[2] The then home secretary Jack Straw alluded to this curious feature during the passage of the Political Parties, Elections and Referendums Bill in 2000: 'It is something of a paradox, then, that so little statutory recognition has so far been given to the central role played by political parties in the political life of this country' (*HC Debates*, 10 January 2000, vol. 342, col. 34).

No tradition of representation has ever had a total grip on political practice. The relevance of different traditions waxes and wanes (Beer 1965; Marquand 2008). The dominant post-1945 Collectivist type of politics has long been under threat from trends of partisan dealignment and party fragmentation, and an older Liberal tradition, with its emphasis on individual MPs acting as representatives for individual constituents, has arguably become more important in recent years. Up until the 1960s, constituents made relatively few demands of their MPs (Norton and Wood 1993). Today, however, MPs perform a much larger constituency role, and being a 'good constituency member' is probably more important today than at any other point in the modern era of mass democracy. Compared with members of the US Congress, British MPs still lack the power and influence to 'bring home the pork' for their constituents, but they are certainly expected to represent their constituents more assiduously than Burke would have liked. MPs also face considerable local demands to work for their constituents full time. Some MPs still enjoy extensive outside interests, but it is much harder to justify extra-parliamentary employment these days. No serious politician can afford to risk claims of being a part-time MP.

At the same time, the changing practices of representation also potentially create new areas of ethical concern. Because of their growing constituency workload, for instance, MPs have acquired more facilities and resources, including expenses and allowances, to enable them to discharge their parliamentary duties. It almost goes without saying that an expanded system of expenses and allowances increases the opportunities for abuse. Rules and regulations have had to develop accordingly. To some extent, such rules have diluted the traditional concern with the conflict of interest problem. But such rules have also reinforced an official preoccupation with what might be termed financial honesty in politics. The discourse of British political ethics is still fixated on the proper use of those resources that come with holding public office, and on ensuring that such resources are used in the public interest and not for private gain. This fixation is also apparent in the institutional arrangements put in place to maintain high standards.

Maintaining high standards

In contrast to an enduring preoccupation with financial conflicts of interest, the ethical landscape of British politics has changed markedly in recent years in terms of the institutional arrangements for maintaining high standards of conduct. A simple, but useful, way of conceptualising these changes is suggested by Michael Atkinson and Maureen Mancuso (1992). Comparing practice in the British House of Commons and the US Congress, they identified two typical institutional strategies: the 'etiquette' and 'edict' approaches. An etiquette system, such as was found in the House of Commons, is one in which regulation largely relies on informal, unwritten norms. There may well be some bodies overseeing conduct, but they tend to operate in an advisory capacity, and there are no established penalties for contravention of the rules (Atkinson and Mancuso 1992: 12). An edict system, on the other hand, is one in which regulation is based primarily on a system of general, public rules, usually accompanied by 'an institutionalised system of standards, investigation and sanction' (Atkinson and Mancuso 1992: 3). This latter approach was best exemplified in US political practice.

In addition to being viewed as ideal types, the edict and etiquette systems can also be viewed as poles at either end of a continuum. At one end of this continuum lies formal, public and extensive regulation; at the other, lies informal, private and less onerous regulation. Recent changes in the institutional features of British political ethics can be understood in terms of movements along this continuum. With the partial exceptions of electoral conduct – which have been regulated through statute since the late nineteenth century – and local government – which saw its statutory central regulator, Standards for England, axed as part of the 2010 Coalition government's drive to cut the number of quangos – virtually every other part of the British political system has seen a clear shift towards more formal ethics regulation.

The key moment of change in recent history was arguably Prime Minister John Major's decision in 1994 to establish an independent Committee on Standards in Public Life (the Nolan Committee after its first chairman, Lord Nolan, a law lord). Its primary remit was to examine contemporary 'concerns about standards of conduct of all holders of public office', with a view to making 'recommendations as to any changes in present arrangements which might be required to ensure the highest standards of probity in public life'. Other commissions and tribunals had been established in the past, usually to examine specific scandals, but these were disbanded once their work had been done. The Nolan Committee was different. Its remit was ongoing. For some of those involved in its creation, the Committee was expected to provide advice only when called upon by the prime minister, but the Committee quickly developed an identity and purpose of its own. It has since become a permanent and active feature of the political landscape, and its recommendations have affected both public office holders, including MPs, peers, ministers and civil servants, as well as political parties (Doig 2006). Following the Committee on Standards in Public Life's (1998) fifth report, for example, Parliament passed the Political Parties, Elections and Referendums Act 2000, which established a new statutory framework that required parties and candidates to register donations above certain thresholds with a new statutory regulator, the Electoral Commission.

We focus particular attention on the changing practice at Westminster as it relates to individual holders of political office (see Gay and Leopold 2004). Apart from serving to illustrate the general national trend, it is also the area of principal relevance to our study. Starting with the House of Commons, historical practice was to leave the management of standards as far as possible to individual MPs (Williams 1985: 35–53). The House was habitually and culturally averse to any form of intervention that might tread on MPs' toes. In 1971, responding to a question about Members' outside interests, the then Leader of the House, William Whitelaw, set out a perfect statement of the conventional wisdom:

I think that there is widespread support in this House for the view that it is right to rely on the general good sense of hon. Members rather than on formalised rules ... I believe that is the view of many right hon. and hon. Members. (*HC Debates*, 3 March 1971, vol. 812, col. 1704)

There were, of course, some rules relating to MPs' conduct, set out in resolutions, in standing orders and in *Erskine May*, Westminster's handbook of parliamentary practice, but these rules generally related to the etiquette of Parliament. The exceptions stemmed from the minimalist concern with financial conflicts of interest, and included requirements that MPs should not take bribes and should avoid contractual relationships that limit their independence, but should declare relevant interests in parliamentary proceedings. The House, moreover, lacked any body specifically charged with monitoring MPs' conduct.

If self-regulation operated at the individual level, it also operated at the corporate level. For constitutional reasons, both Houses of Parliament exercised 'exclusive cognizance', which meant that they enjoyed responsibility for interpreting and managing standards of conduct within their own precincts (Drewry and Oliver 2004). MPs could be arrested in their private capacity – they did not have personal legal immunity – but their conduct as MPs was not a matter for the courts. Until relatively recently, politicians' normative commitment to keeping regulation in-house was immense. It was sometimes defended on constitutional grounds and the need to protect Parliament from executive and judicial intrusion. It was sometimes defended on practical grounds, and the fact MPs knew best the ethical demands of the job and were in the best position to judge conduct. It was also defended on moral grounds and the claim that self-regulation motivated politicians to pursue the highest standards of integrity. All three may have been true, but the practice undoubtedly insulated MPs from the opinions and preferences of those they served, and perhaps contributed to the creation of a distinctive ethical culture at Westminster (Mancuso 1995).

Since the 1970s, arrangements have shifted gradually towards an edict approach to standards management. In 1975, the House instituted a Register of Members' Interests, in which MPs were expected to list any financial and other interests that might be thought to influence their parliamentary behaviour, and a Select Committee on Members' Interests, comprising MPs, to oversee the new system. Then, following the first report of the Committee on Standards in Public Life (1995), MPs instituted a code of conduct for the first time, a new Select Committee on Standards and Privileges and a new post of Parliamentary Commissioner for Standards. The Commissioner would henceforth investigate allegations of misconduct, the bulk of which, in the event, would relate to the rules concerning the registration and declaration of outside interests (Allen 2011). The overall structure retained the House's 'exclusive cognizance', in that MPs would retain the final say in cases of misconduct, although there would now be a semi-independent ethics adviser and investigator.

More recent developments have shifted arrangements even further along the etiquette–edict continuum. In the wake of the 2009 expenses scandal, Parliament established a new statutory Independent Parliamentary Standards Authority (IPSA) for administering and monitoring

MPs' pay and expenses. The initial legislation that created IPSA also contained provisions for a statutory code of conduct for MPs and a new statutory commissioner for parliamentary investigations, and it would also have given IPSA the responsibility of overseeing the registration of MPs' financial interests. In the event, IPSA's remit was limited to the matter of pay and expenses. Otherwise, the post-1995 system of a code and commissioner, located in a general framework of corporate self-regulation, was retained.

If arrangements in the House of Commons have shifted towards a more 'edict' approach to regulating standards, so too have arrangements in Westminster's other chamber, the House of Lords. The Lords finally instituted its own register of interests in 1995, a code of conduct in 2001, and its own independent Lords Commissioner for Standards to investigate alleged misconduct in 2010. As with arrangements in the Commons, the new structures in the Lords exist within a framework that still respects the chamber's 'exclusive cognizance'. The new regime also remains focused primarily on conflicts of interest and the perceived threat that they pose to legislative integrity.

In the British political system, holders of ministerial office are expected to be members of either the House of Commons or House of Lords, and they are subject to the standards and rules associated with the chamber in which they sit. Yet ministers have also always been bound by more stringent rules than mere backbenchers, reflecting their greater capacity to influence public policy. These rules, like those in the Commons and Lords, have tended to focus on financial propriety and conflicts of interest. From 1906, for example, ministers were obliged to divest themselves of all outside business and commercial interests (Platt 1961). Sometimes leading and sometimes following wider trends, the regulation of ministerial conduct has also seen a gradual shift towards an edict approach. Thus, Clement Attlee, when prime minister in 1945, had the rules governing ministers' conduct codified in a specific document, *Questions of Procedure for Ministers*, which John Major first made public in 1992, and which Tony Blair renamed as the *Ministerial Code of Conduct* in 1997 (Baker 2000). Blair later agreed to appoint an Independent Adviser on Ministers' Interests, an individual charged with providing advice to government ministers on the handling of their private interests, and investigating, at the instigation of the prime minister, allegations that individual ministers have breached the ministerial code. Developments in the regulation of ministerial conduct have always been complicated by the prime minister's constitutional role in deciding, ultimately, whether an individual can continue in ministerial office or not. It remains the case that when a minister is alleged to have acted improperly, politics rather than ethics determine his or her fate.

The gradual, and sometimes grudging, institutional changes in Britain's ethical landscape have been driven by a number of factors. One factor has been a general demand for rules and codification in almost all areas of social activity, or what Calvin Mackenzie (2002: 54) calls 'the relentless momentum for "more ethics"' in his analysis of similar changes in the United States. This momentum takes different forms in different countries, yet the push to have more formal regulatory arrangements in respect of politicians' conduct seems to be an 'international phenomenon' (Atkinson and Bierling 2005: 1004). Mackenzie (2002: 112–13) suggests a syllogism that underpins the mood:

Public faith in the integrity of government is essential in a democracy to ensure public support for the policies of government. Integrity can be enhanced by clear and vigorously enforced rules regulating the behavior of government employees. The more of those rules there are and the more they guide and constrain the actions and decisions of public employees, the higher will be the level of government integrity and the greater will be public support for the government.

Regulation is thus a good, and this assumption makes it politically costly, if not impossible, to oppose. When it comes to British politicians' conduct, for example, it seems to be taken for granted that more rules and more external oversight will improve actual standards of conduct and public confidence in their integrity.

Other pressures that are more specific to Britain stem from long-term changes in the nature of political life. British politics is increasingly home to 'career' politicians (King 1981; Riddell 1993; Cowley 2012). Politicians are also now perceived to be full-time public office holders. In the House of Commons, MPs were unpaid until 1911. They regarded themselves, and were regarded by many others, as private citizens performing a public service, and even the law was unclear on whether they were holders of public office. Now, of course, MPs are expected to be full-time, paid parliamentarians. Though it has taken decades, the ambiguity that once surrounded their place in public life has almost entirely gone. They are all individual holders of public office. In the House of Lords, peers are still not paid a regular salary, but the House also now recognises that it is a public body performing a public function, and not just a club for the eldest sons of eldest sons. As members of a public institution, peers must be bound by appropriate standards.

A related pressure for change in the institutional landscape comes from the general expectations surrounding public institutions as corporate bodies. There is considerable pressure for the Commons and the Lords to be opened up to public scrutiny. This demand partly reflects the pull of wider ideas about institutional public 'transparency', as embodied in the Freedom of Information Act 2000, and partly the push of demands by politicians and journalists for more information. Parliament has done much in recent years to 'engage the public with its work and activities' (Kelso 2007: 364). The opening up of the Commons and the Lords, first through radio and television coverage, then through a greater online presence, has arguably made both chambers less insular. The implications of all this openness, both volitional and coerced, have almost certainly been noted by MPs and peers. They need to be ever more mindful of acting in a way that maintains public confidence. With their actions under so much scrutiny, it is doubly important for them to be seen to be doing the right thing.

Yet another general pressure for more ethics regulation comes from recent constitutional changes in Britain (King 2007). Some of these changes are legal: thus, the doctrine of parliamentary sovereignty, which underpins the exclusive cognizance of the Commons and the Lords, remains formally intact, but Britain's membership of the European Union means that it resembles more than ever a legal fiction. Some of these changes are normative: thus, the incorporation of the European Convention on Human Rights into British law has forced MPs and peers to consider whether their own procedures meet its high procedural standards (Drewry and Oliver 2004). It has even become more common to question the Houses' right to exclusive cognizance. And some of these changes are behavioural: thus, an increasingly assertive judiciary seems to be less deferential in dealing with politicians. For example, the decision of the courts in 2010 to proceed with the trials of a number of MPs and peers charged with abusing their official expenses signalled a decisive break with long-held beliefs about judicial non-interference in parliamentarians' conduct. As a result of all these changes, politicians' collective confidence in their right and ability to regulate exclusively and informally their own conduct has almost certainly diminished.

A final set of pressures that have driven changes in ethics regulation are perhaps the most obvious: the occurrence of scandal. Scandals tend to provide the most proximate trigger for change. As one commentator has noted: 'Virtually all progressive moves on legislative ethics have been prompted by political scandals, and in particular by a confluence of individual political scandals that point to a systemic problem' (Kaye 2005: 48). Whatever the long-term pressures for reform, politicians have usually acted to change things only in the face of intense media, political and public demands that often follow from high-profile cases of misconduct. The next section examines this final behavioural feature of British politics' ethical landscape.

The prevalence of misconduct and scandal in British politics

As we saw in Chapter 2, the prevalence of actual misconduct is likely to be a major systemic factor in shaping citizens' beliefs about their elected representatives' integrity. But as we also saw, it is likewise very difficult, if not impossible, to measure objective levels of misconduct. Such difficulties inevitably pose problems for anyone wishing to model the relationship between objective conditions and perceptions. They do not prevent ordinary citizens from forming their own judgements, however.

If the attitudes of political elites are anything to go by, then British politics is generally conducted according to high standards of conduct. A notable feature of the ethical landscape has been politicians' confidence in their probity, at least since the successful elimination of widespread electoral corruption in the late nineteenth century (O'Leary 1962). At the beginning of the twentieth century, the future Liberal prime minister Henry Campbell-Bannerman told MPs: 'We in this country have happily been free for two or three generations from any imputation of mercenary or corrupt motives on the part of our public men, a thing which can be said of few other countries' (quoted in Searle 1987: 1). Half a century later, Clement Attlee observed: 'public administration in this country and public life in this country stand unrivalled in their high standards of service and incorruptibility' (quoted in Robinton 1970: 249). At the beginning of the twenty-first century, a committee of MPs reported how its 'witnesses were convinced that public life in the early twenty-first century was cleaner than it had been before' (Public Administration Committee 2007: 6).

Such confidence may well be justified. Britain has traditionally scored well in cross-national surveys of corruption, and commentators at home and abroad have often praised British politicians' ethical record (Getz 1966: 152; Shaw 1990: 91; Adonis 1997: 104–5). Many members of the public also express confidence in the general integrity of the country's politics, at least when they are asked to compare overall levels of corruption in Britain with elsewhere, as the quote from one of our focus group participants at the start of this chapter illustrates. Yet, in truth, misconduct is a recurring feature of British political life, just as it is a recurring feature of political life everywhere.

Before we turn to some of the recent cases of misconduct that have afflicted British politics, a few words should be said about the way in which most citizens come to learn of them. Citizens' exposure to politicians is largely mediated, and their exposure to political misconduct is almost entirely mediated. Very few members of the public ever experience political misconduct or corruption first hand. Instead, they almost always learn of it from the media. Journalists and media organisations are obviously major players on the ethical landscape of British politics. They are major players in the sense of sometimes helping to expose political wrong-doing and bringing it to public attention. They are also major players in the sense of framing and shaping much of the information about politicians that reaches the public. In both respects, journalists play a vital democratic role. But their behaviour, and the way in which they report politics, has come in for considerable criticism in recent years.

On the one hand, various commentators have identified a general 'dumbing down' in political reporting (Franklin 1997). News has come to be viewed as a product designed and 'processed' for a particular market, and packaged in a way that makes smaller demands on the audience. The detail of political processes, and the complex trade-offs that politicians have to consider, tend to be discarded in the name of brevity. On the other hand, the way in which journalists perceive their democratic role also appears to have changed in recent decades. Some elements of the media appear increasingly confrontational in their relationship with politicians, and a critical, if not anti-politician, line often 'frames' political reporting (Lloyd 2004). Writing at the start of the twenty-first century, a professor of mass communications suggested that political journalism had entered an 'age of contempt' in which confrontational and, at times, derisive coverage was contributing to a 'process which is degrading democracy's institutions and undermining political representatives' (Barnett 2002: 400). In a similar vein, Tony Blair (2007) spoke out just before leaving office against Britain's 'feral' media. The reasons why political reporting has changed are many and complex, but the consequences for what citizens learn about politics are simple: British citizens are all too often presented with the warts but not the all of politics.

Contemporary news coverage may be systematically unfriendly towards politicians, but critics of the media must nonetheless acknowledge that politicians often give journalists plenty of material on which to build critical stories. A potted history of past scandals and misconduct will serve both to illustrate the variety of wrong-doing that has occurred and to highlight those cases that may well have shaped the beliefs of our survey respondents and focus group participants.

More often than not in the modern era, it has been politicians' relationships with money that have given the greatest cause for concern (King 1986), reflecting and perhaps reinforcing the conventional emphasis in British political ethics on financial conflicts of interest. The early twentieth century, for example, witnessed a spate of financial scandals in Britain, notably the Marconi affair of 1912, when three Liberal ministers purchased shares in the American Marconi company despite the fact that its English sister company was a beneficiary of a government contract, and, later, the sale of honours scandal of 1922 (Searle 1987: 172–200). There were surprisingly few such scandals in the years immediately before and after the Second World War. Of these, the case of John Belcher stands out. Belcher was a junior minister at the Board of Trade who, in 1949, was found to have accepted a number of small gifts despite knowing they were intended to secure favourable treatment (Roodhouse 2002). He immediately resigned from ministerial office and from the House of Commons.

A very different kind of misconduct dominated the headlines in the early 1960s, one that involved sex rather than money. In 1963, John Profumo, the Secretary of State for War, resigned from Harold Macmillan's government and the House of Commons after lying to MPs about the nature of his relationship with a prostitute, Christine Keeler (Irving *et al.* 1963). More conventional concerns about money resurfaced in the early 1970s following revelations that John Poulson, a Yorkshire architect, had used financial and material inducements to curry favour and secure contracts (Doig 1984). Those implicated in his web of corrupt relationships included local councillors, civil servants, various public-sector employees and several MPs, including the serving Home Secretary, Reginald Maudling. It was probably the most significant case of financial impropriety to hit British politics in the postwar era and created something of a 'moral panic' among elites. Poulson was eventually imprisoned, as were a number of local politicians and senior officials, while Harold Wilson's government established a Royal Commission on Standards of Conduct in Public Life.

Plenty of individuals were embroiled in their own private scandals during the ensuing years, but it was another two decades before Britain experienced another moral panic about the integrity of its political class. In the early 1990s, a series of scandals coalesced into the general phenomenon of 'sleaze' and generated a massive crisis of confidence in the integrity of Parliament, the Conservative government and British public life in general (Ridley and Doig 1995). Sleaze was a vague notion connoting a general laxity in the moral standards of those in public life. It embraced all sorts of alleged wrong-doing, some of it very serious, some of it less so.

Some of the scandals that contributed to the image of sleaze in public life were sex scandals. Between September 1992 and June 1996, no fewer than nine members of the Conservative government resigned over allegations about their private lives. Other scandals of the era were more substantial. They included alleged government misconduct, most notably the 'arms to Iraq' affair, in which the Conservative government was accused of endorsing the sale of arms by the British company Matrix Churchill to Saddam Hussein's Iraq, of misleading Parliament and of being willing to allow innocent people – in this instance three Matrix Churchill executives – to be imprisoned for activities that the government had condoned. There were also serious scandals in local government, the most notable being the Conservative-led Westminster City Council's attempts to alter the social composition of the borough for electoral purposes. Yet it was a number of financial scandals involving MPs that did most harm to public confidence during this time. Concerns about MPs' business links and relations with lobbyists had been raised intermittently in previous decades, but a sudden spate of allegations suggested systemic financial impropriety and ethical failure at Westminster. Of these allegations, much the most serious were the 'cash for questions' scandals, involving Neil Hamilton, Tim Smith and others, which suggested that MPs were prepared to accept money for tabling parliamentary questions (Doig 1996).

Ahead of the 1997 general election, the Labour Party's new leader, Tony Blair, made hay at the expense of the scandals involving Conservative politicians. As part of his campaign to distance himself from the era of Tory sleaze, Blair promised that his party would be 'purer than pure' when in government (King 2002: 29). It was not long, however, before his party and his colleagues were embroiled in scandals and allegations of misconduct.

Some of the transgressions involving New Labour politicians were standard run-of-the-mill scandals involving individual politicians. Ron Davies, the Welsh Secretary, was forced to resign from the government in 1998 following a 'moment of madness' with another gentleman on Clapham Common. Peter Mandelson, one of the co-architects of New Labour, was obliged to resign twice from the government, once in 1998 for failing to declare a large interest-free loan from another minister and again in 2001 for allegedly improperly trying to help an Indian businessman with a passport application. (He was subsequently exonerated on the second count.) David Blunkett was also twice obliged to resign from the government, first in 2004 over allegations that he had sought to speed up the visa application of his lover's nanny, and again in 2005 over allegations of a conflict of interest surrounding his past business activities. Nothing about these actions was distinctively New Labour.

Other transgressions suggested systemic ethical failings. One area of concern that Labour made its own after 1997 was that of 'spin' (Doig 2005). Attempts to control and manage media and public relations are a natural part of politics and government. However, they create their own problems when taken to extremes, and New Labour took news management to a whole new level in British politics. Spin became a term that summed up ethical disquiet about Labour's general approach to governing in much the same way that sleaze had summed up disquiet about the earlier Conservatives. The public felt it was being misled. By 1999, one survey found that 82 per cent of respondents agreed that ministers quite frequently sought to mislead the public by claiming that they were spending new money on public services or taking new initiatives when they were not (King 2002: 23). Even greater controversy surrounded the government's use of spin ahead of Britain's involvement in the 2003 invasion of Iraq. Again, large sections of the public felt they had been misled.

Another problem area for Labour concerned the issue of party funding. British political parties receive relatively little public subsidy and instead rely largely on voluntary contributions to fund their activities. Unfortunately for them, mass memberships, a major source of their income, have gradually shrunk, obliging all parties to seek income from other places. Almost inevitably, political parties, especially the two major parties, have come to rely heavily on fewer wealthy donors. Sometimes, the behaviour and conduct of donors has damaged the reputations of parties by association. The Conservatives, for instance, have benefited greatly in recent years from the largesse of a wealthy businessman, Lord Ashcroft; questions about his tax affairs, however, encouraged opponents to charge the Conservatives with being unscrupulous vis-à-vis those from whom they accepted money. At other times, it is the lengths to which donors go to conceal their contributions that cause concern. In 2007, for instance, the *Mail on Sunday* published allegations that a wealthy Labour donor, David Abrahams, had donated large sums of money to the party in other people's names.

The reliance on wealthy donors also fuels concerns that some individuals are able to wield considerable influence on party policy. In November 1997, barely six months after New Labour had won the general election, it emerged that Bernie Ecclestone, the billionaire and Formula One ringmaster, had donated £1 million to the party in January 1997. It also emerged that he had met with Tony Blair in October in a bid to persuade the government to exempt Formula One racing from a planned ban on tobacco advertising, and, moreover, that after this meeting the government had granted the requested exemption. Once the story became public knowledge, the Labour Party returned the money, and the government invited the Committee on Standards in Public Life to examine the issue of party funding. Blair even went on television to defend his conduct and declared: 'I'm an honest guy'.

Two particularly significant scandals tarnished the last years of New Labour's time in office. The first was the so-called 2006 'loans for peerages' scandal, when newspapers alleged that the Labour Party had received a large number of secret loans from benefactors who were subsequently nominated to membership of the House of Lords.

The practice of rewarding benefactors with political honours is technically legal, providing that the reward is coincidental, but there cannot be any evidence of a quid pro quo. The practice is also something in which all major parties have engaged, more or less discretely. David Lloyd George's fairly indiscrete exercise of prime ministerial patronage to confer honours on party donors prefigured the 2006 affair and led to the Honours (Prevention of Abuses) Act 1925. Eighty years later, another prime minister was implicated. Under other rules enacted by the Labour government, loans, unlike donations, did not need to be registered; yet the spirit of the legislation was undoubtedly opposed to such activities, and the appearance of a quid pro quo was exacerbated by attempted secrecy. Labour's principal fundraiser, Lord Levy, was one of several individuals close to Tony Blair to be arrested by police, and Blair himself was interviewed twice by police. No one was ever charged, but the damage to Labour's and Blair's reputations was considerable.

The second major scandal to tarnish New Labour's last years in power was the explosive 2009 MPs' expenses controversy, with which we introduced Chapter 1. It was not specifically a Labour scandal, but a parliamentary one: every party had MPs implicated in the widespread misuse and abuse of parliamentary expenses. Nor was it a scandal entirely unheralded. Apparently isolated incidents of impropriety had been coming to light since the start of the new millennium (Allen 2011). Among those implicated at an early stage was the Home Secretary Jacqui Smith, who was accused in early 2009 of taking advantage of Parliament's second-home allowance scheme. She was later found to have breached the House of Commons' code of conduct.

The real drama began on 8 May 2009, when the *Daily Telegraph* began publishing previously secret details of all MPs' expenses and allowances claims (Winnett and Rayner 2009). These details had been leaked by a disgruntled – or public-spirited – parliamentary official, and exposed a pattern of claims by MPs that were not always in keeping with the spirit of the rules. Many of the reported claims, for things like biscuits, certainly seemed petty, but were in fact in keeping with the spirit of the rules. MPs were given allowances to cover the costs of running their offices and to attack MPs for claiming for items consumed by staff was, on the face of it, unfair and unreasonable. Other claims, for items such as a duck house, gardening work and even bags of manure, were less clearly in accordance with an allowance system that was intended to enable MPs to perform their representative duties by maintaining addresses in London and their constituencies. Yet other claims were clearly contrary to the spirit of the rules, such as those by MPs who sought to 'flip' or re-designate their main address in order to redecorate their properties at public expense. And yet more claims suggested fraud, such as those by MPs who sought to claim for the interest on mortgages already paid off. In some cases, the police agreed. Criminal charges would be brought against four Labour MPs – David Chaytor, Jim Devine, Eric Illsely and Elliot Morley – and two Conservative peers – Lords Hanningfield and Taylor.[3] All six men were imprisoned for varying amounts of time.

Conclusion

Thanks to the expenses scandal, the subject of politicians' conduct was a particularly live issue ahead of the 2010 general election and in the months when our surveys were fielded. Those who responded to our questions are unlikely to have been untouched by the extensive and sometimes excessive news coverage that surrounded the affair. But our respondents' attitudes, and the significance of their attitudes, need to be located against the backdrop of a broader ethical landscape. This landscape is both similar and different to the landscape of a hundred years ago or even fifty years ago. In terms of the norms that shape elite-level conduct, it is similar in that many of the fundamental principles of behaviour remain, even if specific expectations have changed. In terms of the institutional arrangements in place for promoting high standards among politicians, it is remarkably different. There are established agencies whose sole purpose is to monitor and regulate conduct; there were no such agencies a century ago. Most ethics rules and the bulk of regulatory activity remain focused on politicians' use of official resources for public not private ends, but there are much more of both, especially at Westminster.

---

[3] In the years after the scandal, charges would be brought against other Labour parliamentarians, including Margaret Moran, who was convicted and given a two-year supervision order in December 2012, and Denis MacShane, who was convicted and jailed for six months in December 2013.

There remains, however, one further dimension of Britain's ethical landscape about which this chapter has been largely silent: the public's response to scandal and their perceptions of integrity. It is this feature of political ethics that preoccupies the next four chapters and to which we now turn.

4 | *Expectations and the scope of ethical judgements*

T HEY SHOULD set out their political stall with a vision of society, and we'd grant them a lot of licence if they stick to that, and not shift with the wind.

(Male focus group participant, Egham)

As we saw in the last chapter, money has been central to many of the major scandals that have rocked British politics, up to and including the 2009 expenses controversy. Money has never been considered the only cause of impropriety, of course, but it has long been viewed as the principal cause, and not without some justification. For similar reasons, protecting the integrity of political processes from the potentially corrupting influence of financial benefits has preoccupied legal and institutional attempts to promote high standards of conduct amongst Britain's political elite.

In different ways, these two features of the wider ethical landscape – the inevitable cases of political misconduct and the narrow institutional focus on conflict of interest – both point to the subject of this chapter: citizens' expectations of politicians' behaviour. On the one hand, citizens' expectations are likely to be a major factor in their evaluations and perceptions of political conduct and their response to alleged impropriety. Integrity evaluations are based in part on prior beliefs about what constitutes appropriate or desirable conduct. If we are fully to understand such judgements at an individual level, we obviously need to know something of the expectations that inform them. On the other hand, systematic variations in expectations may help to explain aggregate-level disaffection with the general conduct of politics. As has been reported in the context of other liberal democracies, citizens often disagree with political elites as to what is actually acceptable behaviour among elected representatives (Jackson and Smith 1996; McAllister 2000; Atkinson and Bierling 2005). Such disagreement may help to explain why politicians continue to engage in practices that violate popular norms of ethical behaviour. As Ian McAllister (2000: 35) notes: 'If voters' expectations about the proper conduct of politicians are continually frustrated, then it has the potential to undermine public confidence in the democratic system as a whole.'

There may, however, be even more fundamental differences between citizens' and politicians' expectations that help to explain general dissatisfaction. These differences concern the perceived scope of 'political ethics', that is to say, what types of political activity and behaviour are considered appropriate for ethical judgement. As we saw in Chapter 2, there is a tendency in modern political practice to ring-fence some aspects of conduct within the domain of 'normal politics'. Yet it may well be the case that what politicians take for granted and regard as 'normal politics' is commonly subject to some kind of ethical judgement by citizens. Such differences of opinion and viewpoint may have particularly important implications for the success or failure of official attempts to regulate standards in public life. If such attempts are underpinned by a conception of ethics that is considerably narrower than the public's, then conduct that the public dislikes and judges to be unethical will continue to slip through the net of regulation.

The chief purpose of the chapter is to chart some of the general expectations that citizens have in respect of their politicians. In the process, it also explores individual-level cognitive features of the apparent gap in British politics between citizens' aspirations for how their politicians should behave and their perceptions of how politicians actually behave. The remainder of the chapter is divided into four parts. The next section describes the broad expectations that citizens have about the scope of ethics. The third section examines the relative weight that citizens attach to public conduct vis-à-vis private behaviour, and the fourth section examines the relative weight attached to probity and honesty vis-à-vis political competence and performance. The final section explores differences between citizens' and elite expectations by examining their responses to possible malfeasance. Throughout, we explore some of the factors that help to explain why different groups of citizens seem to have different expectations concerning political conduct.

The scope of political ethics

There are considerable methodological difficulties associated with studying popular beliefs about political ethics. Most of these difficulties reflect the general limitations associated with standard social science methods. As students of public opinion know, it is challenging to develop valid measures of attitudes: surveys and interviews can take us only so far in ascertaining what people think. But there are also distinctive problems associated with the study of ethical beliefs and evaluations. At a fundamental level, researchers in this area are likely to have relatively sophisticated and structured ideas about 'ethical' conduct and corruption, which are informed by their knowledge of both political practice and the extensive normative literature on polit-ical ethics. These ideas may in turn impose unrealistic assumptions about the way in which other people view politicians' conduct and think about questions of political rights and wrongs. They may even lead to unrealistic assumptions about what constitutes an ethical issue. There is no guarantee that other people's beliefs will be structured in such ways, or that they even view the same issues that the researcher does in ethical terms. As a number of survey-based studies have dem-onstrated, there are often differences in how people respond to dubious conduct, with some people seeing normal politics where others see corruption (Peters and Welch 1978; Redlawsk and McGann 2005). In much the same way, members of the public may also see links between different sorts of ethical issues that are not apparent to the researcher.

Although there is evidence of some structure to citizens' beliefs about political ethics (Peters and Welch 1978), it is also the case that more sophisticated elite-level attempts to classify ideas about ethics do not always accurately reflect what the public thinks. As we saw in Chapter 3, the Committee on Standards in Public Life sought to enumerate 'Seven Principles of Public Life' in its first report. Yet later research commissioned by the Committee found that the public's expectations of officials' conduct were somewhat broader than that encompassed by the principles (see also Chapter 8). Although the research found that 'the Seven Principles largely succeed in articulating what the public expects of the ethical framework within which those in public office work', it also suggested that:

the public has a wider set of concerns that go beyond the scope of the Principles. These wider concerns include a broader sense of honesty than is implied in the 'Honesty' Principle, as well as attributes such as financial prudence, competence and 'being in touch' with what the general public thinks is important. (Committee on Standards in Public Life 2008: 10)

Any research into citizens' understandings of political ethics needs to retain a degree of open-mindedness. Our assumptions about citizens' expectations and beliefs were grounded in previous political science and social psychology research into people's ethical judgements about political conduct. After all, it makes little sense to adopt a purely inductive approach, which may well lead to a proliferation of poorly structured concepts and categories lacking in internal logic. However, in order to tease out the patterns of citizens' ethical judgements, we also undertook some exploratory qualitative research in respect of citizens' expectations and beliefs. This research took the form of a number of open-ended focus group discussions (see Chapter 1 for details), which took place towards the start and end of our project. Such research allowed for a high degree of flexibility in our approach to exploring citizens' beliefs about politicians' conduct and political integrity. It was also a useful reality check in respect of how people beyond the narrow world of academic political science think about these things.

With that last point in mind, one of the most interesting findings to emerge from these focus groups was a tendency for people to understand political ethics in a way that varies considerably from the views that seem to inform elite groups, including, it must be said, many political scientists. As set out in Chapter 3, official and institutional engagement with the issue of standards in public life has grown out of long-standing concerns with preventing bribery and blatant self-serving behaviour, and with regulating financial conflicts of interests. Standards have been conceptualised in narrow terms. Underpinning this conceptualisation has been a certain understanding of the role of elected representatives that emphasises the ideals of public service and representatives' independence of judgement, and that interprets ethical conduct largely in terms of how politicians' use public resources. For many members of the public, however, 'standards in public life' is a concept that embraces not only politicians' use of public resources, but also *individual* and *collective* policy accountability and political discourse. Politicians' use and misuse of official resources may be judged in ethical terms, to be sure, but so too may the substance and tone of everyday political conduct.

A sense of citizens' somewhat broader conceptualisation of the scope of standards in public life is suggested by a number of comments from our focus group participants. As one woman in our Hackney group stressed: 'We all have standards we agree to. We agree you should not lie, hide anything, use public money for yourself ... that goes all the way through politics, it's just a matter of enforcing it.' For this participant, as for so many others, the emphasis on discursive honesty was both a prime concern and a taken-for-granted precept. Her views were echoed by another woman at the same venue:

I'd like my elected representatives to do what they said they would do. And while I don't care about sexual scandals, if a politician had been elected on a platform of sexual probity, and was then found in breach of such behaviour, that would be appalling. Like the local Labour MPs here, who preach equality and then send their children to private schools.

For many citizens, therefore, apparent double standards and the inconsistency between politicians' words and deeds are likely to be judged in terms of right and wrong. Integrity is, at least in part, a matter of consistency.

In some discussions, conduct that most politicians and commentators would probably recognise and accept as normal politics was also singled out for disapprobation. In particular, a number of focus group participants highlighted politicians' tendency to make promises that they might not be able to fulfil. As one man noted at one of the Egham focus groups: 'They [politicians] should set out their political stall with a vision of society, and we'd grant them a lot of licence if they stick to that, and not shift with the wind.' Or, as a woman noted during one of the Bradford focus groups, 'They promise things that never materialise. Sometimes they have good ideas and they don't turn them to fruition.' Such comments suggest a deep reluctance by some of the participants to permit politicians any scope for adjusting their positions, even when circumstances change. Such comments may also reflect a deeper anger and sense of mistrust aimed at politicians; indeed, pre-existing negativity towards politicians and formal politics may well foster unrealistic and unrealisable expectations that are doomed to be unmet.

At the end of several of our focus groups, we asked participants specifically to discuss what they thought might be done to promote public confidence in the integrity of politicians and what changes to the political system might be introduced to that end. Once again, the ensuing comments pointed to a much broader conceptualisation of ethics and integrity than that which tends to permeate elite-level practice, as the following three responses illustrate:

Honesty at all costs. (Man, Egham)

They should stop fighting amongst themselves, and show people they'll do what they said they would. (Woman, Bradford)

For them to stand up for what they believe in and to make decisions that they feel are correct, even though it is against party lines, but it is in the best interest of the constituents. They should stand by their convictions, not their political gains. (Man, Egham)

At the same time, it was clear that most participants in our focus groups had limits to what they regarded as the scope of political ethics and integrity. In particular, it was quite apparent that most people drew the familiar distinction between politicians' purely private behaviour and their public deeds, and that they tended to discount the former. As participants in three different focus groups reasoned:

If you like the food in a restaurant, you would not care about the chef having an affair. The same goes for politicians. (Man, Colchester)

In the 80s a lot of conservative politicians were sexually sleazy, but that for me was irrelevant. They should not leave for that, but for what they do in their jobs … Churchill was another example: he was an alcoholic, he smoked too much, a manic depressive, but he did a reasonable job. (Man, Egham)

In cases where somebody is in the news for being, for example, a philanderer, that does not concern their professional integrity. When it comes to the laws, and the rules and their conduct in office, that's different. There have been cases where politicians have resigned over personal issues, which had no bearing on their office. That should not be a concern. (Man, Egham)

For a few individuals, the division between public and private deeds was absolute. As a woman in one of our Bradford focus groups put it: 'They can do whatever they want in their private lives. It's not fair that people should be involved in their private lives.' But not everyone shared this absolute view. As shown in the quote above from our Hackney focus group, some participants criticised inconsistencies between politicians' private and public positions. In the words of another woman:

It does matter if I have elected someone on the basis of their higher moral standards, and they go on and do something [like having an affair] and it comes out, it does matter. (Woman, Egham)

For others, meanwhile, if politicians brought their personal lives into politics, it made their private behaviour 'fair game' for public criticism (Man, Colchester).

By and large, however, the discussions in our focus groups suggest that most people's conception of political integrity does not generally extend to such things as politicians' sex lives or drinking habits. But it remains the case that many members of the public seem to set great store by what might be termed ideological or discursive integrity. They expect politicians to have clear values, to make promises that they can and will keep, and to keep their word when in office. Such comments also again illustrate the importance that many people attach to straight-talking: the dark arts of political 'spin', the tendency of many politicians to avoid giving straight answers to questions, and the use of other deceptive or evasive forms of language all potentially fall within the scope of standards in public life. For many citizens, such conduct is a matter of right and wrong. People have expectations about the ethical use of official resources; they also have expectations about the ethical use of words.

Politicians are not like other citizens

If many citizens have a somewhat inclusive conception of the appropriate scope of standards in public life, what value do they attach to the holding of political office? As we saw in both Chapters 2 and 3, political thought and practice have long tended to assume that there is a special moral status attached to holding public office or even undertaking to perform a public role. As Alan Rosenthal (1996: 15) observes: 'When a person holds public office, which is a public trust, we expect more from him or her than we expect from ourselves.' Such ideas certainly seem to resonate among the wider public. Indeed, one of the clearest messages to emerge from both our qualitative and quantitative research was that the British people expect their politicians to behave according to considerably higher standards than they apply to their peers.

Such expectations are well illustrated by several comments made during the course of our focus groups:

I'd like to think of politics as of any profession. You don't expect a doctor to do a certain thing that contravenes the medical profession. Or a police officer who is supposed to uphold the law will be punished even more than other persons. It's the same for politicians. They are on a higher level. I accept that they are human, but there's limit. (Woman, Egham)

If you go for elected office, if you are expecting to serve your constituents, you should at least uphold a higher standard ... If you are deemed to be corrupt, what's the hope for the rest of us? (Man, Egham)

If you place yourself in a position to rule, you should be better and provide a better example ... If somebody acts as my guide, they should be better than me. (Woman, Hackney)

Sometimes the expectations had a more 'material' foundation. For one woman, who was from a relatively deprived area in Bradford, elected politicians had to set an example because they were well rewarded for their work: 'If you get paid the amount of money they do, you expect higher standards.'

For some of our participants, the 'moral threshold' crossed by politicians (Hampshire 1978: ix) precluded any compromise in the pursuit of high standards. On occasion, the focus group discussions touched upon the familiar 'dirty hands' conundrum when politicians may need to break some rules in order to do a greater good. Few of those who took part in our discussions were convinced by this argument, however. The following exchange between a man and a woman in our Colchester focus group is characteristic of the views we encountered:

Woman: There's a suggestion that politics is just a dirty business ...
Man: it shouldn't be ...
Woman: But it is. The point is, if we accept that politics is a dirty business, do we not want dirty politicians?
Man: But it should not be dirty, and if you just accept that it is, you're just defending it.
Woman: But politicians do not operate in a moral vacuum. It must be a difficult position to be in, having to make those decisions.
Man: Judges manage. They have to enforce the law, even when they may not agree with the law.

Another common theme that emerged during the focus group discussions related to whether politicians themselves held each other to higher standards than those they represented. Many of the comments we heard suggested a widespread perception that most political institutions actually held their members to *lower* standards than would be tolerated in everyday life. As the following quotes illustrate, there were frequent grumbles that politicians were getting away with acts that ordinary people would be punished for:

In our own personal lives we have to declare things, like tax returns, and incur heavy penalties if we don't. It just doesn't wash with me when someone says 'I'm too busy'. There are rules to abide by. Accountability and transparency are critical in life, and they should lead by example. (Woman, Hackney)

If I fail to pay my taxes, I would be punished for it. Elected politicians should not be treated differently. (Man, Colchester)

The politicians are so far above the people, they have their own rules. Politics have run wild. There is no system, they govern themselves. (Woman, Hackney)

They're supposed to show people respect [but they behave by] different sets of rules. We'd get imprisoned for acting like that [fraudulently claiming expenses] and they don't get punished for anything. (Woman, Bradford)

The last quote is particularly noteworthy since the comment was made after police had charged several MPs and peers with false accounting. Politicians do sometimes get punished for breaking the law, but the perception that they hold themselves to different standards seems to be fairly deeply ingrained (see Chapter 8).

The results of our three surveys shed further light on citizens' tendency to attach a moral premium to the holding of political office. In each of our three waves, we asked respondents whether they thought that elected politicians should be held to the same standards of honesty and integrity as the average person or to much higher standards of honesty and integrity.[1] Answers were given on a 1–5 scale, where 1 denoted 'the same standards' and 5 'much higher standards'.

Figure 4.1 shows how people responded to this question across all three waves. To control for compositional effects, we limit our analysis to only those individuals who responded to all three surveys, a sample of 681.[2] As the answers to this question make clear, the weight of opinion clearly fell in the upper portion of the scale: the overwhelming majority in all three waves – 60.7 per cent, 75.2 per cent and 58.0 per cent, respectively – answered with either 4 or 5 on the five-point scale.

---

[1] The complete wording of this question is set out in the Appendix.
[2] The respective frequencies for all respondents in each particular wave were only very marginally different. Limiting our analysis in this way does not affect the general pattern of over-time changes.

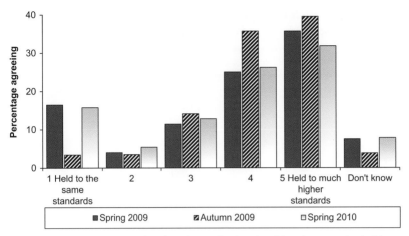

Figure 4.1 Expectations of political standards: should politicians be held to the same standards or to higher standards?

Note: The original wording of the question is included in the Appendix

Most members of the public clearly believe that their elected representatives should be judged according to much higher standards than other citizens. The changes over time also suggest that events can have relatively dramatic, if short-lived, effects on popular expectations. In the autumn 2009 survey, which followed the furore surrounding the *Daily Telegraph*'s coverage of MPs' expenses and allowances claims, the general preference for much higher standards was considerably greater than in spring 2009, and there was a notable thirteen-point drop in the proportion of respondents who said that politicians should be held only to the same standards as the average person. By the time of the final survey in spring 2010, however, popular positions had apparently reverted to the same levels as in the previous spring. According to these measures, the expenses scandal had little long-term impact on what people expected of their political leaders.

The pattern of responses reported in Figure 4.1 suggests that there is a relative consensus among large sections of the British public that the ethical bar for politicians ought to be set much higher than for the average person. At the same time, however, a substantial proportion of respondents did not hold this view. What might account for the variation? To answer this question, it is necessary to explore those factors that might drive citizens' expectations. Since we are primarily

Table 4.1 *Expectations of political standards: should politicians be held to the same standards or to higher standards?*

Attribute		Mean score
Gender	Men	3.7
	Women	3.6
Age	18–34	3.3
	35–54	3.6
	55+	3.9
Education	Graduate	3.6
	Non-graduate	3.7
Household income	Less than £20,000	3.7
	£20,000–£39,999	3.5
	£40,000+	3.7
Personal morals	More moral than average	3.8
	Less moral than average	3.4
Reported attentiveness	Most or some of the time	3.7
	Only now and then or hardly at all	3.5
Party identification	Conservative	3.7
	Labour	3.5
	Liberal Democrat	3.8
	Other	3.6
	Non-identifier	3.6
Total		3.6

Notes: Mean score by attribute, autumn 2009.
Statistically significant differences are discussed in the main text.

concerned with explaining expectations among our sample, we focus exclusively on responses to the first wave of survey, a sample of 1,388. Table 4.1 reports a simple analysis of these responses: it breaks down the mean score for responses to the question about politicians' relative standards of honesty and integrity by various individual-level attributes that have been found in previous studies to be associated with attitudes towards corruption and political ethics. Since answers were recorded on a 1–5 scale, the highest possible score for any group is 5, which would indicate unanimous agreement that politicians should be held to very much higher standards. The lowest possible score for any group is 1, which would indicate unanimous agreement that politicians should be held to the same standards as the average person.

The most obvious set of factors to begin with are those fixed at birth. Previous comparative research into the determinants of ethical beliefs suggests that older people and women tend to judge conduct according to higher standards than younger people and men (Jackson and Smith 1996; Mancuso *et al.* 1998; McAllister 2000; Redlawsk and McCann 2005). This accords with popular notions of women being social custodians of morality, and of older people having stricter views than their younger counterparts. In respect to our data, there was a marked difference between age groups that accords with the previous findings. As Table 4.1 shows, younger people (those under 35) tend to hold politicians to more 'ordinary' standards than older people, with those in the oldest age group (over 55) holding politicians to the very highest standards. The mean scores for each age group were all significantly ($p < 0.01$) different from each other. When it comes to gender, however, we find no statistically significant differences between men and women in their expectations concerning politicians' relative standards.

Other attributes that might shape citizens' expectations are those acquired in life, especially in schools and in the workplace. Evidence from the United States suggests that individuals' socioeconomic status, as measure by their education and income, can affect their ethical beliefs (Redlawsk and McGann 2005). The intuition behind these findings is that those with higher socioeconomic status may be able to empathise more with politicians, with whom they may have more in common from professional and economic points of view, than do people at lower socioeconomic levels. Empathy may then translate into more 'realistic' standards and greater tolerance of ethically dubious behaviour. When we break down our respondents by education and income, however, we find no statistically significant differences in their tendency to support the suggestion that politicians should behave according to much higher standards. Socioeconomic status may affect responses to other questions, as we will see, but it does not appear to shape beliefs about the relative standards of politicians in these bivariate analyses.

Citizens' expectations of political elites may also be affected by their general level of engagement with formal political processes, as this may condition understanding of how politics work and what the job of an elected representative involves (Allen and Birch 2011, 2012). To this end, we examine the impact of two sets of political attributes: respondents' reported attentiveness to what goes on in government and public affairs, and their sense of party identification. When it comes to attentiveness to public affairs, respondents who followed events most or some of the time seemed to expect higher standards from their politicians than those who followed events only now and then or hardly at all. The difference in the mean scores for each group was statistically significant ($p < 0.01$). There were also some partisan differences in expectations. The mean score for Labour identifiers was significantly ($p < 0.01$) lower than the mean score for both Conservative and Liberal Democrat identifiers. Given that there were apparently no ideological influences on respondents' expectations (not reported), it is possible that Labour partisans' expectations were influenced by their party being in government at the time: they were perhaps willing to cut politicians a little more slack as a result. The differences between other partisan groups were not significant.

The final set of individual-level attributes we explore relate to respondents' 'private' ethical beliefs, specifically their personal morals. The rationale for doing so is straightforward. We would expect individuals who are more tolerant of behaviour that breaches social norms to be more tolerant of misconduct by politicians. Our measure of respondents' personal morals relates to whether they thought three different behaviours could always be justified or never be justified, including: avoiding a fare on public transport; telling a lie if it is in your interest; and claiming government benefits to which you are not entitled. These are in some senses correlates of the combination of discursive integrity and honesty in the use of resources that we are analysing in political life, and they are designed to reflect common, but morally dubious, misdemeanours that most people are likely to have contemplated and evaluated as part of their moral development. Responses were recorded on a 0–10 scale, where 0 was labelled 'can never be justified' and 10 was labelled 'can always be justified'. Responses were combined in an additive scale to create a summary measure of personal morality, more specifically a tolerance of ethically ambiguous personal behaviour (this scale had a Cronbach's alpha of 0.71). Once again, we divided respondents on the basis of whether their tolerance of dubious behaviour was above or below the mean (23.4 on the 0–30 scale), that is, whether their personal morals were higher or lower than average.

On the basis of the mean scores reported in Table 4.1, beliefs about morality in private life may well be a factor in explaining expectations of politicians. As expected, respondents who were more demanding of themselves and their peers in everyday life were also more demanding of their representatives. The difference was statistically significant ($p < 0.01$). Although a difference of 0.4 on a 1–5 scale is not all that great, it does indicate that private ethical beliefs almost certainly affect citizens' public expectations.

Probity or performance?

Most Britons clearly expect their politicians to act according to higher standards of conduct than apply in everyday life. Yet relying on questions that refer only to standards and neglect other attributes that politicians might be expected to possess risks painting an unrealistic portrait of citizens' expectations. After all, judgements about political conduct are not made in isolation from the reality in which elected representatives interact with those they serve. An obvious question that arises is how much conduct really counts when it comes to evaluating politicians. Is it all about the means or do the ends matter? It is entirely plausible that other attributes, such as politicians' performance and their ability to deliver preferred social, economic and political out-comes matter as much to people, if not more, than ethical niceties.

There is little evidence to support such a supposition, however. When asked to evaluate the relative importance of ethical probity in comparison with other political qualities, virtually all our focus group participants argued in favour of high standards, even if this led to less governmental effectiveness. There were, of course, some who favoured competence or performance over moral purity, such as a male partici-pant in our Colchester focus group who said: 'if they take money but still do their job, I don't really care. If somebody is honest but ruins everything, I would not want him.' But such views were the exception. The majority view was captured neatly by another man in the same focus group who considered the trade-off before opting for honesty: 'If he was dishonest with me but ran the country effectively . . . his place as an elected official is not to be dishonest with me, not at my expense.'

Responses to our survey provide clearer evidence of the relative weight attached to probity over performance. To get at the balance of opinion on the matter, we asked two differently worded questions in successive waves of our study. The first question, posed in autumn 2009, invited respondents to evaluate the potential trade-off between having honest politicians, on the one hand, and successful and

Expectations and the scope of ethical judgements

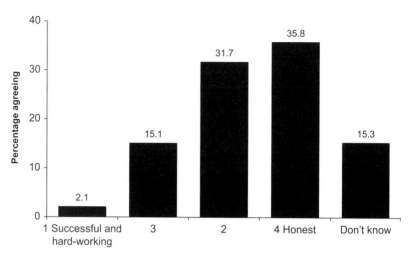

Figure 4.2 Successful and hard-working or honest politicians? spring 2009
Note: The original wording of the question is included in the Appendix.

hard-working politicians, on the other. Responses were recorded on a
four-point scale to avoid what Philip Converse (1995: xv) terms 'the
Problem of the Overstuffed Middle': respondents were forced to pick a
position (or else answer 'don't know'). The distribution of responses to
this question is reported in Figure 4.2. When forced to choose, most
people clearly plumped for having politicians who were honest, even
if they were less successful and hard-working. Over a third of our
respondents placed themselves at the extreme 'honesty' end of this
scale, with almost another third leaning in the same direction. Fewer
than in one-in-five respondents clearly indicated some preference for
having 'successful and hard-working' over honest politicians, and a
tiny proportion expressed the most extreme version of this view. It is
perhaps also worth remarking on the sizable minority of respondents
who chose not to answer this question: over 15 per cent responded
'don't know'.

In our second wave, which was fielded in autumn 2009, we posed a
slightly different question, which was designed to capture a similar
trade-off. To avoid the potential confusion that may have arisen in
some respondents' minds over the double-barrelled phrase 'successful
and hard-working', we asked respondents to balance the relative
importance of 'honesty' and politicians' ability to 'deliver the
goods'. We also asked our respondent to give their answer on a more

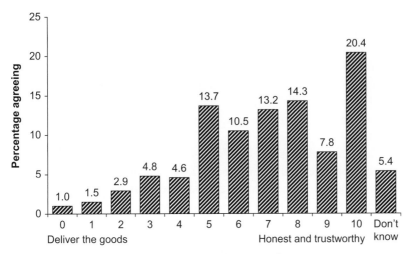

Figure 4.3 Deliver the goods or honest and trustworthy? autumn 2009
Note: The original wording of the question is included in the Appendix.

finely graded 0–10 scale, where 0 meant it was more important to have politicians who could deliver the goods and 10 meant it was more important to have very honest and trustworthy politicians. The distribution of responses is presented Figure 4.3, which is generally comparable to the distribution shown in Figure 4.2 (although the large number of respondents placing themselves in the middle is illustrative of Converse's point). As before, most people tended towards express-ing a preference for honesty, suggesting that this general preference is robust to variations in question wording: some 66.2 per cent of respondents located themselves to the right of the midpoint in Figure 4.3, compared with 67.5 per cent who did so in Figure 4.2. Most of those who indicated some preference for honesty over the ability to deliver the goods located themselves close to the midpoint, which suggested a reluctance to sacrifice probity for performance.

In order to explore the issue of what might explain the variation in preferences for honesty or performance, we go back to the same set of individual-level attributes that we introduced in the previous section, including age, gender, income, attentiveness to politics, par-tisanship and personal morals. Rather than presenting a table of mean scores broken down by personal attribute, we instead present the results of a multivariate regression model, which enables us to look at the independent effect of each explanatory factor while controlling for the impact of others. The dependent variable is the answer to the question reported in Figure 4.3. We focus on the second of our forced-choice questions, since the eleven-point scale used is more appropriate for ordinary least squares (OLS) regression and is more straightforward to interpret. Our independent variables are generally based on the same questions that structured the analysis in Table 4.1.[3]

The results are presented in Table 4.2; each coefficient represents the expected change on the eleven-point scale (where a higher score reflects a preference for honesty over competence) that would result from a one-point increase in the respective independent variable's unit of measurement. We start with the demographic variables. The gender variable, in keeping with much previous research, shows that men were significantly more likely to prefer delivery to honesty: simply being a man moved a respondent over half a point down the scale. Younger people, those under 35, were also significantly more likely to choose an ability to deliver the goods over honesty, in much the same way that younger people were less likely to expect politicians to behave according to higher standards than ordinary people. Among the socioeconomic variables, income exerted a weakly significant influence on expectations: having an income of over £40,000 slightly depressed preferences for honesty over competence. Among the other variables, three were statistically significant: a respondent's personal morality (their tolerance of ethically dubious behaviour in daily life), and identification with the Conservative and Liberal Democratic parties, all of which were associated with a greater preference for competence over honesty. As might be expected, moral laxity in private life is associated with a lesser demand for upright politicians, as is identification with what were then the main parties of opposition. The latter finding can perhaps be linked to a strong desire on the part of Conservative and Liberal Democratic partisans to see a change in the direction of policy-making after thirteen years of Labour rule.[4]

---

[3] Details of variable construction can be found in the Appendix. All the independent variables in this model are taken from the first (autumn 2009) wave of the survey, in order to minimise potential endogeneity.

[4] This model draws on a total sample of 791 autumn 2009 respondents, of which 161 (20.1 per cent) failed to respond to the income question. Given that the resulting model includes only 66 per cent of the respondents in the wave (once

Table 4.2 *Deliver the goods or honest and trustworthy? autumn 2009*

Variables	Coefficients
Gender: male	−0.55**
	(0.21)
Age: under 35	−1.16***
	(0.28)
Age: 55+	0.37
	(0.25)
Education: graduate	0.18
	(0.23)
Income: under £20,000	−0.02
	(0.24)
Income: £40,000+	−0.57*
	(0.26)
Personal ethical tolerance scale	−0.19***
	(0.06)
Attentiveness to public affairs	−0.03
	(0.11)
Conservative identifier	−0.70*
	(0.31)
Labour identifier	−0.28
	(0.31)
Liberal Democrat identifier	−0.90*
	(0.40)
Other party identifier	−0.36
	(0.37)
Constant	8.41
	(0.44)
Adjusted R^2	0.16
N	521

Notes: OLS regression.
* $p < 0.05$, ** $p < 0.01$, *** $p < 0.001$; cell entries are coefficients, standard errors are in parentheses.

small amounts of missing data on other variables are taken into consideration), we re-ran the model without the income variables. In this second model (not shown) the significance and magnitude of the other variables remains largely unchanged. The only noteworthy difference is that in this larger sample the variable designating age over 55 is significant ($p < 0.01$) with a magnitude of 0.59 (a finding that is consistent with expectations).

The tendency of most people to express a preference for honesty over competence when asked to choose between attributes a politician might possess is thus modulated by several factors. Yet before moving on it makes sense to pause in order to consider possible interpretations of this slightly odd finding. One might justifiably wonder whether most people 'really' want to be served by honest leaders even at the expense of effective service delivery, or whether their responses to this question simply represent frustration at what they see as poor behaviour by elites. The design of the research subtending our analysis does not allow us to provide an entirely conclusive answer to this question, but our mixed-methods approach is somewhat helpful in this regard. Certainly, when we probed our focus group participants on their responses to this question – which we had not anticipated would be so categorical – they were generally adamant in the view that honesty 'really' was what they preferred. There are several ways in which this reaction can be understood. It may be that it is a 'true' normative preference in the sense that, in an ideal world, this is what they would like, but that in practice they are often obliged to base their actions (including voting behaviour) on a more pragmatic set of considerations. Alternatively, it could be that most people have not thought through the implications of their stance, nor have they grappled with concrete 'dirty hands'-type scenarios. Finally, it might be that many people have a poor understanding of the job of a politician, believing most elected representatives to be mere 'lobby fodder', and failing to understand the need for political skill. Be that as it may, our research has provided clear evidence that most British people, when prompted, are willing to express a preference for elite honesty over competence.

Taking together all the evidence marshalled so far, it is clear that the British public expects a considerable degree of integrity from its politicians. There are variations in expectations, with older citizens and those with stricter personal moral codes expecting even higher levels of honesty from their representatives, but even the young and those with more permissive personal codes are quite demanding. We are obliged to conclude that most British people appear to want politicians to be 'whiter than white', even at the expense of performance.

'Black', 'white' and 'grey' conduct

Different people have different expectations about appropriate standards of conduct in political life. Some differences are more significant than others, however, and perhaps the most significant difference of all is one not discussed in the preceding section: the potential gulf between what citizens ask of politicians' conduct, on the one hand, and what politicians expect, on the other. From an outsider's perspective, there may well be an apparent consensus within a society as to what is considered right and what is considered wrong. If someone from a society where bribes and backhanders are part of everyday political life were to visit Britain, British voters and politicians alike could well appear to be entirely united in their rejection of such overt forms of corruption. Yet, upon closer attention, that same visitor might begin to notice subtle and perhaps not so subtle differences in specific ideas about appropriate conduct. The devil of political ethics lies in the detail.

The extent to which citizens and politicians share the same expectations and beliefs about appropriate conduct is an empirical question. In a famous contribution to the academic literature on political corruption, Arnold Heidenheimer (1970) proposed a simple typology of corruption on the basis of the interactions of mass and elite opinions. Corruption came in three monochrome colours: 'black', 'white' and 'grey'. When citizens and politicians alike agreed that behaviour was extremely improper, such conduct was deemed to be black. Alternatively, behaviour that was held to be marginally unethical by both elites and the public was deemed to be white. In between the objects of such agreement existed grey corruption, behaviour that only one of the groups felt to be extremely corrupt, but which the other did not. The notion that elites and masses will both be unified in their ethical orientations is hugely implausible, to which the variations already reported in this chapter bear witness. Moreover, Heidenheimer's typology extends only in the direction of foul play; when it comes to political ethics, the interaction between elite and mass opinion could usefully be extended in the other direction. After all, standards in public life address both sinning and doing good, and there may be general differences not only in what behaviour should be prohibited, but also in the conduct that is considered desirable and virtuous. Set within this context, 'white' conduct might more usefully be re-conceptualised as behaviour that both politicians and voters agree is extremely virtuous.

An emphasis on corruption and the 'foul play' side of things has dominated empirical research into politicians' and voters' beliefs about ethics. Within this comparatively small body of work, all the evidence suggests that there are often systematic differences in what politicians and citizens think is acceptable conduct. Thus, available comparative evidence indicates that political elites tend to be less critical than the general public of certain actions, notably favouritism (McAllister 2000; Atkinson and Bierling 2005). Such differences are thought to follow the development of elite norms and practices for dealing with the realities of political life and reflect a degree of elite socialisation (Jackson and Smith 1996; Rush and Giddings 2011). Elites are more likely to be tolerant of morally dubious behaviour and to subscribe to the 'dirty hands' view of politics as a business that requires 'hard choices' and at times unsavoury means to achieve the ends demanded by constituents. Citizens, by contrast, are prone to retain their more stringent and possibly even unrealistic expectations. Hence, as one Australian study concluded, 'for politicians, some scenarios are gray corruption; for voters, all are black' (Jackson and Smith 1996: 33).

The standard approach in the political science literature for exploring differences between politicians' and citizens' ethical values is to conduct surveys of both. In particular, it has become common to present different groups with identical descriptions of hypothetical behaviour and ask them to judge what they see (see, *inter alia*, Welch and Peters 1977; Peters and Welch 1978; Jackson and Smith 1996; Atkinson and Bierling 2005). The obvious advantage of this approach is that it enables researchers to measure different groups' direct response to the same information. It is also an approach that we have used and reported on in greater detail elsewhere (see Allen and Birch 2012). For our present purposes, a short summary of our methods and findings will suffice. In essence, we included in our first survey, which was fielded in autumn 2009, nine hypothetical scenarios (see Table 4.3) that had earlier been included on the 2005 British Representation Study (BRS), a survey of candidates who stood for election in the 2005 general election. These scenarios were themselves adapted from an earlier study of MPs' ethical beliefs (Mancuso 1995). All respondents, whether voters or candidates, were asked how corrupt they felt each scenario was. Their responses were recorded on a seven-point scale, where 1 represented 'corrupt' and 7 represented 'not corrupt'. Because the 2005 BRS questionnaire was sent to all candidates, including incumbent MPs seeking re-election, it was also possible to disaggregate 'elite' opinion further into MPs and other candidates.

Table 4.3 *Hypothetical scenarios of ethically ambiguous behaviour*

Scenario	Description given to respondents
Campaign	A cabinet minister promises an appointed position in exchange for campaign contributions.
Contract	A cabinet minister uses his or her influence to obtain a contract for a firm in his or her constituency.
Gift	At Christmas, an MP accepts a crate of wine from an influential constituent.
Honour	A major company makes a substantial donation to the government party. Later, the chair of the company is given an honour.
Planning	A local councillor, while chair of the planning committee, authorises planning permission for property owned by him or her.
Retainer	An MP is retained by a major company to arrange meetings and dinners in the House of Commons at which its executives can meet parliamentarians.
School	An MP uses his or her position to get a friend or relative admitted to Oxford or Cambridge, or some other prestigious institution.
Secretary	An MP hires a spouse or other family member to serve as his or her secretary.
Travel	An MP is issued a first-class airline ticket as part of a parliamentary delegation. He or she exchanges the ticket for an economy fare and pockets the difference.

Note: Adapted from Mancuso (1995).

Table 4.4 reports responses to the various scenarios ranked by the percentage of voters who said that the act was corrupt, interpreted as a score of 1, 2 or 3 on the seven-point scale (Mancuso 1995). Table 4.4 also reports the corresponding responses of candidates and incumbent MPs. Looking across the columns, we can see a clear consensus in respect of some of the acts. For example, when it comes to the chair of a council's planning committee authorising planning permission for property owned by him or her (Planning), or a cabinet minister promising an appointed position in exchange for campaign contributions (Campaign), or an MP helping to get a friend or relative admitted to Oxford or Cambridge (School), or an MP exchanging a first-class ticket for an economy fare and pocketing the difference (Travel), there is virtual unanimity among politicians and citizens alike that the acts described were corrupt. For each of these scenarios, about nine out of

Table 4.4 *Percentage of public, candidates and MPs saying each scenario is corrupt*

	Public (%)	Candidates (%)	MPs (%)
Planning	95.7	97.0	97.8
Campaign	93.4	97.5	97.9
School	90.2	92.4	89.6
Honour	91.0	80.2	63.0
Travel	88.2	90.2	93.6
Contract	75.6	66.3	66.7
Retainer	71.8	70.0	57.4
Secretary	54.2	16.0	15.2
Gift	52.2	36.6	34.8

Note: The data are based on a weighted sample of voters, MPs and candidates that brings together 2005 British Representation Study data and our own.

ten respondents judged the behaviour to be corrupt. The behaviour was consistently recognised by all respondents as breaching widely held normative standards prohibiting blatant self-serving conduct and using public office to advance narrow private interests.

On the other five scenarios, opinion was more obviously divided. Each of these scenarios described an act that the public generally said was a good deal more corrupt than did politicians. They also described acts on which there was a degree of inter-elite disagreement. Indeed, for two of the scenarios, those referring to the chair of a company being given an honour (Honour) and an MP being retained to arrange meetings and dinners in the House of Commons (Retainer), there were considerable differences. Incumbent MPs were much less likely than other candidates to describe as corrupt a party donor being honoured – a gap of over 17 percentage points – and an MP being retained to organise dinners – a gap of over 12 percentage points.

The discrepancy between citizens and politicians was especially marked when it came to the situations describing an MP hiring a spouse or other family member to serve as his or her secretary (Secretary) and an MP accepting a crate of wine from an influential constituent (Gift). In both cases the public was divided, but a small majority rated the act as corrupt. The politicians surveyed were for the most part unwilling to describe these acts as corrupt. As such, these were the only two scenarios that might be understood as constituting 'grey' corruption within Heidenheimer's typology. The actions described in these two scenarios represent potential, if ambiguous, conflicts of interest, so it is not even the case that members of the public are subscribing to a broader conception of corruption in these instances. Clearly, most candidates and MPs did not see anything particularly untoward in an MP accepting a small gift from a constituent when there was suggestion of a quid pro quo. Meanwhile, the employment of spouses and other relatives, though occasionally controversial, has long been common practice among politicians. While some elites clearly disapprove of the practice, most do not regard it to be corrupt. What we appear to be witnessing with these examples is simply a tendency among members of the British public to describe as unacceptable conflicts of interest that most members of the political elite would not see as problematic.

There are a number of possible reasons for such discrepancies (see Allen and Birch 2012). It may, for example, be that politicians and other citizens have different 'everyday' understandings of right and wrong that colour their view of ethical matters in politics. Or it may be that politicians acquire a different view of the scope and aims of politics and their own role in the polity, which might then imply different views of what is appropriate conduct. Finally, politicians may form different understandings of what is practical in political life, given the various demands placed upon them and the rewards they are given for their labours. All of these potential differences in perspective and expectations may combine to yield wide discrepancies in what is expected of politicians and what is held to be acceptable conduct on their part.

We finish this chapter, however, by presaging the focus of the next. In particular, we look to ascertain whether there were any systematic differences in how members of the public judged the scenarios reported in Table 4.3. A principal component analysis of responses to the nine scenarios suggested two underlying factors structuring responses.[5] Five of the scenarios – Travel, Campaign, School, Honour and Planning – loaded on the first factor, with the other four – Retainer, Secretary, Gift and Contract – loading on the second. The obvious theme underpinning the two dimensions seems to be the degree of ethical ambiguity

---

[5] The first factor explained 28 per cent of the variance in the data; the second factor explained 22 per cent.

inherent in each. The first dimension covers the first five rows in Table 4.4, the second dimension the bottom four rows. To put yet another spin on Heidenheimer's typology, it seems that some conduct can be considered 'black' if public opinion is unanimous about its impropriety, and other conduct can be considered 'grey' when there is much less of a consensus.

By creating composite scales that bring together the 'black' and the 'grey' scenarios, as defined solely on the basis of citizens' responses, it becomes possible to see whether there are any systematic differences in how members of the public responded to more or less ambiguous conduct and what individual-level factors were driving their evaluations. To this end, we first created two additive scales, which we standardised on a 1–7 scale where 1 denoted less corrupt and 7 more corrupt (we inverted the original scale). The first of the new scales, which we term 'grey' conduct, was the sum of responses to the Retainer, Secretary, Gift and Contract scenarios divided by four. The second scale, which we term 'black conduct', was the sum of responses to the Travel, Campaign, School, Honour and Planning scenarios divided by five.[6] Our next step was to model these two scales using OLS regression and the same predictor variables that we employed in Table 4.2. The results of the analysis are reported in Table 4.5.[7]

What is immediately apparent from the two models is that lax personal ethics was associated with a lesser tendency to label both 'grey' and 'black' behaviours corrupt (as it was preferences for competence over honesty in Table 4.3). Yet there were also notable differences in the models for grey and black conduct. The only other factor with a significant association with evaluations of grey conduct was low income, with those whose household incomes fell below the £20,000 mark being somewhat more critical of ambiguous conduct. By contrast, gender and age (but not income) were associated with evaluations of black conduct. Men and younger people tended to take a less stringent stance on generally accepted corrupt behaviour, whereas women and those over 35 tended to be more damning in their judgements. These findings herald points to which we will return in later chapters.

---

[6] The first scale had a Cronbach's alpha of 0.62, which suggested questionable internal reliability by conventional standards, but we proceeded on the basis of the underlying theory. The second scale had a Cronbach's alpha of 0.73, which suggests acceptable internal reliability.

[7] A pair of regressions based on factor scores yielded broadly similar results.

Table 4.5 *Explaining responses to 'grey' and 'black' conduct, spring 2009*

	'Grey' conduct	'Black' conduct
Gender: male	−0.12	−0.13*
	(0.09)	(0.05)
Age: under 35	−0.23	−0.22***
	(0.12)	(0.07)
Age: 55+	−0.06	0.02
	(0.11)	(0.06)
Education: graduate	−0.01	−0.00
	(0.10)	(0.06)
Income: under £20,000	0.40***	0.10
	(0.11)	(0.06)
Income: £40,000+	0.07	0.08
	(0.11)	(0.06)
Personal ethical tolerance scale	−0.07**	−0.12***
	(0.03)	(0.01)
Attentiveness to public affairs	−0.03	0.04
	(0.05)	(0.03)
Conservative identifier	−0.26	−0.05
	(0.14)	(0.08)
Labour identifier	−0.24	−0.06
	(0.14)	(0.08)
Liberal Democrat identifier	−0.20	−0.19
	(0.18)	(0.10)
Other party identifier	0.18	0.03
	(0.17)	(0.09)
Constant	5.27	6.60
	(0.19)	(0.11)
Adjusted R^2	0.05	0.15
N	797	830

Notes: OLS regression.
* $p < 0.05$,** $p < 0.01$,*** $p < 0.001$; cell entries are coefficients, standard errors are in parentheses.

Conclusion

Differences in expectations, both among citizens and especially between citizen and their elected representatives, may have important consequences. In contemporary British politics, such differences almost certainly help to explain why citizens hold their politicians in such low esteem. It is impossible to please everyone all of the time, but if there are significant differences in what people expect, it may become much harder for elites to be, or even appear to be, responsive to citizens' concerns. The evidence presented in this chapter shows clearly that Britons expect high standards of conduct from their politicians, and that this tendency is most pronounced among those who hold themselves to a high moral bar. For many members of the public, being a politician carries with it an additional set of obligations to those placed on citizens in everyday life. In this respect, citizens' expectations are largely in keeping with elite-level norms about the distinctiveness of public office. At the same time, the evidence also suggests that citizens' expectations are sometimes at odds with politicians' own. Not only is the public's understanding of what constitutes ethical behaviour more all-encompassing than that generally understood by politicians and other elites, but the public is also more critical in their judgements of behaviour that falls within the traditional bounds of conflict of interest. Coming to terms with variations in how people understand political ethics and what they expect of their politicians is a necessary step on the road to understanding fully how citizens judge political conduct. The task of the next chapter is to explore this process in greater detail.

5 | *How people judge political conduct*

T HE DECISION has to be made in the best interests of the people, not the politicians.

(Male focus group participant, Egham)

In the previous chapter we found that the British public is a demanding master, holding its elected representatives to very high standards. In this chapter we consider how members of the public go about the task of evaluating political conduct in practice and how their judgements are affected by the information to which they are exposed. Our starting point is the somewhat puzzling observation that most people appear to have little difficulty making up their mind about politicians. Though the vast majority of the public has almost no direct contact with elite politics or experience of what the day-to-day job of an MP, or minister or any other elected politician involves, they nevertheless find the task of judging the behaviour of political actors relatively straightforward. We are so used to reading about survey results on confidence in politicians that this fact does not at first seem extraordinary. But on further thought, the facility with which people judge their leaders' professional actions is rather odd, given the many unusual features of political roles and the complex challenges faced by those who perform them. The analyses presented in this chapter are devoted to understanding aspects of how ordinary members of the public go about this task.

Since political conduct and misconduct is largely mediated, it is crucial to understand just how information reaches people. One piece of the puzzle is how the information presented to people shapes responses. The other piece is the way the mass media 'mediate' the information people employ to make up their minds. This chapter is structured around these two themes. It first considers how common norms shape and frame ethical evaluations, drawing on three survey experiments that enabled us to manipulate precisely the information that respondents received. It then considers how the source of information affects reactions to ambiguous actions undertaken by politicians, using some of the data on acts of 'grey' corruption with which we were familiarised in Chapter 4.

Political norms

Chapter 3 detailed a variety of traditions through which political life in Britain has developed. The focus group evidence in Chapter 4 then showed how these traditions are reflected in the sort of things people say about politics and politicians when asked to discuss their attitudes. The traditions we have discussed can be translated into a series of discrete norms that are commonly employed to make sense of political conduct and misconduct. From the analysis in the previous two chapters, we distil three particularly salient norms that recur repeatedly: role-specific norms; the norm of legality; and the norm of public benefit. Despite the conceptual gap we have established between popular and elite conceptions of the scope of political ethics, these three broad norms can be expected to be shared by both groups alike. Let us examine each of these in turn.

Role-specific norms

The first strategy for evaluating political conduct is to understand ethical misconduct as deviation from a given role.[1] As shown in Chapter 3, arguably the most important norm guiding elite conduct in the British context is what Thompson (1995) terms 'independence', or avoidance of conflict of interest: representatives should act in the public interest, which should be placed above and kept at a distance from personal or partisan interests.

Legality

The norms of law and rule conformity represent a common-sense approach to standards in public life. Conforming with laws and conforming with rules are arguably two distinct norms, since the law, the sum of measures passed by publicly accountable bodies, has an

---

[1] Several previous empirical studies of ethical reasoning have also put emphasis on role-specific norms (Dolan *et al.* 1988; Alvarez and Brehm 2002; Redlawsk and McCann 2005).

authority that exceeds normal institutional rules. Nevertheless, we view them here as one, since the distinction between law-breaking and rule-breaking involves differences of degree rather than differences of kind. The important common denominator is that behaviour should accord with that which is written down.[2]

One might view the legality norm as a baseline approach that requires little active judgement. In this sense it might even be seen as morally neutral, as it does not invoke the moral principles of the individual employing it, save the basic principle of rule of law. It is also noteworthy that individuals accused of impropriety in public life sometimes defend their actions on the basis that they acted within existing rules. For example, a number of MPs caught up in the expenses scandal of 2009 used legalistic arguments to defend their expenses claims. One MP, the Employment Minister Tony McNulty, defended his conduct by noting that 'It's not against the rules', though he was candid enough to add 'though I suppose you might say that is the Nuremberg defence' (Watt 2009).

Public benefit

A third common lens through which the actions of politicians are viewed in the media is constituency benefit or benefit to the general public. According to this norm, politicians are expected to deliver public goods, either for their own parliamentary constituents or another group or interest that they represent. Actions which bring substantive benefits to a large number of people are perhaps more likely to be viewed in a favourable light. This approach has a long lineage, and is perhaps most commonly and obviously associated with the political left, though in the British context it also chimes within certain strands of One Nation Toryism, which is based on a sense of *noblesse oblige* (Leach 2009). This approach might also be termed distributional, in that the ethics of a particular situation are evaluated on the basis of *cui bono*. An act of partiality that benefits a deprived

---

[2] Yet, as with all rules of thumb, such a judgement may not lead to the 'right' answer (Kuklinski and Quirk 1998). In this instance, judgements drawing on rules could be biased, since rules can be bad. Judgements drawing on laws could also be biased, since laws can be bad too. As many others have pointed out, corruption and illegality are not the same thing; the corruption of politics can proceed through the law.

sector of society will be evaluated differently from the same act that would benefit a rich group. If the behaviour in question brings substantive benefits to otherwise deprived groups, the behaviour might be condoned even if it involves minor breaches of the law or role-specific norms.[3]

Evidence of the work of norms

To test the role of norms in shaping evaluations of ethically ambiguous political conduct, we fielded three survey experiments in the autumn 2009 wave of the B/CCAP. Experimental techniques are being used increasingly frequently in political science (Margetts and Stoker 2010); but they have not yet (to our knowledge) been used by scholars of British political ethics. Our experiments took the form of vignettes, each of which included a description of an action taken by a politician. Respondents were required to judge the propriety of the behaviour described. A control group was provided with only the basic scenario, and eight treatment groups were each presented with different combinations of additional information designed to reflect the three norms hypothesised to condition ethical reasoning: approaches based on legal, role-specific and public-benefit norms.

The information pertaining to role-specific norms reflected either a lack of conflict of interest or politically motivated manipulation of the situation (version A), or an implied conflict of interest or politically motivated manipulation (version B). The information pertaining to the norm of law conformity was presented in such a way that one version of the vignette (version A in Tables 5.1(a), 5.1(b) and 5.1(c)) suggested that the action in question conformed to legal and other codes to which politicians are subject, and the other version (B) signalled clear law- or rule-breaking. The information about the scale of the public benefit reflected either an outcome that suggested that the action taken was justified on the basis of its consequences (version A) or suggested that the action was unjustified or motivated by considerations of gain for those represented (version B).

The three vignettes were designed to reflect three different types of ethically ambiguous behaviour that occur in political life and may be

---

[3] Some previous studies of attitudes towards political ethics have found that the identity of those who benefit from the actions of a politician and the nature of the benefit received affects judgements of that action (Chibnall and Saunders 1977; Johnston 1986, 1991; Dolan *et al.* 1988; Frohlich and Oppenheimer 2000).

Table 5.1(a) *Structure of vignette 1's experimental manipulations*

Former minister Bill Lane, who recently left the government, is employed by a consultancy company, which successfully bids for a lucrative government contract ...

Manipulations	Versions	Hypothesis
Legality norm	A: Before taking up the consultancy post, Lane first sought the advice of the government's Advisory Committee on Business Appointments, which decided the new job was acceptable. B: Lane first sought, but then ignored, the advice of the government's Advisory Committee on Business Appointments, which said he should not take the job, and took up the consultancy post anyway.	Behaviour more corrupt when Lane ignored the Committee's advice.
Role-specific norm	A: During the bidding process, Lane spent a lot of time talking to his friends still in government. B: During the bidding process, Lane took great care to avoid any contact with his friends still in government.	Behaviour more corrupt when Lane talked to his friends still in government.
Public-benefit norm	A: Lane's consultancy company won the contract with a bid that was the cheapest and represented the best value for money for the taxpayer. B: Lane's consultancy company won the contract, even though its bid was the most expensive and did not represent the best value for money for the taxpayer.	Behaviour more corrupt when the winning bid was the most expensive.

reported in the news: employing political connections for personal gain (vignette 1);[4] politically motivated favouritism or cronyism at public expense (vignette 2); and politically motivated decision making at

---

[4] In a recent paper, Andrew Eggers and Jens Hainmueller (2009) have demonstrated that some MPs (particularly those who have sat on the Tory benches) have indeed added considerably to their personal wealth through activities of this sort.

Table 5.1(b) *Structure of vignette 2's experimental manipulations*

MP Susan Barnes helps a firm whose headquarters is in her constituency ...

Manipulations	Versions	Hypothesis
Legality norm	A: Barnes writes a letter to the Minister for Trade and Industry asking the minister to intervene to save the firm. B: Barnes shows the firm confidential government documents that give it a competitive advantage. In so doing she breaches the Official Secrets Act.	Behaviour more corrupt when Barnes breaks the law
Role-specific norm	A: The firm has for several years made regular donations to Barnes' party. B: The firm has never made any donations either to Barnes or to her party.	Behaviour more corrupt when firm has made donations to party
Public-benefit norm	A: Closure of the firm would result in the loss of 1,200 jobs. B: Closure of the firm would result in the loss of twelve jobs.	Behaviour more corrupt when fewer jobs at risk

public expense (vignette 3). The first vignette involved a former minister, the second involved a sitting MP, and the third an incumbent minister. The three scenarios thus reflect variation in the types of actor involved, the actions involved, and the level at which the action takes place (there are also a number of other variations in the information contained in the supplementary cues, the consequences of which will be discussed below).

The baseline information provided in the first vignette was the following: 'Former minister Bill Lane, who recently left the government, is employed by a consultancy company, which successfully bids for a lucrative government contract.' To test the law-conformity heuristic, respondents not in the control group were told: 'Before

Table 5.1(c) *Structure of vignette 3's experimental manipulations*

In the run-up to a general election, engineers discover that a small amount of radioactive material has leaked into the ground from a military installation. The Minister of Defence issues a 'gagging order' preventing publication of details of the leak ...

Manipulations	Versions	Hypothesis
Legality norm	A: The minister acts in full accordance with standard departmental procedures. B: The minister acts in total disregard for standard departmental procedures.	Behaviour more corrupt when minister disregards procedures.
Role-specific norm	A: The manufacture of nuclear weapons at this site is a major issue in the election campaign. B: The manufacture of nuclear weapons at this site is central to the nation's defence policy.	Behaviour more corrupt when nuclear weapons are an election issue.
Public-benefit norm	A: The leak is a risk to public health. B: The leak is very small and represents no risk to public health whatsoever.	Behaviour more corrupt when the leak is a risk to public health.

taking up the consultancy post, Lane first sought the advice of the government's Advisory Committee on Business Appointments, which decided the new job was acceptable/unacceptable.' The importance of perceptions of role-specific norms in shaping judgements was probed by providing additional information on the minister's willingness to manipulate his political contacts: 'During the bidding process, Lane took great care to avoid any contact with his friends still in government'; or 'During the bidding process, Lane spent a lot of time talking to his friends still in government'. Finally, the relevance of the size of any public benefit was operationalised by means of the following pair of contrasting statements: 'Lane's consultancy company won the contract with a bid that was the cheapest and represented the best value for money for the taxpayer'; or 'Lane's consultancy company won the contract, even though its bid was the most expensive and did not represent the best value for money for the taxpayer.'

The second vignette centred on the conduct of 'MP Susan Barnes' who 'helps a firm whose headquarters is in her constituency'. The importance of legality considerations in this instance was explored by telling respondents either that: 'Barnes writes a letter to the Minister for Trade and Industry asking the minister to intervene to save the firm'; or that 'Barnes shows the firm confidential government documents that give it a competitive advantage. In so doing she breaches the Official Secrets Act'. The extent to which role-specific norms were a factor in shaping judgements was measured by varying whether there was a partisan benefit surrounding the MPs' actions: 'The firm has never made any donations either to Barnes or to her party'; or 'The firm has for several years made regular donations to Barnes' party'. The importance of the wider public benefit was manipulated by telling respondents that: 'Closure of the firm would result in the loss of 1,200/twelve jobs'.

The third vignette revolved around the following scenario: 'In the run-up to a general election, engineers discover that a small amount of radioactive material has leaked into the ground from a military installation. The Minister of Defence issues a "gagging order" preventing publication of details of the leak.' Additional information designed to test the importance of the law-conformity norm took the form of two alternative statements: 'The minister acts in full accordance with standard departmental procedures'; or 'The minister acts in total disregard for standard departmental procedures'. Role-specific considerations were manipulated in two statements, one that implied the minister was acting for the government on behalf of the country, the other that the minister was engaging in party politics: 'The manufacture of nuclear weapons at this site is central to the nation's defence policy'; or 'The manufacture of nuclear weapons at this site is a major issue in the election campaign'. Finally, information about the public benefit was varied by telling respondents that: 'The leak is very small and represents no risk to public health whatsoever'; or 'The leak is a risk to public health'.

The various permutations of these alternatives resulted in eight different treatments in addition to the control. The sample was allocated at random to one of the nine groups. Before we report how participants in our survey responded to these vignettes, however, it is worth noting how some of our focus group participants responded to them. Rather than presenting different versions of the vignettes to the group, we introduced the scenarios and gradually provided further information, asking participants to reflect on the information. Their reactions gave us confidence that the various manipulations prompted the sort of normative considerations we were interested in testing.

In one of our Egham focus groups, for example, the moderator first introduced the 'MP Susan Barnes' vignette, telling the group: 'She helps a firm, based in her constituency. Is that right or wrong?' One male participant noted: 'if they are in her constituency, and it is right and proper, of course she should', and another added that creating jobs for her constituents 'should be part of her role'. At the same time, the group was generally clear that the MP's role was one of serving the public and not herself: one man wanted to 'make sure she does not have any personal gains herself', and another man said the action might be okay 'as long as she's not gaining from it'. When the group was asked if Barnes' writing a letter to the Trade and Industry Minister, asking him to intervene to save the firm made any difference, it was pointed out that 'she's representing her constituents … it's part of her job'. Such contributions suggested that the vignette did indeed prompt role-specific considerations.

Other responses from the same group also gave us confidence that the vignette was prompting judgements based on normative considerations of public benefit and legality. Following the initial discussion just described, the moderator asked the group to 'imagine that the firm has, for years, made donations to her party. Does that affect your judgement?' One male participant immediately suggested the need to consider what help Barnes provides to the firm: 'If the help encourages the business to create more jobs in the area, maybe it's not an issue. But if the firm influences the lawmaking process for *its* benefit, there will be a query.' Another added: 'maybe other companies in that constituency donated to the party because people voted that way, and she helped them all. Then it's ok. But if they're the only ones, then you might see more of a problem.'

The moderator then provided one further piece of information to the group: 'imagine now that Barnes shows the firm confidential government documents, which give it a competitive advantage, so breaching the Official Secrets Act. Does that affect your judgement?' One of the women participants immediately answered with reference to the legality of the MP's actions: 'certainly, if it breaks the rules and regulations'. Another woman added straight away: 'it relates back to the moral standing of the person. They should at least obey the rules . . . if nobody obeyed the rules, society would go wild.' She was followed up by a man who alighted on the fact that Barnes had 'access to that information, it's her moral and legal obligation to make sure that it is secure. To take advantage of it is wrong.'

How did survey respondents respond to our vignettes? After being shown a version of each of the vignettes, respondents were asked to evaluate the acceptability of the action of the politician on a scale of 0 to 10. They were then asked two comprehension questions in order to test that the vignettes were understood by the respondents in the intended way.[5] Respondents were also asked to evaluate how 'corrupt' the action of the politician was on a scale of 0–10, as we were interested in knowing to what extent ethical acceptability equated in the popular mind with corruption, or whether respondents distinguished between actions that were unacceptable, but nonetheless were not 'corrupt'. Corruption is, of course, a contested concept, but the notion of corruption, though problematic, confronts individuals with the starkest of ethical judgements about what is right and wrong in the practice of democratic politics.

---

[5] For the three scenarios, we asked respondents: (i) whether Lane had broken official rules before taking up the consultancy post; (ii) whether Barnes had broken the law when she helped the firm; and (iii) whether the Minister of Defence correctly followed departmental procedures. In all three cases, the mean evaluation of each scenario was significantly more unacceptable ($p < 0.001$) for those responding that the rules or law had been broken, suggesting that the respondents were correctly influenced by this experimental manipulation. For the Lane scenario, we also asked respondents whether they thought Lane's personal contacts in government were a major factor in his company winning the contract, to test whether or not there was an appropriate manipulation of the scenario in terms of key decision makers performing their role in the public interest. The scenario was significantly more unacceptable ($p < 0.001$) among those who thought Lane's personal contacts were a major factor. Similarly, the mean evaluation of the ministerial gagging order scenario was also significantly more unacceptable ($p < 0.001$) among those who thought the minister was motivated by electoral considerations. In both cases, the results suggest respondents were appropriately influenced by the manipulations. Finally, we tested the appropriateness of the public-benefit manipulation in the Barnes scenario by asking respondents whether the firm's fate would greatly affect the local economy or not. Those who thought the fate of the firm would greatly affect the local economy found the scenario significantly less unacceptable ($p < 0.001$), which, one again indicated that respondents were being appropriately influenced by the experimental manipulation.

The many differences between the situations presented in the vignettes preclude precise comparisons of normative effects; in other words, direct comparison of reactions to a violation of the Official Secrets Act and violation of the norm that politicians should not give preferential treatment to party donors is not possible due to the inevitable variations in intensity of reaction elicited by different pieces of contextual information. Nevertheless, if we see patterns emerging across diverse scenarios, we can have more confidence that variations in responses reflect differential propensities to respond to the norms invoked by the informational cues contained in the vignettes. It is to this type of analysis that we now turn.

Results

The results of these experiments illustrate key features of citizens' normative beliefs and how they judge political conduct. An overview of responses to the question on the 'acceptability' of a politician's actions is presented in Tables 5.2(a), 5.2(b) and 5.2(c). The results strongly suggest that all three of the norms identified are employed by respondents in evaluating the ethical conduct of politicians, and in all cases the results are in the expected direction: respondents judge a politician's action to be less acceptable when it violates legality, role-specific and public-benefit based norms. Moreover, the accumulation of violations is associated in all three cases with a monotonic increase in perceived deviation from acceptability. Those actions that simultaneously violate all three norms are judged most severely, with mean scores of 8.0, 8.3 and 8.2 in vignettes 1 (former minister Lane holds consultancy), 2 (MP Barnes helps firm) and 3 (Minister of Defence issues gagging order), respectively. Meanwhile, those actions without any suggestion of norm violation are least likely to be judged unacceptable by respondents, with mean scores of 4.4, 3.0 and 5.3 for the three respective vignettes.

The results based on the question of the 'corruptness' of a politician's actions, presented in Tables 5.3(a), 5.3(b) and 5.3(c), are in most respects similar, though the variations between categories are smaller. The scenarios in which all three norms are violated received mean scores of 7.1 (former minister Lane holds consultancy), 7.3 (MP Barnes helps firm) and 7.9 (Minister of Defence issues gagging order). The corresponding scores for the scenarios in which

Table 5.2(a) *Effects of scenario characteristics on 'unacceptability' of former minister Lane's actions in vignette 1*

Scenario version	Lane spent a lot of time talking to his friends still in government	Lane avoided contact with his friends still in government
The Advisory Committee on Business Appointments ruled ...		
The new job was acceptable	6.9 (0.23) N = 149	5.1 (0.22) N = 183
Lane should not take the job.	7.6 (0.19) N = 188	6.9 (0.18) N = 187
The contract was ...		
The cheapest and represented the best value for money for the taxpayer	6.9 (0.21) N = 163	5.3 (0.19) N = 202
The most expensive and did not represent the best value for money for the taxpayer	7.6 (0.20) N = 174	6.9 (0.21) N = 167
Advisory Committee ruling and contract		
Job was acceptable, contract was best value	6.5 (0.32) N = 68	4.3 (0.27) N = 103
Job was acceptable, contract was not best value	7.3 (0.31) N = 81	6.1 (0.33) N = 80
Should not take the job, contract was best value	7.2 (0.27) N = 95	6.2 (0.25) N = 99
Should not take the job, contract was not best value	8.0 (0.25) N = 93	7.63 (0.22) N = 88

Notes: Mean score, 0–10 scale.
Mean responses for treatment groups. Lower scores indicate that respondents found vignette more unacceptable. Values in parentheses are standard errors.

the manipulations were aligned to suggest no violation of any of the three norms were 4.9, 3.1 and 5.0.

Together, these findings suggest that even in their most benign forms, actions commonly carried out by politicians are judged by many

Table 5.2(b) *Effects of scenario characteristics on 'unacceptability' of MP Susan Barnes' actions in vignette 2*

Scenario version	Firm made regular donations to party	Firm never made donations
Legality of Barnes' actions		
Writes a letter to minister	5.0 (0.21)	3.5 (0.23)
	N = 161	N = 175
Breaches Official Secrets Act	8.0 (0.18)	7.8 (0.21)
	N = 215	N = 165
Closure of the firm would result in . . .		
The loss of 1,200 jobs	6.5 (0.23)	5.3 (0.29)
	N = 191	N = 166
The loss of twelve jobs	7.0 (0.21)	5.9 (0.26)
	N = 185	N = 175
Legality and consequences of closure		
Writes a letter, 1,200 jobs at stake	4.9 (0.29)	3.0 (0.30)
	N = 84	N = 84
Writes a letter, twelve jobs at stake	5.0 (0.29)	4.0 (0.32)
	N = 77	N = 91
Breaks law, 1,200 jobs at stake	7.7 (0.29)	7.6 (0.34)
	N = 107	N = 82
Breaks law, twelve jobs at stake	8.3 (0.20)	7.9 (0.27)
	N = 108	N = 83

Notes: Mean score, 0–10 scale.
Mean responses for treatment groups. Lower scores indicate respondents found vignette more unacceptable. Values in parentheses are standard errors.

members of the public as somewhat dubious, even corrupt. However, people do respond systematically to additional informational cues, and the variations in response accord with our predictions as to the effects of different norm violations.

In order to obtain a more precise picture of the relative impact of the different norms on patterns of ethical judgement, we carried out a multivariate analysis of evaluations of the 'acceptability' and 'corruptness' of the politicians' actions in each of the three vignettes. In each case, respondents were coded according to whether they received a 'positive' or 'negative' version of each vignette, and these codings were used to create the independent variables of interest.

Table 5.2(c) *Effects of scenario characteristics on 'unacceptability' of Minister of Defence's actions in vignette 3*

Scenario version	Issue in election campaign	Central to nation's defence
Abidance by rules		
Acts in accordance with rules	6.8 (0.22)	6.2 (0.21)
	N = 170	N = 188
Acts in total disregard for rules	7.7 (0.20)	6.9 (0.17)
	N = 182	N = 169
Risk to public health		
Leak is no risk whatsoever	6.5 (0.22)	5.9 (0.23)
	N = 179	N = 176
Leak is a risk	8.0 (0.19)	7.2 (0.20)
	N = 175	N = 181
Following rules and risk to public health		
Follows rules, leak is no risk	6.0 (0.29)	5.3 (0.31)
	N = 95	N = 92
Follows rules, leak is a risk	7.8 (0.31)	7.1 (0.27)
	N = 75	N = 96
Disregards rules, leak is no risk	7.1 (0.32)	6.5 (0.33)
	N = 84	N = 84
Disregards rules, leak is a risk	8.2 (0.24)	7.3 (0.30)
	N = 99	N = 85

Notes: Mean score, 0–10 scale.
Mean responses for treatment groups. Lower scores indicate respondents found vignette more unacceptable. Values in parentheses are standard errors.

These variables were entered into a number of regression models, together with relevant interaction terms, as is conventional in the analysis of factorial vignettes of this type. Since the dependent variables in all cases take the form of a 0–10 scale, we use OLS regression.

The models presented in Table 5.4 show the impact of normative considerations on the acceptability of political conduct among our survey respondents. The results largely confirm the results of the bivariate analyses reported above. Though not all the coefficients achieve conventional levels of statistical significance, ethical

Table 5.3(a) *Effects of scenario characteristics on 'corruptness' of former minister Lane's actions in vignette 1*

Scenario version	Lane spent a lot of time talking to his friends still in government	Lane avoided contact with his friends still in government
The Advisory Committee on Business Appointments ruled ...		
The new job was acceptable	6.4 (0.20) $N = 149$	5.3 (0.17) $N = 183$
Lane should not take the job	7.0 (0.17) $N = 188$	6.4 (0.17) $N = 187$
The contract was ...		
The cheapest and represented the best value for money for the taxpayer.	6.4 (0.19) $N = 163$	5.5 (0.16) $N = 202$
The most expensive and did not represent the best value for money for the taxpayer	7.0 (0.18) $N = 174$	6.4 (0.19) $N = 167$
Advisory Committee ruling and contract		
Job was acceptable, contract was best value	5.9 (0.29) $N = 68$	4.9 (0.21) $N = 103$
Job was acceptable, contract was not best value	6.9 (0.28) $N = 81$	6.0 (0.27) $N = 80$
Should not take the job, contract was best value	6.8 (0.24) $N = 95$	6.2 (0.22) $N = 99$
Should not take the job, contract was not best value	7.1 (0.25) $N = 93$	6.7 (0.26) $N = 88$

Notes: Mean score, 0–10 scale.
Mean responses for treatment groups. Lower scores indicate respondents found vignette more corrupt. Values in parentheses are standard errors.

judgements are found to be conditioned by all three norms. Variations in context from vignette to vignette are reflected in the different weight attached to the different informational cues. The strongest reaction is elicited by 'MP Susan Barnes' when she is described as having violated

Table 5.3(b) *Effects of scenario characteristics on 'corruptness' of MP Susan Barnes' actions in vignette 2*

Scenario version	Firm made regular donations to party	Firm never made donations
Legality of Barnes' actions		
Writes a letter to minister.	4.9 (0.18)	3.4 (0.21)
	N = 161	N = 175
Breaches Official Secrets Act	7.5 (0.17)	7.0 (0.22)
	N = 215	N = 165
Closure of the firm would result in …		
The loss of 1,200 jobs	6.4 (0.20)	5.1 (0.26)
	N = 191	N = 166
The loss of twelve jobs	6.3 (0.20)	5.2 (0.25)
	N = 185	N = 175
Legality and consequences of closure		
Writes a letter, 1,200 jobs at stake	4.8 (0.26)	3.1 (0.30)
	N = 84	N = 84
Writes a letter, twelve jobs at stake	4.9 (0.25)	3.6 (0.29)
	N = 77	N = 91
Breaks law, 1,200 jobs at stake	7.6 (0.22)	7.2 (0.29)
	N = 107	N = 82
Breaks law, twelve jobs at stake	7.3 (0.25)	6.9 (0.32)
	N = 108	N = 83

Notes: Mean score, 0–10 scale.
Mean responses for treatment groups. Lower scores indicate respondents found vignette more corrupt. Values in parentheses are standard errors.

the Official Secrets Act. This is not surprising, given that the violations of the legality norm that figure in the other scenarios involve disregard for internal governmental codes and procedures with which residents are less likely to be familiar and which, more importantly, lack the moral weight of law. Nevertheless, violation of legal norms is in two of three cases strongly associated with a less favourable view of the actions depicted in the vignettes. The exception is the 'Minister of Defence' vignette, where the public-benefit considerations associated with the danger associated with a radioactive leak appear to trump other factors.

Table 5.3(c) *Effects of scenario characteristics on 'corruptness' of Minister of Defence's actions in vignette 3*

Scenario version	Issue in election campaign	Central to nation's defence
Abidance by rules		
Acts in accordance with rules	6.0 (0.22)	5.5 (0.20)
	N = 170	N = 188
Acts in total disregard for rules	7.2 (0.20)	6.6 (0.21)
	N = 182	N = 169
Risk to public health		
Leak is no risk whatsoever	5.8 (0.21)	5.9 (0.21)
	N = 179	N = 176
Leak is a risk	7.4 (0.20)	6.1 (0.20)
	N = 173	N = 181
Following rules and risk to public health		
Follows rules, leak is no risk	5.4 (0.27)	5.0 (0.29)
	N = 95	N = 92
Follows rules, leak is a risk	6.8 (0.34)	5.9 (0.26)
	N = 75	N = 96
Disregards rules, leak is no risk	6.4 (0.31)	6.8 (0.27)
	N = 84	N = 84
Disregards rules, leak is a risk	7.9 (0.23)	6.4 (0.31)
	N = 99	N = 85

Notes: Mean score, 0–10 scale.
Mean responses for treatment groups. Lower scores indicate respondents found vignette more corrupt. Values in parentheses are standard errors.

The association between evaluations of acceptability and the scale of any public benefit is less consistent in the other two vignettes. The fact of having been implicated in the award of a contract to the 'wrong' bidder causes 'former minister Lane' to be very poorly regarded by respondents, whereas the relevance of the number of jobs at stake in the constituency of 'MP Barnes' appears to be less of an issue.

The impact of information intended to manipulate role-specific considerations in respondents' evaluations of political conduct is more difficult to evaluate. The self-serving action of 'former minister

Table 5.4 *The role of norms in shaping evaluations of unacceptability*

Variable	Vignette 1 (Lane)	Vignette 2 (Barnes)	Vignette 3 (Minister)
Negative version of legality norm	0.92**	3.58***	0.28
	(0.304)	(0.33)	(0.34)
Negative version of role-specific norm	1.23***	0.86**	−0.23
	(0.34)	(0.33)	(0.33)
Negative version of public-benefit norm	0.86**	−0.04	0.85**
	(0.32)	(0.32)	(0.33)
Negative version of legality norm x negative version of role-specific norm	−0.42	−0.74	0.55
	(0.40)	(0.40)	(0.42)
Negative version of legality norm x negative version of public-benefit norm	0.41	0.40	−0.26
	(0.40)	(0.40)	(0.42)
Negative version of role-specific norm x negative version of public-benefit norm	−0.29	0.25	0.69
	(0.40)	(0.40)	(0.42)
Constant	5.35	3.99	6.36
	(0.19)	(0.20)	(0.21)
Adjusted R^2	0.09	0.30	0.04
N	801	799	799

Notes: 0–10 scale.
* $p < 0.05$, ** $p < 0.01$, *** $p < 0.001$; cell entries are coefficients; standard errors are in parentheses.

Lane' and the donation-motivated behaviour suggested in the 'MP Barnes' scenario both have a statistically significant impact on evaluations of acceptability, whereas the suggestion of electoral motivation in the gagging order vignette did not elicit any significant response. This may be due to the fact that in the first two cases money was at stake, and material gain is judged more harshly than potential electoral benefit.

Broadly similar findings are evident in the models of evaluations of 'corruptness' presented in Table 5.5, though with two important exceptions. The first exception is that when it comes to labelling an action as corrupt, legality consistently proves to be by far the most significant factor. This suggests that corruption evaluations are in

Table 5.5 *The role of norms in shaping evaluations of corruptness*

Variable	Vignette 1 (Lane)	Vignette 2 (Barnes)	Vignette 3 (Minister)
Negative version of legality norm	0.69**	3.13***	0.63*
	(0.27)	(0.31)	(0.32)
Negative version of role-specific norm	0.50	0.76*	−0.79*
	(0.30)	(0.31)	(0.31)
Negative version of public-benefit norm	0.55	−0.43	−0.30
	(0.28)	(0.30)	(0.31)
Negative version of legality norm x negative version of role-specific norm	−0.04	−0.48	0.46
	(0.35)	(0.37)	(0.40)
Negative version of legality norm x negative version of public-benefit norm	−0.23	−0.07	−0.04
	(0.35)	(0.37)	(0.40)
Negative version of role-specific norm x negative version of public-benefit norm	0.15	0.34	1.82***
	(0.35)	(0.37)	(0.40)
Constant	5.56	4.14	6.11
	(0.17)	(0.19)	(0.20)
Adjusted R^2	0.04	0.26	0.06
N	801	799	799

Notes: 0–10 scale.
* $p < 0.05$, ** $p < 0.01$, *** $p < 0.001$; cell entries are coefficients; standard errors are in parentheses.

some senses a narrower type of ethical judgement than evaluations of 'acceptability'. The second exception concerns the coefficients for the Minister of Defence's 'gagging order' vignette, where there is evidence of strong interaction between role-specific and public-benefit norms. The large coefficient on the interaction term between these two variables indicates that when respondents were presented with the 'negative' version of the role-specific manipulation (the minister was acting as an office-seeker rather than as a public servant) but the 'positive' version of the public-benefit norm (there was no risk to public health), the former actually led to a slight *decrease* in the extent to which the action was judged corrupt, perhaps because respondents were willing to see this as 'politics as usual'. However,

when respondents were presented with the 'negative' version of both
norms (the minister was acting as an office-seeker and the leak presented
a risk to public health), they were considerably more likely to judge the
action 'corrupt'. Thus, electioneering is not in and of itself believed to be
especially problematic, but it is strongly condemned when it clashes with
the public interest and leads politicians to sacrifice the latter in order to
increase their electoral prospects.

The experimental exercise conducted by means of fictitious vignettes has demonstrated that when evaluating information presented
to them, people respond to established political norms. The results
of this analysis also demonstrate that the context associated with
different behaviours conditions the norms that are most salient in
different situations. When the situation involves a threat to national
public health, as in the 'Minister' vignette, the public interest norm
assumes considerable significance, whereas when an important legal
norm is violated, as in the Barnes vignette, then legality takes on
greater importance. Legality also rises in salience when it is a matter
of labelling an act 'corrupt'.

The medium and the message

So far in this chapter we have established that political norms common
in British society shape the way in which political conduct is interpreted by members of the public. We turn now to consideration
of how details of such conduct reach people and whether the medium
through which they are conveyed is associated with people's judgements. There is ample evidence of subtle normative effects in all media
communication: the way in which events are presented and the
semantic lens used to make sense of them have been found to affect
the judgements people make (Gamson and Modigliani 1989; Zaller
1992; Nelson and Kinder 1996). Drawing on this literature, we can
posit that the media frame the actions of politicians in certain ways,
generally negative ways, and that these frames help to shape the way in
which people come to evaluate that conduct.

Most people in the contemporary age get the vast majority of their
information about politics from the mass media, and it is reasonable to
assume that people evaluate politicians largely on the basis of what
they see on television, hear on the radio and read in the papers. Most
journalists and editors, for their part, are happy to provide a steady

supply of information on the misconduct of the political elite. Newspapers take great delight in splashing across their front pages stories of political wrong-doing and impropriety. Barely a week goes by without a story being printed that involves ethically dubious behaviour on the part of a minister or an MP, or a member of some other political institution. From stories of affairs of an adult nature, to shocking cases involving the misuse and abuse of office, the British public can, and a sizeable number of them do, read all about it. In the first quarter of 2009, for example, newspapers reported, among other things, certain members of the House of Lords offering to amend legislation for money (Calvert *et al.* 2009); a certain MP engaging in a 'sex romp' with a mystery brunette in his House of Commons office (Prince 2009); and a husband of a senior minister trying to claim the cost of watching porn on his wife's parliamentary expenses (Roberts 2009). And all this before the *Daily Telegraph* began publishing details of every MP's expenses claims (Winnett and Raynor 2009).

Members of the British public, like citizens in other liberal democracies, are thus frequently called upon to judge the propriety of their politicians' conduct by virtue of what they read in the newspapers and on the Internet, and what they see on television, or hear on the radio. Or, perhaps more accurately, given the almost contemptuous way in which journalists and editors often describe the behaviour of politicians (Barnett 2002; Lloyd 2004), members of the public are required to judge the validity and veracity of media allegations of impropriety. Needless to say, even when a story or event is not explicitly framed as an ethics issue, some citizens may consciously or subconsciously form a judgement about the propriety of a politician's behaviour.

In the autumn 2009 wave of our survey, we took the opportunity of a high-profile recent scandal to ask our survey respondents directly about what they thought of the way the media depict politicians. Specifically, we asked them whether they thought media coverage of the expenses scandal had been fair and balanced; they were asked to rate coverage on a 0–10 scale, where a lower score corresponds to greater fairness and balance.[6] The mean rating was 4.0, indicating that overall, people are

---

[6] The precise question wording was as follows: 'You may have read or heard a lot earlier this year about MPs' claims under Parliament's second-home allowance scheme. Some people thought the press coverage was fair and balanced. Other people thought the coverage was not fair and balanced. Using the scale of 0 to 10,

Table 5.6 *Media consumption patterns in the B/CCAP sample,
spring 2009*

	Number	%
Newspaper:		
Daily Express	32	3.8
Daily Mail	80	9.5
Daily Mirror/Record	61	7.2
Daily Star	11	1.3
Sun	148	17.7
Daily Telegraph	43	5.1
The Guardian	35	4.2
The Independent	12	1.4
The Times	57	6.8
Glasgow Herald	11	1.3
Other paper	99	11.8
Television news:		
BBC News	604	69.4
Channel 4 News	172	19.8
Channel 5 News	100	11.5
ITN News	372	42.7
Sky News	143	16.5
Newsnight	210	24.1

Note: The data in this table are based on answers to the following questions: 'Which
daily morning newspaper do you read most often?' and 'Which, if any, of the
following have you watched on television in the last seven days?' Data are drawn
from the spring 2009 wave of the B/CCAP survey.

prepared to accept the information they receive through the media
about the probity of politicians and their conduct.

As can be seen from the data in Table 5.6, people obtain their news
from a wide variety of sources. The BBC television news was the only
news source accessed by more than half our sample, and only three
sources (all television news programmes) were named by as many as
one in five of our respondents at the time the first wave of our survey
was conducted.

where 0 means the press coverage was fair and balanced and 10 means the press
coverage was not fair and balanced, where would you place your views?', mean
response.

The question that concerns us here is *how* citizens' ethical judgements of politicians are shaped by the media that people consume (consideration of the impact of the media on *what* people think will be taken up in Chapter 6). It has become a virtual commonplace in writing about political conduct that the media are in large part to blame for the low regard in which politicians are held (e.g., Oborne 2005: 229–45; Stoker 2006: 127–30; Riddell 2011: 109–33; Flinders 2012: 142–69). At the same time, scholars have often struggled to find 'media effects' in other aspects of attitude formation and behaviour (McAllister 2000; Newton 2006). Though it might seem clear to some that people's views are shaped by the media sources they access, most analyses have found that information derived from the media largely confirms and reinforces existing views (Zaller 1992; Newton, 1999; Bennett and Iyengar 2008).

The power of the media was acknowledged by many of our focus group participants, who allude to 'media malaise'-type arguments. Several expressed the opinion that the media are more active than previously in publicising wrong-doing by politicians, for example:

That's why people feel that politicians are more corrupt now than they used to be. It's because people are more educated now. And also the media are more likely to report that sort of behaviour. Back in, say, the 50s, there was more deference towards politicians, both from the people and the newspapers. They were probably the same as today, we just did not know about it. (Man, Colchester)

But people differed in their normative evaluation of the media's perceived power. For some participants, the media have too much influence in choosing what is important and in shaping people's views:

In this country we have lost sight of the power that the media have. Some politicians have been publicly persecuted because of their private lives. Look at how gay politicians have had to suffer. But when you have people like Jeffrey Archer, who went to jail for lying about being with a prostitute ... people don't care about that. That's his business, and not part of our standards ... I think the media have too much influence in setting the standards, we don't have a say in that. (Woman, Hackney)

I wonder about the lack of integrity, and whether it is really that big. A lot of it is press-generated. Perhaps they do not focus on the things that matter, like crime and the economy. They would rather have headlines on sexual scandals than on crime casualties. (Man, Colchester)

Others in our focus groups viewed the media as playing an important and positive role in scrutinising politics and holding leaders to account:

> If it takes a newspaper to publish something for them to react, then it makes you feel like they are hiding something. At the end of the day they are supposed to represent us. One thing annoys me more than anything in politics: there's a bad story in the press, we contacted X department and nobody was available to comment. They are perfectly happy to comment when it is to their advantage. (Man, Egham)

> When the public cries out, the media will take up what the public said, because most of the time politicians don't listen to us. It is when the media publish these issues that politicians will succumb. (Man, Hackney)

When it comes to making up their mind about the behaviour of politicians, there is very limited evidence from our investigations that media consumption is strongly associated with how people form ethical judgements. The data presented in Table 5.7 show the relationship between news media consumption and evaluations of the three most contentious of the scenarios analysed in Chapter 4: the Retainer ('An MP is retained by a major company to arrange meetings and dinners in the House of Commons at which its executives can meet parliamentarians'), the Secretary ('An MP hires a spouse or other family member to serve as his or her secretary') and Gift ('At Christmas, an MP accepts a crate of wine from an influential constituent') scenarios. These were the three scenarios that fewer than three-quarters of our sample judged 'corrupt'. The basic idea is that if exposure to news media does affect the way in which people judge political conduct, and especially exposure to the ways in which different newspapers and broadcasters habitually frame their coverage of politics, then we would expected to see some differences in response to the three ethically ambiguous scenarios.

The figures in Table 5.7 are the mean corruptness scores for each scenario by news source (although it needs to be borne in mind that most respondents accessed more than one source). The readers of the *Daily Express*, *Daily Star*, the *Sun* and *The Independent* newspapers were, on average, more condemnatory of each scenario than other respondents, as were the viewers of news programmes on the BBC and Channel 4. By contrast, the readers of *The Guardian* and viewers of television news on Channel 5, Sky and BBC's *Newsnight* were consistently less severe than average in their judgement of the behaviours described. The other media sources generated mixed results.

Table 5.7 *Media consumption patterns and corruption judgements*

	Retainer	Secretary	Gift
Newspaper:			
Daily Express	5.5	4.9	5.2
Daily Mail	5.3	4.1	4.3
Daily Mirror/Record	5.2	4.5	4.6
Daily Star	5.5	4.4	5.2
Sun	5.3	4.8	4.4
Daily Telegraph	5.0	3.7	4.6
The Guardian	5.1	3.4	4.0
The Independent	6.2	5.3	4.5
The Times	4.6	4.2	3.6
Glasgow Herald	5.7	3.4	4.3
Other paper	5.3	4.5	4.4
Television news:			
BBC News	5.3	4.3	4.4
Channel 4 News	5.4	4.3	4.6
Channel 5 News	5.2	4.3	4.3
ITN News	5.3	4.4	4.3
Sky News	5.0	4.1	4.2
Newsnight	5.2	4.1	4.2
All	5.3	4.3	4.4

Note: The figures in the cells are mean scores on a scale of 1–7 where a higher number represents an evaluation of greater corruptness. Data are drawn from the spring 2009 wave of the B/CCAP survey.

Multivariate analysis (not shown), which included the same control variables used in Tables 4.2 and 4.5, finds readers of *The Independent* to be more critical of the Retainer and Secretary scenarios, whereas *Sun* readers were more critical of the Secretary and Gift scenarios, all else considered. Channel 4 viewers were slightly more critical of the Gift scenario. It is difficult to know how to interpret these findings, and they certainly do not conform readily to expectations that one might hold on the basis of stereotypes associated with the traditional left–right or tabloid–broadsheet distinctions. We will return again to media effects in Chapter 6, but for now we must conclude that exposure to certain sources of news alone is insufficient to account for how people make ethical judgements of political conduct. In other words, the message matters more than the medium.

Conclusion

This chapter has considered how people approach the task of evaluating politicians. Having examined the principal sources of information about politics, we have come to the conclusion that the way in which people judge ethically ambiguous actions is not greatly influenced in any direct or obvious way by the source of the news to which they are generally exposed. Rather, we have found that a common set of political norms related to political roles, conformity with the law and the public good play an important role in making sense of politicians' actions for people and helping them to judge those actions. This provides evidence that people anchor their assessment of politicians in their own experience and their own understanding of the world, rather than in conceptual categories specific to political life. We must be cautious in drawing conclusions from the results of the individual vignettes we examined, as responses to these hypothetical situations will undeniably be conditioned by the contextual details presented and will never reflect precisely the relevance of the abstract principle which a vignette is designed to embody. However, the overall pattern that emerges from the different experiments presented here confirms the role of culturally embedded norms in shaping popular reactions to political conduct.

Having considered the conceptual maps that people have of political ethics, as well as the ways in which they go about forming judgements about politicians' actions, we turn now to what is in some senses the core concern of any study of this topic: what the British people actually think of their politicians and the sort of factors that structure their beliefs and perceptions.

6 | *What people think of their elected politicians*

I THINK WHAT we see is the tip of the iceberg.
(Female focus group participant, Hackney)

Having grappled in the last chapter with the way in which British citizens approach the task of evaluating the ethical conduct of their elected representatives, we turn now to consideration of *what* people think about political conduct and their perceptions of the extent to which their leaders live up to the standards they hold for them. The content of people's integrity perceptions is on the face of it quite amenable to examination. Yet the question of what drives people's sceptical orientations has proved to be more difficult for scholars to ascertain. This is a topic on which there has been considerable prior research, both in the British and the comparative contexts. There is overwhelming evidence to suggest that most people in democratic states are critical of politicians and view them as having a tendency to act according to low ethical standards of conduct (Listhaug 1995; Norris 1999, 2011; Pharr 2000; Dalton 2004; Davis *et al.* 2004). In seeking to make sense of this finding, the political psychology literature can help us to develop a finding we touched upon briefly in Chapter 2: the common belief that political corruption is widespread, even in democracies and even in the absence of concrete evidence to that effect. In the 1970s, Amos Tversky and Daniel Kahneman identified a number of ways in which human perceptions are systematically biased (Tversky and Kahneman 2000). Two of these, 'availability' and 'adjustment and anchoring', are particularly useful in helping to understand why it is that so many people perceive politicians to be corrupt.

'Availability' is the tendency to make generalisations about the frequency of a class of events from information that comes immediately to mind (Kahneman and Tversky 2000: 11–14). The role of the availability bias in driving popular perceptions of political conduct is clearly evident in the tendency of people to believe that most politicians are corrupt. The media regularly report cases of politicians' misconduct and other transgressions, whereas the myriad routine acts of public service carried out on a daily basis by our elected representatives are less commonly reported. When people are asked to evaluate the ethics of their elected representatives, recently received accounts of misconduct are most likely to be the first thing that comes to mind. Though a few swift calculations would most likely be sufficient to make someone realise that the number of serious scandals in any given political cycle is far less than the number of people holding elected roles, the availability bias helps to account for why the regularity of political scandals is often enough to make people believe that most politicians are corrupt. We return to this point in Chapter 8.

The bias caused by 'adjustment and anchoring' can further explain this tendency. As conceptualised by Kahneman and Tversky, adjustment and anchoring is the tendency when making evaluations of magnitude to start from an anchor point related to cues or personal experience, and adjust somewhat, but insufficiently, in the direction of anticipated variation. The 'anchor' thus biases their estimate (Tversky and Kahneman 2000: 14–18). For example, most people hold jobs that yield them a modest salary (the mean salary in 2010 when our fieldwork was completed was just under £26,000) and give them only moderate amounts of discretion over the tasks they perform. They must typically account for their performance at frequent intervals, and there are strict rules governing their conduct, ethical and otherwise. In contrast, most high-level positions, whether in the political or corporate world, afford their holders far more discretion and greater pay. Politicians themselves are unlikely to perceive that they are over-paid and unaccountable, whereas many members of the public are likely to come to this conclusion if they anchor their evaluation of what they read or hear about politicians in their own roles. Such apparent unaccountability and extravagance can all too easily translate into perceptions of corruption.

Understanding the effects of availability and anchoring can thus help us to make sense of the common finding that far more people believe politicians to be corrupt than is likely to be the case. Nevertheless, this cursory analysis leaves many features of contemporary British integrity perceptions still to be explored, not least the types of malfeasance that are viewed most unfavourably by the public, and which types of politician are seen as being most prone to engage in misconduct. It also leaves to be explored the important issue of possible systematic differences in citizens' condemnation of elected representatives' apparently unethical behaviour.

Most previous research has addressed the third of these features, and there is a growing body of evidence of how both country- and individual-level factors can structure perceptions of conduct, as seen in Chapter 2. As far as country-level variables are concerned, several aspects of the British political system help to explain why the public might be discontented with elite performance. For a start, the voting system used to elect MPs breeds lower levels of congruence between public opinion and policy outcomes than is the case in other countries, in that there is a lower degree of correspondence between the positions of policy-makers and that of the median voter (Powell 2000: 240–6; Powell and Vanberg 2000; McDonald *et al.* 2004). Moreover, levels of income inequality are also higher in Britain than they are in many continental European countries, and income inequality has been shown to increase corruption perceptions (You and Khagram 2005).

As for the possible individual-level factors associated with integrity perceptions, previous research has identified several demographic, attitudinal and behavioural characteristics that are linked to perceptions of ethics, especially corruption. Age (Davis *et al.* 2004; Blais *et al.* 2005; McCann and Redlawsk 2006; Allen and Birch 2011) and gender (McCann and Redlawsk 2006; Allen and Birch 2011) have been found to be associated with perceptions of misconduct, with older people and women tending to be more critical in their evaluations of political elites. Several studies have also found that education levels (McManus-Czubińska *et al.* 2004; McCann and Redlawsk 2006) and socioeconomic status affect beliefs about proper and improper conduct (Johnston 1986; Jackson and Smith 1996; Davis *et al.* 2004; Redlawsk and McCann 2005). The general finding is that people with higher socioeconomic status are less critical of politicians. Normative attitudes towards political malpractice have also been identified in several studies as factors that magnify people's perception of wrong-doing (Grødeland *et al.* 2000; McManus-Czubińska *et al.* 2004; Redlawsk and McGann 2005; Allen and Birch 2011). In addition, partisanship has been found to have a variety of effects on evaluations of political ethics (Davis *et al.* 2004; Blais *et al.* 2005; McCann and Redlawsk 2006; Allen and Birch 2011). We might also expect perceptions of misconduct to be conditioned by media consumption, and that those members of the public who consume certain types of media (tabloid newspapers and television as opposed to broadsheets) will tend to have an inflated perception of the levels of elite misconduct. It also may be the case that people's evaluations of the ethical conduct of leaders is coloured by their views of those leaders' performance in office, as suggested by Paul Whiteley and colleagues (Whiteley *et al.* 2013). Following the 'performance politics' approach (Clarke *et al.* 2009, 2011), we can therefore anticipate that evaluations of politicians will be conditioned by people's assessments of what recent governments have delivered for themselves and for the country in material terms.

This chapter assesses the relevance of these factors as it explores key features of contemporary perceptions of political ethics in Britain. The next section considers overall ethical evaluations, while the third section charts popular perceptions of change over time, including a tendency to view past political conduct in somewhat more positive terms. The fourth part of the chapter shifts its focus to perceived differences between categories of elite, including elected politicians versus other public elites, local versus national politicians, and politicians from different political parties. The final part looks at how people evaluate different types of misconduct and the forms of wrong-doing about which they are most concerned.

In it for themselves? Overall perceptions of politicians

Our focus group and survey evidence confirms the findings of numerous other studies: the British public is generally unimpressed with the moral fibre of those who govern and represent them. Starting with the focus groups, the transcripts of those we conducted provide a good flavour of the views that people hold, as well as the language in which they express them. The following extracts are typical of the comments were heard:

We know that power corrupts, and some go into politics for their own career ... I think it's wider than just enforcing standards, because people are in it for lots of different things. (Woman, Hackney)

People get into politics to get something out of it for themselves, rather than to work for the country... People use politics to make money. (Man, Colchester)

Politicians always badmouth each other, which is something I dislike in politics. (Man, Colchester)

It seems politics has become a career rather than a mission. Personal gain has taken over representation and civic duty towards one's constituents. (Man, Colchester)

One thing that annoys me more than anything in politics: there's a bad story in the press, 'we contacted department X and nobody was available to comment'. They are perfectly happy to comment when it is to their advantage. (Man, Egham)

There is no ideology, and from that point of view, there's less honesty. Parties used to have an ideology, and they were honest with that. (Man, Egham)

They don't live in the real world. They live in a fantasy world. (Woman, Bradford)

There were some individuals, of course, who disagreed and declined to accept the prevailing popular wisdom. But even such minority voices failed to deliver ringing endorsements of Britain's political classes:

I don't think our government lacks integrity or is corrupt. Maybe a few individuals. But if it does not affect the government as a whole, I don't care about it. Perhaps the government lacks charisma. (Man, Colchester)

It is noteworthy that the complaints articulated in these comments reflect the broader understanding of political ethics that we considered in Chapter 4. The British public is generally disturbed by what it sees as venal and self-serving behaviour, but it also appears to be equally disturbed by the 'spin', apparent inconsistencies and lack of ideological accountability which they attribute to politicians.

In order to obtain a summary measure of how people feel about the integrity of Britain's political elite, we asked respondents in all three waves of our survey a general question designed to tap their basic perceptions of the ethical standards of conduct of politicians: 'Overall, how would you rate the standards of honesty and integrity of elected politicians in Britain today?' At all three points in time, the majority of respondents tended to express an unfavourable view of politicians, as shown in Figure 6.1, with nearly two-thirds consistently answering either 'somewhat low' or 'very low'.[1] Hardly anyone was

---

[1] These and the other data in this chapter are based on respondents who took part in all three surveys, in order to ensure comparability over time.

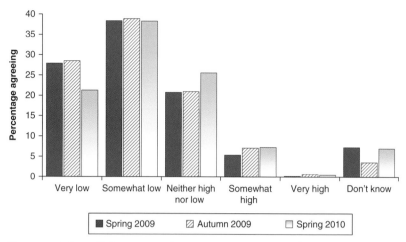

Figure 6.1 Overall honesty and integrity perceptions of elected politicians
Note: The original wording of the question is included in the Appendix.

prepared to credit their leaders with 'very high' standards – less than 1 per cent of respondents at all three points in time. And in all three cases, 'somewhat low' was the modal category, consistently accounting for nearly 40 per cent of respondents. It is thus clear that the British public has a rather jaundiced view of those entrusted to run the country.

The figures do vary slightly over the successive waves of our survey, however, suggesting that citizens' evaluations of politicians are influenced by events. When we consider these changes in the light of the May 2009 media frenzy surrounding MPs' expenses, which broke in the press shortly after the first survey was completed, it appears that this episode had a mildly *polarising* effect on views. Contrary to what we might at first expect, there was no pronounced downward shift in people's opinion of their elected leader several months after the frenzied coverage abated. True, a marginally larger proportion of our respondents held a negative view in autumn 2009 (when 67.4 per cent of respondents said that politicians' standards were 'somewhat low' or 'very low') than in spring 2009 (66.3 per cent). But a slightly larger proportion of our respondents also expressed a positive opinion in the wake of the media frenzy: 5.6 per cent tended to express a favourable view in the spring 2009 survey compared with 7.8 per cent in the autumn 2009 survey.

The lack of any clear decline in evaluations may well be due to the fact that the public already held politicians in very low regard at the time of our first survey. Although it preceded the *Daily Telegraph*'s decision to publish leaked details of all MPs' claims, a number of allegations and abuses had come to light in the months before the survey was fielded (see Chapter 3). Moreover, the Committee on Standards in Public Life had previously announced an inquiry in March, and in April Gordon Brown had taken to YouTube to deliver a personal message promising reforms. In other words, expenses were very much on the agenda before our first survey, and a number of problems and abuses had already been given a thorough public airing before the scandal proper broke. To a large extent, the media frenzy may have confirmed what people already suspected. We may also be observing in our results the well-established phenomenon of increases in information about a topic polarising views on the subject (Zaller 1992; Lodge and Taber 2013).

The aggregate-level picture of general stability in our respondents' perceptions also conceals a degree of individual-level volatility. Clearly, some individuals did change their minds about politicians in the wake of the frenzied media coverage. In autumn 2009, we asked our respondents directly whether their opinions about the honesty and trustworthiness of MPs had changed following the expenses controversy. In response, 29.5 per cent of respondents, well over a quarter, said they had thought most MPs were honest and trustworthy before the scandal, but now thought most MPs were dishonest and untrustworthy. Not every respondent claimed to have been influenced by the scandal, however. Some 18.3 per cent said that they thought most MPs were honest and trustworthy before the scandal and still thought most MPs were honest and trustworthy now. A larger proportion, 38.0 per cent said they thought that most MPs were dishonest and untrustworthy before the scandal and that they still thought most MPs were dishonest and untrustworthy. In other words, 56.3 per cent of respondents claimed that the expenses scandal did not affect their opinion of MPs' integrity one way or another. A very small proportion, 2.9 per cent said that they now thought most MPs were honest and trustworthy, whereas before the scandal they had thought most MPs were dishonest and untrustworthy. Self-reported changes in views must always be treated with caution, but those reported here do suggest that the expenses scandal had a short-term impact on some individuals' evaluations of British political elites.

In order to get a better handle on the factors that affect views of political elites, it is useful to harness the power of multivariate analysis, which allows us to evaluate the relative importance of different hypothesised causes. Table 6.1 reports a series of regression models that help us account for respondents' overall perceptions of elected politicians' honesty and integrity in all three waves of our survey. Since the dependent variable is a 1–5 scale, we use ordinal logistic regression to estimate the models. The final column of the table models changes in perceptions between the spring 2009 and spring 2010 waves. The dependent variable in this case is simply respondents' 2010 score minus their 2009 score, so that a positive value indicates that respondents' perceptions improved over the year. All four models include both standard demographic control variables and relevant attitudes, including personal ethical standards (operationalised as their tolerance of ethically dubious private behaviour), expectations of politicians (operationalised here in terms of the question we examined in Chapter 4 as to whether or not politicians should be held to higher standards than other people), attentiveness to politics and partisanship. Economic evaluations – of personal economic circumstances as well as the state of the national economy – were included as proxies for political performance. Also included are a wide range of media consumption variables, including the newspaper readership and television news viewership variables we encountered in Chapter 5. Details of variable construction can be found in the Appendix.

The variables that do most of the 'work' in these models are clearly the attitudinal characteristics, including the standards to which respondents hold politicians, attentiveness to politics and party identification (with party identifiers exhibiting a considerably more favourable view of politicians than non-partisans) and economic evaluations. Once these attitudinal factors are taken into consideration, none of the demographic variables exhibits a strong and consistent relationship with perceptions of honesty and integrity. Perhaps more surprising is the lack of any clear association between patterns of media consumption and perceptions of politics. Certainly, there are media variables that are found to be associated in a statistical sense with honesty perceptions, but they vary over time, and they are somewhat difficult to interpret. In comparison with the baseline category of people who read no newspaper, *Daily Mirror* and *Daily Telegraph* readers were more critical of politicians' integrity in spring 2009. In the spring 2010 survey, it was the turn of *Daily Mail*, *Sun* and *The*

Table 6.1 *Modelling overall honesty and integrity perceptions*

Variable	Spring 2009	Autumn 2009	Spring 2010	Change spring 2009-spring 2010
Demographics:				
Gender: male	0.01	−0.29	−0.16	−0.16
	(0.18)	(0.18)	(0.21)	(0.21)
Age: under 35	−0.06	0.30	−0.23	−0.60
	(0.24)	(0.23)	(0.30)	(0.30)
Age: 55+	−0.04	−0.10	0.39	0.54*
	(0.21)	(0.21)	(0.25)	(0.25)
Education: graduate	−0.33	−0.59**	−0.27	−0.08
	(0.19)	(0.19)	(0.23)	(0.23)
Income: under	−0.02	0.15	0.16	0.03
£20,000	(0.21)	(0.21)	(0.25)	(0.25)
Income: £40,000+	0.20	0.30	0.71**	0.40
	(0.22)	(0.22)	(0.26)	(0.26)
Dispositions:				
Personal ethical	0.11*	−0.01	−0.08	−0.00
tolerance scale	(0.05)	(0.05)	(0.06)	(0.06)
Expectations of	−0.14*	−0.15**	−0.17*	−0.14
higher standards	(0.06)	(0.06)	(0.07)	(0.07)
Attentiveness to	−0.01	0.20*	0.33**	0.13
public affairs	(0.10)	(0.10)	(0.12)	(0.12)
Conservative	1.15***	1.25***	0.86**	−0.36
identifier	(0.27)	(0.27)	(0.33)	(0.33)
Labour identifier	1.15***	0.71**	1.02**	−0.22
	(0.27)	(0.27)	(0.33)	(0.32)
Liberal Democrat	1.24***	1.13**	0.24	−0.92*
identifier	(0.34)	(0.33)	(0.43)	(0.44)
Other party identifier	0.16	−0.16	−0.15	−0.25
	(0.32)	(0.32)	(0.38)	(0.38)
Improvement in	0.17	0.09	0.52***	0.28*
personal finances	(0.11)	(0.10)	(0.13)	(0.12)
Improvement in	0.88***	0.50***	0.47**	−0.52**
national economy	(.15)	(0.14)	(0.17)	(0.17)
Media consumption:				
Daily Express reader	−0.80	−0.10	−0.87	0.47
	(0.55)	(0.53)	(0.68)	(0.66)
Daily Mail reader	−0.34	−0.24	−1.20**	−0.62
	(0.32)	(0.32)	(0.40)	(0.40)
Daily Mirror/Record	−1.54***	0.33	−0.34	1.03*
reader	(0.39)	(0.38)	(0.46)	(0.46)

Table 6.1 (*cont.*)

Variable	Spring 2009	Autumn 2009	Spring 2010	Change spring 2009-spring 2010
Daily Star reader	−0.26	1.63	−0.14	−0.05
	(0.88)	(0.87)	(0.90)	(0.91)
Sun reader	−0.24	0.34	−0.97**	−0.76*
	(0.27)	(0.27)	(0.33)	(0.33)
Daily Telegraph reader	−0.89*	0.04	−0.49	0.68
	(0.45)	(0.44)	(0.51)	(0.51)
Guardian reader	0.57	0.66	−0.18	−0.51
	(0.43)	(0.43)	(0.51)	(0.51)
Independent reader	−0.35	0.30	−2.69***	−1.51*
	(0.65)	(0.63)	(0.85)	(0.75)
Times reader	−0.37	0.57	−0.47	0.12
	(0.36)	(0.35)	(0.45)	(0.45)
Glasgow Herald reader	−0.09	0.48	−0.42	0.64
	(0.87)	(0.86)	(1.17)	(1.16)
Other newspaper reader	−0.48	0.32	−0.07	0.40
	(0.28)	(0.28)	(0.33)	(0.33)
BBC News viewer	0.04	0.27	−0.11	−0.01
	(0.22)	(0.22)	(0.26)	(0.26)
Channel 4 News viewer	−0.44	−0.26	−0.08	0.28
	(0.23)	(0.22)	(0.26)	(0.26)
Channel 5 News viewer	−0.21	−0.09	0.10	0.38
	(0.29)	(0.28)	(0.32)	(0.32)
ITN News viewer	−0.07	0.07	0.24	0.34
	(0.18)	(0.18)	(0.21)	(0.21)
Newsnight viewer	0.91***	0.21	0.26	−0.44
	(0.25)	(0.24)	(0.29)	(0.29)
Sky News viewer	0.11	−0.06	0.18	0.01
	(0.21)	(0.21)	(0.24)	(0.24)
N	518	515	367	367
Nagelkerke R^2	0.29	0.20	0.26	0.18

Notes: Ordinal logistic regression.
* $p < 0.05$, ** $p < 0.01$, *** $p < 0.001$; cell entries are coefficients; standard errors are in parentheses. Cut points omitted. These models include only respondents who responded to the overall honesty question in all three waves of the survey. In the autumn 2009 and spring 2010 models, independent variables are constructed on the basis of responses to the spring 2009 survey in order to minimise the possible effects of endogeneity.

Independent readers to express more censorious attitudes. The lack of any readily interpretable pattern in these findings, either in terms of the ideological leanings of the titles or their market positions, suggests that the significant coefficients may well be the result of idiosyncratic factors such as particular news stories printed in the different publications at the time our surveys were conducted. Dummy variables designating tabloid and broadsheet newspaper readership also failed to yield significant results in additional models not shown here.

As far as the effects of television are concerned, few of the relevant coefficients achieved statistical significance. The only clear effect is that of BBC *Newsnight* viewers being more positive about politicians in the spring 2009 survey. This finding may reflect a tendency for more in-depth and 'highbrow' news outlets to make people feel better about politicians. However, since this variable is not significant in subsequent waves, it would be unwise to place too much emphasis on this interpretation.

The model of changes in perceptions, as reported in the fifth column, also yields extremely limited results. The only two variables to reach conventional levels of statistical significance were the media-related variables of *Daily Mirror*, *Sun* and *The Independent* readership, with the former exhibiting a positive sign and the latter two negative signs. Given the lack of obvious patterns in the newspaper variables in the previous models, these findings can undoubtedly be discounted. Insofar as individuals' views of politicians changed during the period under analysis, these changes were evidently distributed nearly randomly across broad groups in the population. The only somewhat puzzling finding is the negative and statistically significant coefficient for sociotropic economic evaluations in the change model, for which we do not have a satisfactory interpretation.

All in all, these results suggest that people's underlying values and attitudes are more important than specific patterns of media consumption in shaping popular ethical judgements of political elites.[2] Those who hold politicians to high standards are more critical, all else considered. This effect is counterbalanced by a tendency for those who invest more time and effort in paying attention to and being involved

2 Our media consumption findings echo those of Ian McAllister (2000), who found in the Australian setting that media consumption was a poor predictor of ethical evaluations, whereas cognitive sophistication predicted such evaluations far better.

in politics having more positive evaluations. More positive views of personal and national economic conditions also appear to cast a rosy tint on evaluations of political leaders. The tentative conclusion one may draw from this is that if people's expectations were lowered and their attention more firmly fixed on public affairs, their views of politicians might improve. The implications of this conclusion are something we shall take up again in Chapter 8.

A tendency to assume decline?

In addition to exploring the dynamics of overall perceptions of politicians' conduct, we were also interested in the question of whether people believed that current standards of elected politicians reflected long-standing traditions of behaviour, or whether they thought that there had been a change in recent years in the standards to which politicians adhere. From the mid-1990s onwards, as we saw in Chapter 3, sections of British political life have been subject to increasingly formalised modes of ethics regulation. Despite, or perhaps because of, these changes, we found a pronounced tendency among both our focus group participants and survey respondents to exhibit a certain nostalgia about years gone by, when politicians were assumed to be altogether more honourable. In the words of some of those who took part in our focus groups:

Before, to be a politician, you'd go into your community. Now technology has changed all that. The balance of standards is tilted towards politicians, who are becoming the aristocracy of the future. (Man, Hackney)

In the past, politicians were more respected, they achieved something for being elected, or they were honourable gentlemen. (Woman, Colchester)

In the past, politicians who got caught red-handed had the decency to resign. Now they don't. (Woman, Colchester)

I remember the case of the Chancellor of the Exchequer resigning because of a leak in his department, even though he wasn't personally responsible for that. Nowadays, that would be incredible. (Man, Egham)

Such sentiments suggest an element of 'golden ageism' in citizens' views of politicians. They also once again show that standards of conduct in political life are often understood in broader terms than those that underpin much of the increased ethics regulation of recent years.

However, not all the voices from our focus groups subscribed to such a nostalgic view. Some individuals sought to dispel what they saw as the myth of falling standards with references to recent changes in politics, society and the media:

That's why people feel that politicians are more corrupt than they used to be. It's because people are more educated now. And also the media are more likely to report that sort of behaviour. Back in, say, the fifties, there was more deference towards politicians, both from the people and the newspapers. They were probably the same as today, we just did not know about it. (Man, Colchester)

[Politicians] deal with a much more media-intensive age, which makes it more difficult not to be aware of things that are going on. Maybe in the past only the headline scandal would have been something that the man in the street would have been aware of. (Man, Egham)

Our survey results confirm that those who see standards as having fallen are in the clear majority. In each wave, we invited respondents to say whether they thought that the standards of honesty and integrity of elected politicians in Britain had been improving in recent years, had been declining, or had stayed about the same. In each wave, a clear majority of respondents said that standards had been declining, as Figure 6.2 shows. Curiously, however, the proportion of pessimists fell moderately over the course of the three surveys, and the proportion

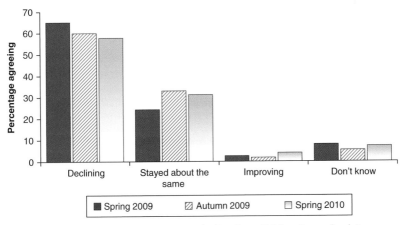

Figure 6.2 Perceived improvement or decline in politicians' standards?
Note: The original wording of the question is included in the Appendix.

of respondents who said standards had improved rose slightly. It is not immediately clear what might explain this trend. A positive interpretation of the changes is that the extensive media coverage surrounding the expenses scandal had the effect of persuading some respondents that only a tiny minority of MPs had in fact acted criminally. A less positive interpretation is that the scandal persuaded some respondents that, actually, politicians had always been crooked and that standards had never been high.

Considering these results, and those in the previous section, a clear gap exists between subjective and objective political conduct in Britain. In the face of much evidence to the contrary (see Chapter 8), most Britons perceive their politicians to be unethical and dishonest, if not outright crooked, even though the overwhelming majority of politicians go through their careers without having been implicated in, let alone having been found to have engaged in, misconduct. It is also the case that very few citizens have direct experience of politicians' misconduct (see Rose and Mishler 2010). In spring 2009, we asked our survey respondents whether they or anyone they knew had ever had first-hand knowledge or experience of wrong-doing by an MP. In response, about 3 per cent of our sample answered 'yes', a proportion somewhat inflated by respondents' liberal interpretation of 'wrong-doing'.[3]

Why, then, do so many people come to hold the view that most politicians are dishonest and lack integrity? We have previously considered the very broad understanding of political ethics held by the British public, and this undoubtedly goes some way towards providing an answer to this question. If much that is 'normal politics' is subject to ethical judgement in the minds of citizens, then a great deal of normal politics may well be judged unethical. We have also

---

[3] An open-ended follow-up question asked respondents to provide details of the wrong-doing experienced. Some of the details given were political in tone, for example, Tony Blair's support for war, John Major's signing of the Maastricht Treaty and the sacking of a local MP from ministerial office. Others referred to inadequate constituency service. Yet others described general discursive dishonesty, for instance, 'did not do what was promised' or 'telling a lie'. Others referred to private misdemeanours, including the local MP having an affair, the local MP setting fire to a hotel and, in the most amusing response, the local MP crashing through a car park barrier when drunk. We cannot verify the veracity of the details, but the information provided leads us to conclude that the figure of 3 per cent of respondents claiming to have had direct experience of wrong-doing by an MP overestimates actual experience.

contemplated the role of the 'availability' and 'anchoring' biases. The popular media plays an important role in enabling these biases. Irrespective of the specific media outlets to which people pay attention, the overall media climate may well create the impression that politicians are not to be trusted. Wrong-doing being far more newsworthy than the efficient and effective discharge of official duties, scandals and political misconduct are far more likely to grace newspaper headlines and news bulletins than the routine dutiful actions that make up the vast majority of most politicians' lives. The same phenomenon applies to perceptions of other headline-grabbing phenomena such as crime, which typically exaggerate actual crime statistics and survey-based reports of the experience of crime.

It may also be that most people believe that there is a large amount of unreported and undiscovered misconduct that goes on in politics. Fed a regular diet of news stories about politicians engaging in improper activity, citizens might well come to the conclusion that, as one of our focus group respondents put it, 'I think what we see is the tip of the iceberg' (Woman, Hackney).

In order to gauge the extent of views such as this, we included a number of questions in our surveys that were explicitly designed to capture the language commonly used by focus group respondents to articulate their views of politics and politicians. The first question, posed in the spring 2009 wave, asked respondents how strongly they agreed or disagreed with the view that the various political scandals reported in the newspapers and on television were 'only the tip of the iceberg' in terms of the misconduct that went on. Table 6.2 summarises responses to this question. It is clear from these figures that a large majority of respondents agree with this view. In total, 77.9 per cent of respondents said they 'strongly agree' or 'tend to agree' with this statement, whereas a paltry 2.6 per cent were prepared to say categorically that they disagreed. This finding gives strong support to the 'availability' theory; most people extrapolate from the information they receive about ethical misconduct and form their views on the basis of behaviour that is (presumably) the exception rather than the rule.

Another question that preoccupied us when puzzling over people's perception of politics was how it is that they account for the behaviour of politicians. Is it to do with the motives they ascribe to politicians? In autumn 2009, we therefore asked respondents to our survey how

Table 6.2 *Percentage agreeing with statements about politics and politicians*

	Reported scandals are 'only the tip of the iceberg' (%)	Politicians are 'in it just for themselves' (%)
Strongly agree	30.9	21.5
Tend to agree	44.2	36.6
Neither agree nor disagree	12.5	23.3
Tend to disagree	2.7	12.8
Strongly disagree	0.3	1.4
Don't know	9.4	5.0
N	1,388	809

Note: Figures in the second column are from spring 2009, figures in the third column are from autumn 2009.

much they agreed or disagreed with the statement that 'politicians are in it just for themselves'. Answers to this question are also presented in Table 6.2. A majority of our respondents agreed with this statement as well; 58.1 per cent agreed that politicians were 'just in it for themselves', whereas only 14.1 per cent disagreed.

Finally, we also sought to establish whether the public holds the political system itself responsible for conditioning the integrity of elected politicians. As the historian Lord Acton once observed in a letter to Bishop Creighton: 'Power tends to corrupt and absolute power corrupts absolutely ... There is no worse heresy than that the office sanctifies the holder of it.' To this end, we presented respondents in the spring 2009 survey with a number of statements that invited them to consider whether personal or systemic factors were responsible for explaining current levels of integrity, and asked them to pick which statement came closest to their view. In response, 30.6 per cent picked the statement, 'The way politics is conducted these days makes politicians less honest and trustworthy than they used to be'; and another 29.1 per cent selected, 'The people going into politics these days are personally less honest and trustworthy than they used to be AND the way politics is conducted these days makes them less honest and trustworthy than they used to be.' By way of contrast, only 13.5 per cent picked the statement, 'The people going into politics these days are personally less honest and trustworthy than they used to be'; and a further 7.6 per cent picked,

'The people going into politics these days are NOT less honest and trustworthy than they used to be and the way politics is conducted does NOT make them less honest and trustworthy either.'[4] Large sections of the public thus seem to share Lord Acton's view of politics. Though many respondents believed that some combination of personal and systemic factors were responsible for a perceived deterioration in political standards, most saw the problem as having a clear systemic component. In short, it seems, the British public is inclined to view politics as being institutionally unethical if not corrupt.

Together, the various findings reported in the previous and present sections allow us to gain a better picture of how people perceive their elected representatives. For many, politicians are primarily motivated by venality rather than by a desire to serve the public; and practices of political life only make them worse. The logical consequence of such beliefs is that most politicians are perceived to be dishonest, even if many of their misdeeds are never revealed, and it is all too easy for large sections of the public to think that general standards of honesty and integrity in political conduct have deteriorated.

Differences between categories of elite

So far we have mainly considered evidence of citizens' views of elected politicians in general. Not all politicians are the same, however, and it is quite possible that citizens' perceptions of the honesty and integrity of political elites vary according to which type of actor is being considered. It therefore makes sense to drill down into people's views in order to ascertain whether the generally critical attitudes evident in answers to the question about overall integrity are reflected consistently in evaluations of politicians in specific roles.

We start by considering responses to a question designed to help discern how people view certain types of politicians in comparison with other public elites. In both the spring 2009 and spring 2010 waves, we asked our survey respondents to evaluate six different types of public actor – government ministers, MPs in general, local councillors, respondents' own local MP, judges and journalists – and to say, using a 0–10 scale, whether they thought that the actor in question was completely honest and trustworthy (a score of 10), or

---

[4] A large proportion of respondents, 19.2 per cent, answered 'don't know'.

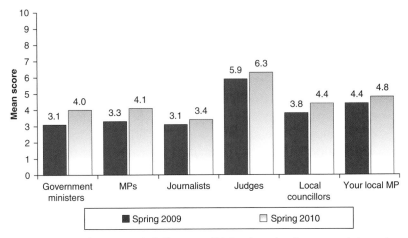

Figure 6.3 Evaluations of different politicians' and other actors' integrity
Note: The data in this figure are mean scores on the 0–10 scale. The original wording of the question is included in the Appendix.

not at all honest and trustworthy (a score of 0). We included judges and journalists as examples of actors that have well-established reputations in British public life. As shown in Figure 1.1, judges are generally held in high esteem and trusted to tell the truth and thus serve as a benchmark of perceived high integrity. Journalists, meanwhile, are generally as distrusted as politicians.

Responses to this question are represented in Figure 6.3 in the form of mean scores. The higher the score, the more honest that group is perceived to be. As expected, all the categories of politicians receive relatively low ratings, as do journalists, whereas judges are, on average, perceived to be somewhat more honest. The results confirm that members of the public can, and do, distinguish between different types of public elite when making ethical judgements, but they do not seem to make a great distinction between government ministers and MPs in general, as the scores for the two categories are fairly similar in both waves. We also find, in confirmation of other studies, that respondents are also more positive about their own MP than MPs in general.[5]

---

[5] For overviews of this topic, see research by Suzanne Parker and Glenn Parker (1993), Margaret Levi and Laura Stoker (2000) and Pippa Norris (2002). See also Pierre Lacoumes *et al.* (2010).

However, before MPs alight on this finding as evidence of good news, it must be pointed out that even evaluations of local MPs are hardly fulsome. There is also little evidence of major change in the time between spring 2009 and spring 2010; and the change we do observe suggests that people evaluated all categories of politician more positively in 2010 than they did in 2009.

The results in Figure 6.3 also show that local councillors are generally said to be more honest and trustworthy than the examples of national-level politicians, ministers and MPs in general that were presented to respondents. Further evidence in support of this finding comes from an additional question that we asked of our survey respondents in spring 2009. When asked whether they thought MPs or local councillors were generally more honest and trustworthy, or whether both groups were about the same, some 56.3 per cent said 'they are about the same', 24.9 per cent said local councillors and just 7.3 per cent said MPs.[6] Among those who discriminated between the two types of elected representative, there was a clear tendency to rate local councillors above MPs: approximately three-and-a-half times as many respondents said they thought local councillors were more honest and trustworthy as said the same of MPs. When it comes to politics, it does seem that proximity tends to breed trust, and that people are more willing to credit local councillors – with whom they are more likely to have had some contact – with higher ethical standards.

As noted in Chapter 2 and again in the introduction to this chapter, a number of studies have found that partisanship and respondents' psychological attachments to parties can shape corruption perceptions and beliefs about political ethics (Davis *et al.* 2004; Blais *et al.* 2005; McCann and Redlawsk 2006). In its simplest formulation, supporters of a given party can be expected to have a more favourable view of fellow partisans, all things being equal. Much is likely to depend on the context, however. It may be that the party or parties in power at any given time are more likely to be held responsible for overall standards of conduct in political life, just as governments are generally held responsible for the state of the economy and other social and

---

[6] The remaining 11.5 per cent answered 'don't know'. The original question was phrased: 'Which group do you think is generally more honest and trustworthy: Members of Parliament or local councillors, or are they both about the same?'

Table 6.3 *Perceptions of different parties' MPs by partisanship,*
autumn 2009

		By party identification		
Which party's MPs are more honest?	All (%)	Conservative (%)	Labour (%)	Liberal Democrat (%)
Conservative	5.2	15.9	0.9	0.0
Labour	4.4	2.8	10.7	0.0
Liberal Democrat	10.9	4.7	8.9	49.3
Other	1.9	0.9	1.3	0.0
No difference between them	68.7	65.4	73.3	45.1
Don't know	8.8	10.3	4.9	5.6
N	791	206	230	81

political conditions (Fiorina 1981; Paldam 1986; Anderson 1995). A party in power may also come to be blamed for specific scandals that occur on its watch. As Angus Campbell and colleagues (1960: 556) note in *The American Voter*: 'when events of the wider environment arouse strong public concern the electorate is motivated to connect them with the actors of politics, typically, with the incumbent party'. And, of course, a party's association with a particular scandal or set of scandals may affect its general reputation. Thus, the various allegations of 'sleaze' levelled at John Major's Conservative Party in the mid-1990s left an enduring mark on the party's image (Norton 1998).

In addition to including measures of partisanship in our multivariate models (see, e.g., Tables 6.1 and 6.5), we also posed a specific question in the autumn 2009 survey that asked respondents to say which political party's MPs were generally more honest. Since the majority of British MPs represent one of three major parties, the response categories included the Conservative Party, Labour Party, the Liberal Democrats and 'other', as well as 'no difference between them'. Responses to this question in total and broken down by respondents' party identification are reported in Table 6.3. Over two-thirds of the sample in total maintained that when it came to levels of honesty, there were no differences between MPs from different parties. Despite being the party of government and thus the potential repository of blame for the expenses scandal, Labour MPs were not singled out for particular opprobrium. When it comes to party identification, there was a slight tendency for Labour and Conservative partisans to rate politicians from their own party more favourably than those from other parties, but in both cases the vast majority saw no differences between MPs of any party. Liberal Democrat supporters were the clear exceptions; over half of this group asserted that their party's MPs were more honest than those of other parties, and only about two in five saw no difference between politicians from different parties.

All told, our findings suggest a tendency for respondents to lump all politicians together, be they local or national representatives, members of one's own party or members of a rival party. There is evidence of a slight tendency to see one's own MP in a more favourable light than MPs as a whole, and to evaluate local politicians more positively than national politicians, but the general tendency is to generalise across all political elites. Most noteworthy perhaps is the lack of a pronounced tendency of our respondents to rate co-partisans more highly than other politicians, which strongly suggests that ideological orientations and ethical evaluations are distinct dimensions of judgement.

Evaluations of different types of misconduct

The evidence presented in Chapter 4 demonstrates that the British public generally has a broad understanding of political ethics. Discursive honesty is at least as important as financial honesty. We can thus conjecture that the negative view of politicians that many citizens hold is shaped as much by an aversion to political 'spin' and a perceived lack of policy accountability as it is by the belief that large proportions of the political elite engage in the more nefarious forms of political misconduct such as bribe-taking and other patently illegal activities. The focus group comments cited above bear this out. As we have already noted, our focus group participants volunteered a wide range of criticisms of politicians when prompted to articulate their grievances, but few of these related to anything that would be considered corruption in the eyes of the law. Many of their complaints centred on issues of honesty, straight talking and commitment to ideological principles.

A suite of questions included in all our surveys allows us to evaluate the relative importance of various types of perceived misconduct,

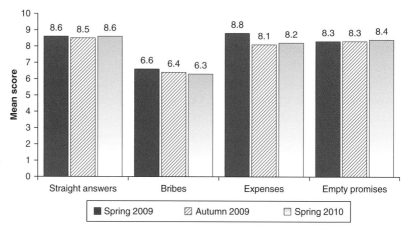

Figure 6.4 Concern with problematic behaviours in British politics
Note: The numbers are mean scores on the 0–10 scale. The original wording
of the question is included in the Appendix.

including those pertaining both to politicians' financial and discursive
integrity. In each survey we asked respondents: 'How much of a
problem is the following behaviour by elected politicians in Britain
today?' The behaviours we listed were: 'not giving straight answers
to questions'; 'accepting bribes'; misusing official expenses and allowances'; and 'making promises they know they can't keep'. Answers
were recorded on a 0–10 scale, where a higher score indicated that
the behaviour was more of a problem.[7] Although the question does
not enable respondents to distinguish between the moral impropriety
of the act and its perceived prevalence, it nonetheless serves as a general
measure of their concern with certain behaviours in contemporary
British politics.

As can be seen from the results in Figure 6.4, respondents generally
tended to view all these behaviours as serious problems in British
politics. In all three waves of our survey the mean scores for all four
of the actions were firmly towards the upper end of the 0–10 scale,
suggesting that most respondents perceived significant problems with
the entire range of misconduct indicators. However, the pattern of

---

[7] The order in which the various actions were presented to respondents was
randomised.

scores also suggests that British citizens do distinguish between different forms of wrong-doing and are more concerned by some than by others. Clearly, the public was least concerned with what lawmakers and political theorists generally reckon to be the most serious form of political abuse, the acceptance of bribes, with average scores only slightly above the mean. The average scores for the other three actions were consistently above 8 on the 0–10 scale. We can thus infer a general tendency among respondents to view expenses fiddling, not giving straight answers to questions and not keeping promises as lesser but more common forms of political misconduct in the British context. Bribery, often held up as the epitome of corruption, is perceived to be less widespread. (As one participant said in one of our Egham focus groups: 'What's the level of corruption is this country? Probably lower than any other society in the world. That's not a bad standard, is it?')

Moving to changes in perceptions, it is curious to note that the mean scores were actually slightly *lower* in the autumn of 2009 than they were in the spring of that year, before the expenses controversy erupted, including the mean rating for 'misusing official expenses and allowances'. This may be due to the fact that the British public had become inured to wrong-doing in the wake of the expenses scandal. Perhaps more likely, it may be that the various allegations that had appeared in the press before the full details of MPs' expenses were published in the *Daily Telegraph* had already heightened sensitivity to this issue, whereas by September, when the second survey was fielded, the public's concerns had turned to other things.

It is also instructive to compare people's overall ratings of the honesty and integrity of politicians with their views on specific forms of abuse. This is what we do in Table 6.4, which reports the mean score on the 0–10 scale for all behaviours by overall perceptions of politicians' honesty and integrity in each wave. Once again, there is a clear distinction between bribe-taking and the three other behaviours, with bribery being judged less problematic by all groups at all time points. The figures also show in all cases that people who say standards are low are also more critical of individual forms of misconduct. What is truly fascinating about the data in this table, however, is that even those who rate politicians' overall standards of honesty and integrity as 'high' still perceive certain behaviours to be problematic. Indeed, with only one notable exception, respondents' expressed

Table 6.4 *Concern about types of behaviour by overall honesty and integrity perceptions*

Type of potentially problematic behaviour	Overall perceived standards of elected politicians' honesty and integrity								
	Spring 2009			Autumn 2009			Spring 2010		
	High	Neutral	Low	High	Neutral	Low	High	Neutral	Low
Not giving straight answers	7.3	8.6	8.9	7.5	8.5	8.9	8.0	8.6	8.9
Accepting bribes	5.1	6.4	7.0	4.6	6.2	7.1	5.0	6.1	6.9
Misusing expenses	6.7	9.0	9.3	6.3	8.3	8.8	6.9	8.3	8.8
Making empty promises	6.8	8.3	8.7	7.1	8.5	8.8	7.6	8.4	8.8

Note: The figures in this table are mean scores on the 0–10 scale. The category listed in this table as 'high' includes the responses 'somewhat high' and 'very high'; the category listed 'neutral' includes the response 'neither low nor high'; the category listed as 'low' includes the responses 'somewhat low' and 'very low'.

concern about 'bribes' in autumn 2009, none of the mean scores for any of the four behaviours in any of the three waves of the survey was below the mid-point of 5 on the 0–10 scale. This suggests that responses to the question about overall honesty do not simply reflect vague generalisations or antipathy to political elites; respondents are equally, if not more, critical when asked far more specific questions about particular misdeeds.

Multivariate analysis again helps us to gain a fuller understanding of the factors that are associated with these evaluations, enabling us to determine whether different sorts of people are likely to express varying levels of concern about distinct types of behaviour in British politics. The dependent variables are the responses to each of the four behaviours – not giving straight answers, accepting bribes, misusing official expenses and making empty promises – as measured in the spring 2009 wave (models from the other waves, not reported, yield very similar results). Since these responses were recorded on a 0–10 scale, we use OLS regression. The independent variables are essentially those we employed in our models of overall honesty and integrity perceptions (Table 6.1), but with simpler media consumption indicators: dummy variables designating tabloid readership and broadsheet or quality newspaper readership.

Table 6.5 reports the results of regression analyses for each of the four actions. As far as the demographic and dispositional variables are concerned, the results recall some of the patterns we saw in attitudes towards overall levels of honesty among politicians detailed in Table 6.1 (although the coefficients in Table 6.5 have the opposite signs, reflecting the different question wording of the dependent variables). Men are somewhat less concerned about all problems than women. Respondents' personal ethics – operationalised once more as their tolerance of ethically dubious behaviour in everyday life – are also associated with their concerns about political conduct: those who are more tolerant of rule-breaking in private are generally less concerned about possible ethical irregularities in political life. There is also a weak association between expectations and expressed concerns. Respondents who expect their elected politicians to be held to higher standards are likely to perceive two of the behaviours, not giving straight answers and misusing expenses, to be more problematic. Meanwhile, attentiveness to politics depresses concern about bribery, undoubtedly reflecting the paucity of reported cases of outright bribe-taking in British political

Table 6.5 *Modelling concern about types of behaviour, spring 2009*

Variable	Straight answers	Bribes	Expenses	Empty promises
Demographics:				
Gender: male	−0.24	−0.63**	−0.37**	−0.25*
	(0.13)	(0.20)	(0.13)	(0.12)
Age: under 35	−0.42**	0.37	−0.09	−0.22
	(0.16)	(0.26)	(0.16)	(0.16)
Age: 55+	0.15	−0.01	0.02	−0.04
	(0.15)	(0.24)	(0.15)	(0.15)
Education: graduate	−0.14	0.38	0.25	−0.07
	(0.14)	(0.22)	(0.14)	(0.14)
Income: under £20,000	0.32*	0.04	0.20	0.35
	(0.15)	(0.24)	(0.15)	(0.15)
Income: £40,000+	−0.02	−0.16	−0.10	0.04
	(0.15)	(0.25)	(0.07)	(0.15)
Dispositions:				
Personal ethical	−0.08*	−0.05	−0.14***	−0.09**
tolerance scale	(0.03)	(0.05)	(0.03)	(0.03)
Expectations of higher	0.09*	0.02	0.13*	0.06
standards	(0.04)	(0.07)	(0.04)	(0.04)
Attentiveness to public	0.10	−0.57***	−0.09	−0.05
affairs	(0.06)	(0.10)	(0.07)	(0.06)
Conservative identifier	−0.13	−0.08	0.31	−0.01
	(0.19)	(0.30)	(0.19)	(0.19)
Labour identifier	−0.18	−0.35	0.04	−0.29
	(0.18)	(0.29)	(0.19)	(0.18)
Liberal Democrat	−0.33	0.11	−0.40	−0.55
identifier	(0.24)	(0.38)	(0.24)	(0.24)
Other party identifier	0.04	0.17	0.05	0.32
	(0.22)	(0.36)	(0.23)	(0.22)
Improvement in	−0.19**	−0.38***	−0.23**	−0.22**
personal finances	(0.07)	(.12)	(0.07)	(0.07)
Improvement in national	−0.41***	0.00	−0.41***	−0.29**
economy	(0.10)	(0.16)	(0.10)	(0.10)
Media consumption:				
Tabloid reader	−0.04	0.63**	0.27*	0.15
	(0.14)	(0.22)	(0.14)	(0.14)
Quality newspaper	0.10	−0.38	−0.22	0.07
reader	(0.18)	(0.28)	(0.18)	(0.18)

Table 6.5 (*cont.*)

Variable	Straight answers	Bribes	Expenses	Empty promises
Constant	9.37	9.24	9.92	9.52
	(0.35)	(0.57)	(0.36)	(0.35)
N	864	790	859	855
Adjusted R^2	0.10	0.10	0.13	0.08

Notes: OLS regression.
* $p < 0.05$, ** $p < 0.01$, *** $p < 0.001$; cell entries are coefficients; standard errors are in parentheses.

life. Positive economic outlooks – both egocentric and sociotropic – tend to have the same impact on concerns about all four types of wrong-doing. Finally, it should be noted that there are almost no evident media consumption effects in any of the models; the only significant media coefficient is the effect tabloid readership evidently has in inducing heightened concern with bribery. If exposure to political information has any impact on perceptions, it is almost certainly by refining prior dispositions that are shaped by values.

Conclusion

This chapter has considered what is in many respects the core issue in the study of political ethics: the content of people's views of their elected representatives. The evidence we have surveyed confirms the findings of previous studies that the British public is less-than-enamoured with its representatives. We have discussed how the well-known psychological biases of 'availability' and 'anchoring' can help to account for these beliefs. We have also seen that most people are unwilling or unable to make nuanced evaluations of different types of politicians, but they are able to distinguish between types of misconduct. In some senses this is not really news; the generally low regard in which politicians are held in Britain is a commonplace of political discourse. Yet the analysis carried out in this chapter has also yielded a number of interesting insights as to the way in which the British public thinks about political morals.

When considering specific forms of wrong-doing, respondents attributed approximately equal weight to 'not giving straight answers to questions', 'misusing official expenses and allowances' and 'making promises they know they can't keep'. Once again, we have further evidence that the public views discursive dishonesty as a form of behaviour that is just as problematic as misconduct involving resources and pecuniary interest. This may well be a basic fact that many elites have failed to grasp; it also suggests that reforms designed to 'clean up politics' by reducing pecuniary abuse will be only partially successful in altering people's view of political ethics, as their understanding also reflects discursive acts that are far more difficult – if not impossible – to regulate and reform. This is a question to which we shall return and consider in some detail in Chapter 8.

Also interesting is the finding that those who exhibit greater levels of political sophistication – as indicated by their attentiveness to politics – are less critical of political elites than others and less prone to seeing wrong-doing as a pervasive aspect of British politics. But before we grapple with the question of what might be done to ameliorate the situation we have described, we shall turn in Chapter 7 to the big 'so what?' question, examining the practical consequences of the evaluations of ethical conduct we have documented in this chapter.

7 | *The political effects of ethical evaluations*

[T HE MPs' expenses scandal] was a manifestation of the decline in morality of the level of representation, from which the general public will then take their lead. The politician will start fiddling his expenses, and then the public will start fiddling his [sic] expenses and the whole system of morality and direction becomes diluted.

(Male focus group participant, Egham)

In the previous chapter, we saw how suspicious most British citizens appeared to be of their elected politicians and of standards of political conduct more generally. We also saw, somewhat surprisingly, that such suspicions were not greatly exacerbated, at least in the medium term, by the frenzied press coverage surrounding MPs' expenses in May 2009. But if citizens are sceptical of their politicians' conduct and integrity, there are also grounds for others to be sceptical about the general importance of such critical attitudes. For a start, politicians as a class have always been distrusted and derided, and yet democratic politics in advanced industrial democracies has still rubbed along. Far larger proportions of citizens regularly vote to choose their representatives than express confidence in their representatives' standards, and most citizens are seemingly content with a representative model of democracy (Hibbing and Theiss-Morse 2001, 2002; Allen and Birch forthcoming). Put another way, dissatisfaction with the standards of politicians' conduct has rarely translated into dissatisfaction with the ideals of democracy or diminished support for the political community. Nor has it resulted in a general lack of compliance with democratic decisions or a refusal to turn to politicians for help and advice (O'Neill 2002).

A related factor concerns the virtual inevitability of politicians being regarded as objects of distrust and derision. Thanks to a free and sometimes investigative press, citizens are bound to learn of politicians who flagrantly misconduct themselves and who, through their behaviour, reinforce existing perceptions. More generally, those who seek responsibility for governing will almost inevitably disappoint those they seek to rule. It is an occupational hazard. Politicians have to take positions across a range of issues, and they also have to compromise. Since virtually no position is universally popular, and since compromise requires politicians to shift position, every citizen is likely to feel disappointed or even betrayed on at least one issue. Some people may be upset with their politicians all of the time; all will be upset some of the time. In the circumstances, it is easy to discount negative perceptions of politicians' integrity as simply background noise.

Further grounds for being sceptical about the importance of politicians' perceived conduct exist in voters' actual behaviour at the ballot box. As Sam Popkin (1991: 99) observes: 'Voters generally care about ends, not means; they judge government by results and are generally ignorant of or indifferent about the methods by which the results are achieved.' There are certainly numerous cases of politicians with dubious personal morals being returned to office, from Lloyd George's victory as the 'man who won the war' in the 1918 British general election to Silvio Berlusconi's successive victories in Italian general elections in the early twenty-first century. Looking to explain the very brief impact that allegations of President Bill Clinton's relations with Monica Lewinsky had on his approval ratings in 1998, John Zaller (1998: 185) highlights the importance of the 'political substance' and the 'delivery of outcomes and policies that the public wants'. A sceptic of the importance of politicians' conduct could also point to the enduring importance of partisanship in structuring citizens' responses to alleged transgressions, as we saw in Chapter 6, and in shaping subsequent behaviour. Individuals' trust in politicians in general may explain little once their sense of partisan attachment is taken into account.

In short, therefore, people's judgements of their rulers' and representatives' integrity and ethics may well be regarded as a minor consideration when compared with other factors, such as the state of the economy, their perceptions of government performance across a range of issues, their ideological predispositions and their partisan attachments. One of our female focus group participants in Colchester articulated this perspective when she said: 'Maybe I'm a pessimist, but I have a dim view of politicians. Ideally, I'd want them to be different, but they're not. And in relation to integrity, I think there are bigger problems. [Integrity] is not a big deal for me.'

At the same time, however, many people would disagree with such views. As we saw in Chapter 2, there is a considerable body of academic research that points to the wider implications of citizens' ethical judgements about politicians in terms of their interaction and engagement with state authorities. Moreover, politicians' ethics and standards of conduct were matters of great importance to the vast majority of those who took part in our surveys and focus groups. Evidence from these sources all pointed to the fact that a large proportion of citizens attach great weight to the conduct of politics and the way their politicians behave. As one of our focus group participants observed when reflecting on the MPs' expenses scandal:

The actual material loss and damage that the scandal had ... was not enormous. It was more the principle that the elected officials that were supposedly abiding by the laws were subverting them for their benefit, undermining your own trust in politicians. It made you question why the public would be expected to pay taxes, and be punished for tax evasion or similar deeds. (Man, Egham)

Other focus group participants linked the perceived decline in politicians' standards of conduct to a likely fall in electoral turnout and a lowering of Britain's international standing. Whatever sceptics might say, therefore, it is important to consider fully the implications of such attitudes and the substantive impact of citizens' perceptions of politicians' conduct on the democratic process.

In this chapter we assess the relationship between Britons' perceptions of political conduct and trust in political actors, on the one hand, and their behaviour and other attitudes, on the other. Together, our findings confirm what many of our focus group participants suggested: that politicians' standards of conduct matter. They matter for how people engage with democratic politics and the policy process, and they matter for how citizens respond to policy outputs and political institutions. The next section accordingly examines the relationship between citizens' integrity perceptions and other attitudes towards the political system. The third section explores the relationship between such perceptions and electoral participation. The fourth section looks at the potential impact of perceptions on the ease with which future public policy may be implemented, and the fifth section examines the extent to which citizens take moral cues from politicians' perceived conduct.

Engagement with politics: attitudes towards the political system

We begin our examination of the effects of citizens' integrity perceptions by exploring the relationship between these perceptions and three indicators of political support: satisfaction with the way democracy works; external political efficacy; and support for the norm that every citizen should vote. All three indicators are frequently associated with higher levels of political participation

As we saw in Chapter 2, students of mass politics conventionally distinguish between more or less specific objects of political support, with political actors at the 'specific' end of the continuum, the wider political community at the 'general' or 'diffuse' end of the continuum, and the political regime somewhere in between (Easton 1965, 1975; Norris 1999, 2011). The first of our indicators, satisfaction with democracy, can be interpreted as tapping support for regime performance (Linde and Ekman 2003). It was derived by asking respondents the question: 'On the whole are you very satisfied, fairly satisfied, a little dissatisfied or very dissatisfied with the way that democracy works in this country?' The second of our indicators, external political efficacy, can also be interpreted as tapping support for regime performance. It measures the extent to which citizens believe that political actors and institutions are responsive to their attempts to exert political influence over them. This indicator was derived from responses to a standard survey item: 'Some people say it makes a difference which party is in government. Others say that it does not make a difference which party is in government. Using the following scale – where 1 means it makes a difference which party is in government and 5 means that it does not make a difference which party is in government – where would you place yourself?'

Our third indicator, duty to vote, can be interpreted as support for a key regime principle, popular participation in choosing governments. As Sarah Butt and John Curtice note (2010: 2), this indicator taps an individual's 'sense of commitment to their country and its democracy'. It has also been shown to be a strong determinant of individuals' propensity to vote in elections (Jones and Hudson 2000; Clarke *et al.* 2009). To measure this sense of commitment, respondents were simply asked how strongly they agreed or disagreed with the proposition that 'It is every citizen's duty to vote in an election.'

Our measure of integrity perceptions and our three indicators of political support all come from data obtained from the third (spring 2010) wave of our panel survey. The integrity perceptions measure is respondents' overall ratings of elected politicians' standards of honesty and integrity (see Table 6.1, above). As the most recent measure of this disposition, it reflects respondents' summative judgement of politicians' conduct over the period in which our surveys were fielded.

Our basic expectations are that citizens' who have greater confidence in their politicians' honesty and integrity are likely to be more satisfied with democracy, to have a higher sense of external efficacy and to be more committed to the norm that every citizen should vote. It is, of course, highly likely that these variables are all related to each other in complex webs of reciprocal causality (Finkel 1985). For instance, perceptions of politicians' ethics almost certainly shape support for regime principles and regime performance, but it may also be the case that support for the regime colours attitudes towards politicians' integrity. Respondents who are more satisfied with the way democracy works may be inclined to judge politicians' ethics more favourably. Moreover, other factors that structure citizens' engagement with politics, such as age, education, media consumption and partisanship, may drive citizens' evaluations of politicians and regime performance together. Partly for these reasons, we confine ourselves for the time being to reporting general patterns of association and simple cross-tabulations of the key variables.

Table 7.1 shows respondents' perceptions of politicians' standards of honesty and integrity with their reported satisfaction with democracy. For ease of presentation, we group together those respondents who said politicians' standards were 'very high' or 'somewhat high', a clear minority, and those who said standards were 'somewhat low' or 'very low'. The relationship between the two measures is clear. Those who tended to rate their politicians' standards as being high were slightly more likely to be very or fairly satisfied with the way democracy works than those whose rated their politicians' standards as being neither high nor low, and very much more likely to be very or fairly satisfied than those who rated their politicians' standards as being low. Alternatively, respondents who tended to evaluate their politicians' more critically were more likely to be dissatisfied with the way

Table 7.1 *Perceptions of politicians' honesty and integrity versus satisfaction with the way democracy works in Britain, spring 2010*

How satisfied with the way democracy works?	Politicians' standards of honesty and integrity			
	High (%)	Neutral (%)	Low (%)	All (%)
Very satisfied	11.9	4.9	3.9	4.8
Fairly satisfied	44.8	49.1	32.2	37.6
A little dissatisfied	34.3	37.2	35.5	36.2
Very dissatisfied	9.0	8.8	28.5	21.4
N	67	226	541	834

Note: The category listed in this table as 'high' includes the responses 'somewhat high' and 'very high'; the category listed as 'neutral' includes the response 'neither low nor high'; the category listed as 'low' includes the responses 'somewhat low' and 'very low'. 'Don't knows' excluded.

democracy works.[1] The relationship between integrity perceptions and satisfaction with democracy remains significant and positive when multivariate analysis is undertaken to control for the effect of demographic and other dispositional variables (not reported).

Table 7.2 reports in a similar format the relationship between integrity perceptions and respondents' sense of external efficacy. The relationship is less clear-cut than that reported in Table 7.1, but there is still an association. Approximately two-thirds of those with a positive or neutral view of politicians' integrity place themselves at the upper end of the efficacy scale (a score of 4 or 5), whereas the number is about half among those who tend to have a low opinion of politicians' standards.[2] Additional multivariate analysis (not reported) confirms a significant positive relationship between the two variables after taking into account a range of other factors.

Finally, Table 7.3 reports the relationship between respondents' perceptions of politicians' ethics and their response to the duty-to-vote

[1] The gamma coefficient for the relationship between integrity perceptions (as measured on the original five-point scale) and satisfaction with democracy was 0.36 ($p < 0.001$). This suggests a significant moderate relationship between the two measures and that they are tapping distinct views.

[2] The gamma coefficient for the relationship between integrity perceptions (as measured on the original five-point scale) and efficacy was 0.19 ($p < 0.001$), suggesting a significant, but modest relationship.

Table 7.2 *Perceptions of politicians' honesty and integrity versus efficacy, spring 2010*

Which party is in government makes ...	Politicians' standards of honesty and integrity			
	High (%)	Neutral (%)	Low (%)	All (%)
1 No difference	6.0	3.9	13.6	10.3
2	16.4	12.2	11.0	11.8
3	11.9	17.8	17.5	17.2
4	14.9	25.7	24.3	23.9
5 A big difference	50.7	40.4	33.6	36.9
N	67	230	536	833

Note: The category listed in this table as 'high' includes the responses 'somewhat high' and 'very high'; the category listed as 'neutral' includes the response 'neither low nor high'; the category listed as 'low' includes the responses 'somewhat low' and 'very low'. 'Don't knows' excluded.

Table 7.3 *Perceptions of politicians' honesty and integrity versus agreement with the statement that 'it is every citizen's duty to vote', spring 2010*

It is every citizen's duty to vote	Politicians' overall standards of honesty and integrity			
	High (%)	Neutral (%)	Low (%)	All (%)
Strongly agree	74.2	44.6	39.7	43.4
Tend to agree	19.7	33.0	34.8	32.6
Neither agree nor disagree	4.5	15.0	14.3	13.8
Tend to disagree	1.5	5.2	5.1	4.4
Strongly disagree	0.0	2.1	6.2	4.8
N	66	233	552	851

Note: The category listed in this table as 'high' includes the responses 'somewhat high' and 'very high'; the category listed as 'neutral' includes the response 'neither low nor high'; the category listed as 'low' includes the responses 'somewhat low' and 'very low'. 'Don't knows' excluded.

question. Those who tended to rate their politicians' standards as high were very much more likely to strongly agree that it is every citizen's duty to vote compared with those who were more equivocal in their judgement, and they were almost twice as likely to agree compared with the most critical citizens. The mirror image of this relationship was evident among those respondents who tended to rate their politicians' standards as being low. A higher proportion of those who judged their politicians' ethics negatively tended to disagree or strongly disagree with the idea that every citizen should vote compared with those whose judgements were neutral or positive.[3] Again, multivariate analysis (not reported) confirms a significant, positive relationship between the two variables after controlling for other factors.

The findings of this brief section largely confirm those of comparative studies: critical attitudes towards the ethical behaviour of political elites depress satisfaction with democracy, external efficacy and a sense of obligation to vote. These effects may well go some way towards explaining the much lamented decline in electoral turnout and other forms of participation in recent years. It is to the direct effects of integrity perceptions on citizens' actual behaviour that we turn now.

Political participation

As numerous studies have shown, a lack of confidence in political institutions is associated with a reduced propensity to participate, whether through conventional or unconventional means (Finkel 1985; Powell 1986; Clarke and Alcock 1989; Norris 2002, 2004; Karp and Banducci 2008; Birch 2010). The basic idea is that, if people distrust the individuals and institutions that represent them and act on their behalf, they will be less motivated to participate in the activities that select them. Our own analysis of the impact of integrity perceptions on participation takes advantage of the timing of our surveys. It focuses on reported behaviour at the time of the 2010 general election, and takes in engagement with the campaign, turnout and vote choice.

Several survey questions posed in spring 2010 enable us to explore the relationship between citizens' ethical evaluations and their engagement with the contemporary 'short' election campaign. Respondents

---

[3] The gamma coefficient for the relationship between integrity perceptions (as measured on the original five-point scale) and duty to vote was 0.17 ($p < 0.001$), suggesting a significant, but modest relationship.

Table 7.4 *Active participation in the 2010 election campaign,
spring 2010*

Activity	Percentage who participated
Worn a badge or sticker for a candidate	0.6
Discussed a candidate with someone	15.9
Went to hear a candidate speak	1.1
Visited a political party's website	3.5
Visited a candidate's website	3.7
Watched a video of a candidate on the Internet	2.4
At least one of the above	19.4
N	933

were asked whether they had recently participated in one of a number
of campaign-related activities, ranging from discussing a candidate
with someone to visiting a party or candidate website. As Table 7.4
makes clear, the proportion of respondents who had done so was
small: only 19.4 per cent of respondents said they had participated in
at least one of the listed activities, the most common of which was
discussing a candidate with someone else. Nevertheless, by examining
those factors associated with participation and non-participation, it is
possible to establish whether citizens' evaluations of their politicians'
conduct played any role in suppressing or promoting political
participation.

The regression model reported in the second column of Table 7.5
examines the impact of citizens' perceptions of elected politicians'
honesty and integrity on their engagement with the 2010 general
election campaign. The model also controls for several other factors
that might be expected to affect levels of participation, including
indicators of cognitive mobilisation, such as education, attentiveness
to public affairs, newspaper readership, partisanship and economic
evaluations, as well as basic demographic variables, including age,
gender and income.[4] It should be noted that we do not include the

---

[4] With the exception of the attentiveness variable, all the indicators come from
the third wave of our survey, which we also use in our models of turnout and
voter choice in the 2010 general election. The attentiveness question was not
asked in the spring 2010 survey, so we use the measure from the spring 2009
survey. Political interest is a slow-changing variable (Prior 2010), and we have no
reasons to assume that it would have changed much over the twelve months.

Table 7.5 *Engagement with the 2010 general election campaign: active participant versus non-participant*

	Politicians overall	Local MP
Integrity perceptions:		
Overall honesty of politicians	0.51***	
	(0.14)	
Honesty of local MP		0.04
		(0.04)
Demographics:		
Gender: male	−0.21	−0.14
	(0.22)	(0.23)
Age: under 35	0.48	0.45
	(0.28)	(0.29)
Age: 55+	0.15	0.22
	(0.27)	(0.28)
Education: graduate	0.17	0.21
	(0.25)	(0.25)
Income: under £20,000	0.13	0.17
	(0.28)	(0.29)
Income: £40,000+	0.19	0.28
	(0.26)	(0.26)
Dispositions:		
Personal ethical tolerance scale	0.02	0.01
	(0.06)	(0.07)
Attentiveness to public affairs†	0.73***	0.73***
	(0.14)	(0.14)
Conservative identifier	0.49	0.73
	(0.42)	(0.45)
Labour identifier	0.67	0.91*
	(0.40)	(0.44)
Liberal Democrat identifier	0.48	0.66
	(0.43)	(0.46)
Other party identifier	0.70	0.84
	(0.45)	(0.49)
Improvement in personal finances	0.16	0.25
	(0.15)	(0.15)
Improvement in national economy	−0.20	−0.07
	(0.12)	(0.12)
Newspaper consumption:		
Tabloid reader	−0.37	−0.51
	(0.26)	(0.27)

Table 7.5 (*cont.*)

	Politicians overall	Local MP
Quality newspaper reader	0.36	0.35
	(0.28)	(0.28)
Constant	−5.42***	−5.26***
	(0.74)	(0.78)
Nagelkerke R^2	0.22	0.19
N	640	605

Notes: Binary logistic regression.
* $p < 0.05$, ** $p < 0.01$, *** $p < 0.001$; cell entries are coefficients; standard errors are in parentheses.
† Attentiveness to public affairs comes from the spring 2009 wave, all other independent variables from the spring 2010 wave. The dependent variable comes from the post-election wave. See n. 4, above.

attitudinal variables discussed in the previous section because it is not clear in which direction the causal arrow runs between them and our principal variable of interest, integrity perceptions. The dependent variable is a simple dummy variable, where 1 means the respondent participated in at least one of the activities described in Table 7.4, and 0 means they did not. Because of its dichotomous nature, we use binary logistic regression.

The multivariate analysis shows that, even after controlling for other factors, positive integrity perceptions were significantly associated with a greater likelihood of engaging with the election campaign. Respondents who tended to think their politicians had higher standards of honesty and integrity were more likely to undertake at least one of the campaign activities. Of the other variables included in the model, only prior political attentiveness was significant. As might be expected, respondents who said they paid greater attention to public affairs were more likely to have participated in some way in the election campaign.

As objects of political support, 'elected politicians' are somewhat general and familiar, if only in the abstract; to use Pippa Norris' Eastonian framework, they arguably straddle the boundary between political actors and regime institutions. Respondents' ethical evaluations of less familiar objects may be expected to have a weaker effect on participation since they are unlikely to arouse strong opinions. Our data enable us to explore this possibility by examining the impact of respondents' evaluations of their own local MP's honesty (see also Figure 6.3, above) on their engagement with the 2010 election campaign. The third column in Table 7.5 reports a model examining such evaluations, which is otherwise identical to that reported in the second column. It suggests that evaluations of local MPs did not have a significant effect on citizens' propensity to engage with the 2010 election. The results give further support to what we found in Chapter 6, that people do distinguish between politicians in general and their own local MPs, and they further suggest that perceptions of the former tend to matter more in structuring popular engagement with politics. Concerns about voters' own representatives' ethics do not generally lower participation; concerns with the ethics of politicians in general do.

Engagement with an election campaign is one thing, but what arguably matters most in a democracy is actual voting behaviour. Citizens' integrity perceptions can be expected to affect their behaviour at the ballot box in at least two respects: perceptions may affect whether or not citizens cast a vote at all; they may also influence citizens' vote choice among those who do turn out. To explore both possibilities, we examine the relationship between our survey respondents' integrity perceptions, as measured in spring 2010, with reported voting behaviour in the May 2010 general election, as measured in an additional post-election survey.[5] Two caveats should be noted, however. First, our analysis is confined to the national-level dynamics of voting behaviour. We do not seek to control for constituency-level factors, which can obviously play an important role in shaping vote choice. Secondly, we do not seek to examine the direct impact of the 2009 MPs' expenses controversy on voting behaviour in the 2010 general election. This issue has already been thoroughly examined in the academic literature, and the general consensus is that the scandal had a surprisingly limited impact, both at the constituency level (Curtice *et al.* 2010; Eggers and Fisher 2011; Pattie and Johnston 2012) and the national level (Clarke *et al.* 2011; Heath 2011).[6]

---

[5] This post-election wave was fielded between 15 and 30 June 2010, and made available to all teams participating in the British Co-operative Campaign Project.

[6] A constituency-level analysis in the 2010 Nuffield election study, for example, found that incumbent Labour MPs who had been seriously implicated in the scandal lost more votes on average than incumbent MPs who had not been implicated, but 'incumbents who had been caught up in the expenses scandal still performed better than non-incumbent candidates who were attempting to defend

Our analysis begins with turnout. Declining levels of turnout in recent general elections have been a notable cause of concern among commentators and politicians. In the early 1950s, over 80 per cent of registered voters cast a ballot on polling. Since the early 2000s, the proportion has been closer to 60 per cent. Various factors have been identified that may explain this decline, including weakening levels of party identification; the emergence of better educated and more highly sophisticated 'critical citizens' (Norris 1999); a decline in civic norms (Clarke *et al.* 2009; Butt and Curtice 2010); the convergence of the main political parties around the 'centre ground' of British politics; and a series of uncompetitive elections in which one party was widely expected to win. At the same time, however, the general decline in turnout has also coincided with a long-term fall in levels of political trust. There are good reasons, therefore, to examine the role of citizens' ethical evaluations of politicians in shaping their propensity to vote.

The two models reported in Table 7.6 examine, separately, the impact of citizens' overall integrity perceptions and beliefs about their own local MP's honesty on turnout in the 2010 election. In both cases we control for the same factors that we controlled for in our analysis of campaign engagement. In both cases, the dependent variable is whether or not respondents said they voted, with a score of 1 indicating that they did vote and a score of 0 indicating that they did not. Since our dependent variable is a dummy variable, we use binary logistic regression.

Our general expectations are that evaluations of the honesty and integrity of politicians in general will have a positive effect on turnout. Respondents who expressed greater confidence in politicians just ahead of the election will be more likely to have voted than those who expressed less confidence. Negative evaluations of politicians' standards of conduct could, in theory, anger people and rouse them to protest. To invoke Albert Hirschman (1970), citizens who are disappointed with their politicians may be inclined to 'voice' their frustration. Yet the bulk of empirical evidence suggests that such

a Labour-held seat' (Curtice *et al.* 2010: 393–4). Meanwhile, Conservative MPs who had been seriously implicated in the scandal saw their own vote share increase by a smaller proportion than incumbent MPs who had not been implicated (Curtice *et al.* 2010: 398).

Table 7.6 *Reported turnout in the 2010 general election: did vote versus did not vote*

	Politicians overall	Local MP
Integrity perceptions:		
Overall honesty of politicians	0.79**	
	(0.27)	
Honesty of local MP		0.13
		(0.08)
Demographics:		
Gender: male	−0.47	−0.53
	(0.41)	(0.44)
Age: under 35	−1.73**	−1.58**
	(0.52)	(0.55)
Age: 55+	−0.72	−0.59
	(0.59)	(0.63)
Education: graduate	0.08	0.54
	(0.50)	(0.56)
Income: under £20,000	0.02	0.40
	(0.46)	(0.51)
Income: £40,000+	0.49	0.31
	(0.52)	(0.53)
Dispositions:		
Personal ethical tolerance scale	−0.30**	−0.22
	(0.11)	(0.12)
Attentiveness to public affairs†	0.87***	1.01***
	(0.22)	(0.24)
Conservative identifier	0.35	0.77
	(0.65)	(0.69)
Labour identifier	−0.20	0.34
	(0.60)	(0.61)
Liberal Democrat identifier	0.88	0.99
	(0.68)	(0.73)
Other party identifier	1.19	0.86
	(0.76)	(0.74)
Improvement in personal finances	−0.16	−0.22
	(0.25)	(0.28)
Improvement in national economy	−0.26	−0.09
	(0.23)	(0.24)
Newspaper consumption:		
Tabloid reader	−0.67	−0.68
	(0.42)	(0.45)

Table 7.6 (*cont.*)

	Politicians overall	Local MP
Quality newspaper reader	0.13	−0.16
	(0.76)	(0.81)
Constant	1.64	1.50
	(1.01)	(1.05)
Nagelkerke R^2	0.29	0.28
N	504	478

Notes: Binary logistic regression.
* $p < 0.05$, ** $p < 0.01$, *** $p < 0.001$; cell entries are coefficients; standard errors are in parentheses.
† Attentiveness to public affairs comes from the spring 2009 wave, all other independent variables from the spring 2010 wave. The dependent variable comes from the post-election wave.

citizens are likely to behave differently. They are prone to 'exit' electoral politics, just as they are prone to exit other forms of participation, as we have seen in respect of campaign engagement. Our expectations concerning respondents' evaluations of local MPs' honesty and turnout build on our findings in respect of campaign engagement. Although knowledge of misconduct by a local MP might be thought capable of mobilising voters, since constituents have a direct opportunity to evict their representative from office, we suspect that most citizens' opinions about their local representative will not be strong enough to affect turnout once other factors are taken into account.

The results, reported in Table 7.6, confirm our expectations. As shown in the second column, even after controlling for other factors that can be expected to mobilise turnout, especially partisanship and attentiveness to politics, integrity perceptions have a (weakly) significant positive effect on whether or not someone later claimed to have voted in the election. Respondents who judged politicians' ethics more favourably in the run-up to polling day were more likely to have voted. Meanwhile, respondents' perceptions of their local MP's integrity were not significant. What is perhaps surprising is that in both models, partisanship seemingly played no role in their decisions whether to vote or not. Prior interest in politics, as measured by the attentiveness indicator, almost certainly washed out the effects of party identification. Otherwise, younger people were significantly less likely to vote in both models, a reflection of this well-known feature of contemporary political life, while those whose personal ethical code was more tolerant of rule-breaking were also less likely to vote in the 'Politicians overall' model. More rigid morals in one's private life may well correlate with a sense of duty and a commitment to civic norms, which, as seen, is known to correlate with higher levels of participation.

The findings in Table 7.6 suggest that citizens' propensity to vote is modestly conditioned by their evaluations of elected politicians. Disillusioned citizens found it difficult to muster the energy to drag themselves to the polls to vote for people they believed to be dishonest. But how did integrity perceptions affect the behaviour of those who did cast a vote on polling day? Our answer to this question focuses on support for the three main British parties, Labour, the Conservatives and the Liberal Democrats. In 2010, the three parties' combined vote share was, at 88.1 per cent, the lowest in any post-1945 general election. Moreover, the decline in their combined appeal from the 2005 election was fully in keeping with a long-term decline in their triopoly at the ballot box. Many of the explanations for the gradual erosion of support for the major parties echo those offered in attempts to explain declining levels of turnout. Thus, one possible explanation voiced from time to time is the loss of trust in elected politicians: voters who are generally sceptical of politicians' integrity increasingly turn to smaller parties out of frustration with the conduct of national politics. One of our male focus group participants in Egham expressed such a sentiment when reflecting on politicians' misuse of their parliamentary expenses: 'If you want to express the disgust over the expense scandal, which party do you vote for? People think that there is little difference on the main issues between the three major parties, and there is no way to express that displeasure.'

The multivariate analyses in Table 7.7 employ binary logistic regression to examine if integrity perceptions influenced whether respondents voted for one of the three major parties (coded 0) or for another party (coded 1). Once again, we examine the impact of respondents' overall evaluations of politicians, as well as of their local MP. We also include the same control variables that we employed in Tables 7.5 and 7.6, but this time we use identification with any one of the three main parties as the partisanship reference category.

Table 7.7 *Reported vote choice in the 2010 general election: voted for minor party versus a 'major' party (binary logistic regression)*

	Politicians overall	Local MP
Integrity perceptions:		
Overall honesty of politicians	–0.87**	
	(0.29)	
Honesty of local MP		–0.17*
		(0.08)
Demographics:		
Gender: male	0.64	0.58
	(0.43)	(0.45)
Age: under 35	–0.37	–0.34
	(0.57)	(0.60)
Age: 55 plus	–0.20	–0.05
	(0.48)	(0.51)
Education: graduate	–0.38	–0.67
	(0.51)	(0.55)
Income: under £20k	–0.49	–0.70
	(0.47)	(0.49)
Income: £40k plus	–0.13	–0.16
	(0.55)	(0.58)
Dispositions:		
Personal ethical tolerance scale	–0.13	–0.05
	(0.11)	(0.11)
Attentiveness to public affairs†	–0.18	–0.17
	(0.21)	(0.22)
Minor party identifier	4.26***	4.03***
	(0.58)	(0.57)
No party identification	2.72***	2.50***
	(0.59)	(0.61)
Improvement in personal finances	–0.07	–0.11
	(0.28)	(0.29)
Improvement in national economy	0.03	–0.04
	(0.22)	(0.22)

Table 7.7 (*cont.*)

	Politicians overall	Local MP
Newspaper consumption:		
Tabloid reader	−0.22	−0.12
	(0.46)	(0.47)
Quality newspaper reader	−0.05	−0.05
	(0.64)	(0.67)
Constant	−1.39	−2.19
	(1.16)	(1.17)
Nagelkerke R^2	0.50	0.48
N	469	447

Note:
* $p < 0.05$, ** $p < 0.01$, *** $p < 0.001$; cell entries are coefficients, standard errors are in parentheses.
† Attentiveness to public affairs comes from the spring 2009 wave, all other independent variables from the spring 2010 wave. The dependent variable comes from the post-election wave.

The results provide clear evidence to support the notion that concerns about politicians' probity weakens support for the three major parties. As the second column shows, the more confident respondents were in politicians' integrity in general, the less likely they were to have voted for one of the minor parties. In this model, the only other significant explanatory variables were the two partisanship indicators. Identification with one of the minor parties was positively signed, as was no sense of party identification. Not surprisingly, respondents in these two categories were far more likely to vote for a minor party compared with those who identified with one of the three major parties. Prior attentiveness, meanwhile, which exerted such a strong effect on turnout, did not exert a direct influence on how those who turned out cast their ballots. Similar findings emerge from the model reported in the third column. For once, evaluations of a local MP's honesty and integrity do have a significant effect on the dependent variable, even controlling for other factors: those who thought their local MP to be more honest in April 2010 were less likely to have voted for a minor party in May 2010, and were more likely to have voted for one of the three major parties. It may be the case that citizens who choose to vote have clearer opinions about their local MP; their greater interest in politics makes them better informed or at least gives them a better sense of their MP's character.

Overall, the evidence presented in this section is clear about the importance of citizens' integrity perceptions in influencing their behaviour. Our survey respondents' perceptions of politicians were correlated with their engagement with, and participation in, the 2010 general election. Distrust of political elites depressed political participation. Among those who participated, distrust of political elites made them more likely to vote for parties beyond those that dominate parliament.

Compliance with policy outputs

Having examined the effects of citizens' perceptions of politicians on their engagement with the political system, we now turn to the effects of such perceptions on policy implementation and leadership. In a famous essay on the British political system, Anthony Birch (1964) highlighted two key obligations incumbent upon rulers in liberal democratic regimes. On the one hand, governments must be responsive to public opinion and take citizens' preferences into account when forming public policy. On the other hand, governments must also be responsible and pursue wise policies, whether or not they meet with popular approval. Meeting these obligations is not easy. As Birch (1964: 21) went on to note:

a government which wishes to pursue consistent policies must continually be arranging compromises between the conflicting demands of sections of the public. It must also, on occasion, initiate policies which it conceives to be in the best interests of the nation, even though they are unpopular. It must educate the public so that they accept the need for compromises and unattractive policies.

Put another way, citizens must be prepared to follow the lead of their elected representatives in a democracy, just as representatives must follow citizens' preferences.

If any government is to educate the public and successfully implement its policies, citizens need to be receptive to political leadership, and they also need to be willing, in general terms, to comply with laws and other instruments of public policy. Policy-makers in Britain and elsewhere have recently begun to embrace the findings of behavioural economics, in particular ideas about how people can be 'nudged' into altering their behaviour through indirect means, such as the way choices are presented (Thaler and Sunstein 2008; John *et al.* 2009). Surprisingly little attention, however, has been paid to whether other attitudes and predispositions, in particular citizens' perceptions of political conduct, impact on their receptiveness to political leadership and willingness to comply with laws. Since integrity perceptions affect citizens' willingness to influence politics through conventional means, such as voting, there are obvious reasons to suppose that such perceptions may also affect their engagement with the system's outputs. As one commentator conjectures: 'If you are widely held in contempt, it is much more difficult for you to engage the sympathy and support of your voters for both the compromises and risks which decisions by government involve' (Riddell 2011: 137).

Our examination of the importance of integrity perceptions on citizens' engagement with outputs begins with a series of survey experiments designed to assess respondents' willingness to follow the lead of politicians. These experiments took the form of three questions that were posed in the third wave of our survey fielded in spring 2010. The first two questions described a hypothetical action by a third party in which a 'difficult' decision was taken concerning the distribution of resources. The first scenario presented to respondents began: 'A large company decides to make a number of its staff redundant in order to protect its other employees' pension scheme.' The second scenario began: 'A local authority decides to close one of its schools in order to invest the money into other schools in its area.' Both questions were intentionally designed to elicit uncertainty in the minds of respondents: although there were likely to be potential losers – the staff made redundant, or the community served by the local school facing closure – the action could nonetheless be justified by recourse to the greater public good. The third scenario was more abstract and referred to a general area of policy disagreement: 'People disagree over whether or not it is a good idea to invest more money in building nuclear power stations.' In this case, the intention was to highlight the existence of an issue on which people took different positions.

For each question, respondents were randomly assigned to one of three groups. The first group were presented with the scenario alone. The second and third groups were given additional information about the position taken on the decisions or issue by different politicians: for a third of respondents, a politician or group of politicians were supportive; for another third, a politician or group of politicians were opposed. For all three scenarios, respondents were asked what they thought of the decisions or issue by indicating their approval on a 0–10 scale, where 0 meant that it was 'a very bad idea', and 10 meant it was 'a very good idea'. Details about the three versions of each scenario are set out in Table 7.8.

The aim of the exercise was to ascertain the extent to which the views of politicians could influence people's opinions. Our expectation was that additional information about politicians' views would cue respondents to be more or less supportive depending on the group to which they had been assigned. As illustrated in Figure 7.1, we expected respondents who were told that politicians were against the decision or proposal (A) to be more likely to say it was a bad idea than respondents who were not given a cue (B). Conversely, we expected respondents who were told that politicians were in favour (C) to be more likely to say it was a good idea compared with the control group (B). The experiment also enabled us to explore how individuals' integrity perceptions affected their responses. To this end, we drew on our questions about how honest and trustworthy respondents said ministers and MPs were in general (see Figure 6.3, above), dividing respondents into those who judged the group to be less honest than average (i.e., answered with a score below the mean score) and those who judged the group to be more honest than the average (i.e., answered with a score above the mean score).[7] We used the resulting variable relating to ministers to analyse responses to the first scenario ('redundancies'), and the variable relating to MPs to analyse responses to the second and third scenarios ('school closure' and 'nuclear power').

In essence, we expected information about the views of politicians – whether in favour or opposed to the proposal – to be more persuasive among respondents who were more trusting of politicians (A_1 and C_1),

---

[7] In practice, respondents were divided into those that gave an answer between 0 and 4, inclusive, on the 0–10 scale, and those that gave an answer of 5 or more. Accordingly, some 459 respondents were classified as judging ministers to be less honest than average, and 393 were classified as judging them to be more honest than average. The respective numbers for MPs in general were 448 and 406.

Table 7.8 *Overview of scenarios employed in survey experiments, spring 2010*

Position taken by politicians	Scenario 1: redundancies	Scenario 2: school closure	Scenario 3: nuclear power
No position (baseline statement)	A large company decides to make a number of its staff redundant in order to protect its other employees' pension scheme.	A local authority decides to close one of its schools in order to invest the money into other schools in its area.	People disagree over whether or not it is a good idea to invest more money in building nuclear power stations.
Politicians support	*Baseline statement plus:* Several government ministers appear on television supporting the decision.	*Baseline statement plus:* The local MP strongly supports the decision.	*Baseline statement plus:* A group of MPs from all parties has recently spoken out strongly in support of investing more money in nuclear power.
Politicians oppose	*Baseline statement plus:* Several government ministers appear on television opposing the decision.	*Baseline statement plus:* The local MP strongly opposes the decision.	*Baseline statement plus:* A group of MPs from all parties has recently spoken out strongly in opposition to investing more money in nuclear power.

Table 7.9(a) *Redundancies scenario*

A large company decides to make a number of its staff redundant in order to protect its other employees' pension scheme	Politicians oppose	Baseline	Politicians support	Support–oppose gap
More than average trust in ministers (mean score)	4.3	4.2	4.8	+0.5†
Less than average trust in ministers (mean score)	4.6	3.7	4.2	−0.4
More trusting–less trusting gap	−0.3	+0.5	+0.6*	
All respondents (mean score)	4.5	3.9	4.5	−0.1‡
N	284	231	259	

Notes: Mean scores on 0–10 scale.
† $p < 0.1$; * $p < 0.05$. Figures have been rounded to one decimal place.
‡ Change less than −0.05. The scores reflect a 0–10 scale, where 0 means the decision is a very bad idea and 10 means it is a very good idea.

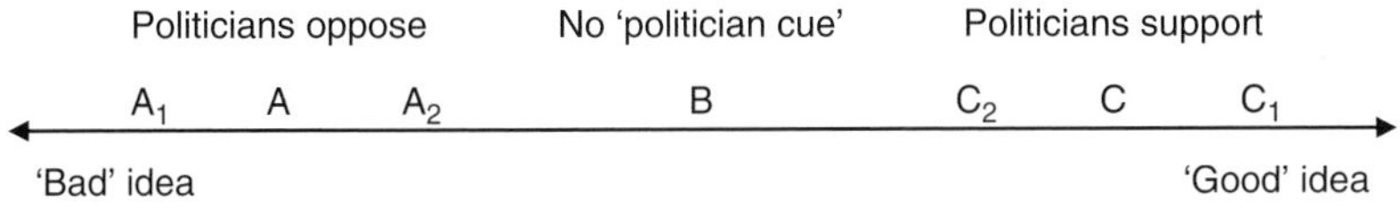

Figure 7.1 Anticipated effects of politicians' views on respondents' support

and to be less persuasive among respondents who tended to think politicians were dishonest (A_2 and C_2). To use simple algebraic formulae, we would expect: C_1-$A_1 > C_2$-A_2. Moreover, we would also only expect significant differences between more or less trusting respondents within the two treatments referring to politicians' positions; since politicians are not referred to in the baseline treatment (although a local authority is referred to in all the 'schools closure' scenarios, a point to which we return), we would not expect there to be a significant gap between more or less trusting respondents (all located at B) who were given this version of each scenario.

The results provide some support for our expectations. In the redundancy scenario, the positions taken by ministers had mixed effects (see Table 7.9(a)). Among all respondents, the mean score for both those who were told that ministers opposed the firm's decision and

Table 7.9(b) *School closure scenario*

A local authority decides to close one of its schools in order to invest the money into other schools in its area	Politicians oppose	Baseline	Politicians support	Support–oppose gap
More than average trust in MPs (mean score)	4.5	5.1	5.7	+1.2**
Less than average trust in MPs (mean score)	4.0	4.5	4.5	+0.5
More trusting–less trusting gap	+0.5	+0.7*	+1.2***	
All respondents (mean score)	4.2	4.8	5.0	+0.8**
N	242	280	247	

Notes: Mean scores on 0–10 scale.
* $p < 0.05$, ** $p < 0.01$, *** $p < 0.001$. Figures have been rounded to one decimal place. The scores reflect a 0–10 scale, where 0 means the decision is a very bad idea and 10 means it is a very good idea.

those who were told that ministers supported it was 4.5. However, among respondents who tended to rate ministers' honesty more positively, the positions taken by politicians did lead to the expected outcome. Being told that ministers supported the decisions elicited a mean score of 4.8, whereas being told that ministers opposed the decision elicited a mean score of 4.3. The gap was small, however, and was only significant by a less stringent threshold ($p < 0.1$), a consequence in part of the small N.[8] Meanwhile, respondents who tended to be less trusting of ministers seemingly rejected politicians' cues altogether: respondents who were told that ministers opposed the decision were on average more supportive than those who were told that ministers supported the redundancies, though this difference is not significant at conventional levels.

The results of the second experiment, the school closure scenario, accorded most closely with our expectations (see Table 7.9(b)). Among all respondents, the position taken by the MP had the anticipated effect on their judgements about the decision to close the local

---

[8] The significance of differences between respondents who received the different treatments was ascertained by creating separate treatment variables for each question and then conducting a *T*-test.

Table 7.9(c) *Nuclear power scenario*

People disagree over whether or not it is a good idea to invest more money in building nuclear power stations	Politicians oppose	Baseline	Politicians support	Support–oppose gap
More than average trust in MPs (mean score)	6.3	6.0	6.2	−0.1‡
Less than average trust in MPs (mean score)	5.6	5.7	5.7	+0.1
More trusting–less trusting gap	+0.6†	+0.30	+0.51	
All respondents (mean score)	5.9	5.7	6.0	+0.1
N	246	264	236	

Notes: Mean scores on 0–10 scale.
† *p* < 0.1. Figures have been rounded to one decimal place.
‡ Change less than −0.05. The scores reflect a 0–10 scale, where 0 means more investment is a very bad idea and 10 means it is a very good idea.

school. When the local MP was opposed to the decision, the mean score was 4.2, and when the local MP supported the decision, the mean score was 5.0. The 0.8 difference between these two scores was statistically significant (*p* < 0.01). More trusting and less trusting respondents also behaved in the expected way: opposition to the closure seemed to encourage both sets of respondents to judge it less favourably, whereas support for the closure encouraged both sets to judge it more favourably. Moreover, the average between the positions was greater among more trusting respondents (1.2) than the less trusting (0.5), in line with expectations.

The third experiment, which used politicians' positions on the issue of further investment in nuclear power to cue responses, returned no statistically significant differences between respondents exposed to MPs' support for further investment and those exposed to MPs' opposition (see Table 7.9(c)). Similarly, there were no differences among more trusting respondents and less trusting respondents. It may be that individuals responded differently to the abstract nature of the question, but it could also well be the case that nuclear power was an issue on which most respondents already had firm views, such that the additional information provided here did not sway them. At any rate, the results from all three experiments suggest that perceptions of politicians' integrity can affect citizens' willingness to follow their lead, especially when it comes to issues on which people are unlikely to have a prior opinion.

Providing a moral lead?

Politicians may seek to persuade citizens through speech-making and taking clear positions on certain issues, but they may also persuade citizens through their deeds as well as their words. Such 'teaching by doing' can be intentional or unintentional, of course; citizens may observe how politicians behave and alter their own conduct in ways that governments may not wish them to.

As seen at the very beginning of this chapter, some of our focus group participants suggested that politicians serve as role models for the public, and if they act inappropriately and break rules, other citizens may follow suit. The fortuitous timing of our surveys around the 2009 MPs' expenses scandal provides something of a natural experiment that allows us to investigate this supposition. Could it be that the widely publicised allegations of widespread expenses fiddling in Parliament led to a loosening of moral standards among the general public? Did large numbers of citizens draw the lesson from MPs' deeds that it was acceptable to act in similar ways in their own walks of life?

We test this possibility by examining changes in responses to a series of questions that sought to tap citizens' private moral standards. We first asked our respondents in spring 2009 whether they thought that three different behaviours could always be justified or never be justified, including: avoiding a fare on public transport; telling a lie if it is in your interest; and claiming government benefits to which you are not entitled (see Chapter 4). Responses were recorded on a 0–10 scale, where 0 meant 'can never be justified' and 10 meant 'can always be justified'. We interpreted this scale as a measure of tolerance for the behaviour in question. We also combined these responses to create a scale of personal morality, which we have used as a control variable in a number of our multivariate analyses. Crucially, we asked our respondents the same questions a year later. Subtracting responses in 2009 from those in 2010 gives us a measure of how respondents' personal morals changed over the year. Although we did not ask respondents to evaluate the acceptability of misusing expenses and allowances in their own workplace, they could conceivably draw a

Table 7.10 *Changes in personal moral standards, spring 2009– spring 2010*

	Mean score on personal morality questions (on 0–10 scale)		
	Spring 2009	Spring 2010	Change
Avoiding a fare	2.1	2.1	+0.1
Telling a lie	3.6	3.9	+0.3
Abusing benefits	1.0	1.0	−0.1‡

Notes: ‡ Change less than −0.05. Only respondents who answered the question in both waves are included in this table. The figures in the second and third columns have been rounded to one decimal point, hence the apparent discrepancy in terms of the change concerning 'avoiding a fare'.

parallel between the 'fiddling' that went on Westminster and other types of money-related impropriety such as fare dodging and abusing the benefits system. If citizens learned unethical truths from the expenses scandal, we would expect the most pronounced changes to occur in respect of these questions.

Looking at the aggregate-level picture, as represented in Table 7.10, there is little evidence of any general loosening of public morals in the wake of the MPs' expenses scandal. Among our respondents who answered the questions in both waves, there was virtually no change in overall levels of tolerance of avoiding a fare on public transport or claiming benefits to which individuals were not entitled. Respondents' willingness to condone lying did increase between spring 2009 and spring 2010, but it is not immediately clear why citizens would become more tolerant of self-interested lying as a result of the expenses scandal.

To analyse the potential impact of the expenses scandal in more detail, it is necessary to look at individual-level changes rather than just the aggregate-level picture. In particular, it is necessary to relate changes in respondents' personal moral standards to changes in their ethical assessments over the same period. Table 7.11 accordingly reports a series of bivariate correlations between changes in respondents' answers to the three personal ethics questions and changes in their perceptions of potentially problematic behaviours in British politics.[9]

[9] The survey items employed for this purpose are those analysed in Chapter 6: 'How much of a problem is the following behaviour by elected politicians in Britain today? ... Not giving straight answers to questions ... Accepting

Table 7.11 *Bivariate correlations: changes in ethical judgements and changes in private morals, spring 2009–spring 2010*

	More tolerant of ...		
Has become more problematic	Avoiding a fare	Telling a lie	Abusing benefits
Misusing expenses	−0.08*	−0.02	−0.11**
Making false promises	−0.09*	−0.03	−0.11**
Not giving straight answers	−0.04	−0.02	0.03
Accepting bribes	0.02	0.04	−0.02

Notes: Bivariate correlations = Pearson's *r*.
* $p < 0.05$, ** $p < 0.01$.

The results show that, in answer to the question as to whether citizens learned unethical truths from the expenses scandal, respondents who thought that the abuse of official expenses had become more problematic were likely to have become less tolerant of avoiding a fare on public transport ($r = -0.08, p < 0.05$) and less tolerant of benefit fraud ($r = -0.11, p < 0.01$). Changes in perceptions of politicians' tendency to make false promises had a similar relationship with three personal ethics variables. There was no significant association between changes in perceptions of the abuse of official expenses and changes in respondents' tolerance of lying. Overall, then, the expenses scandal seemed to make respondents more righteous.[10] It could well be that the scandal reinforced the view that cheating the system is wrong among citizens who became more critical of standards in political life, but that it also served to justify certain transgressions in the eyes of those who were more tolerant of elite misconduct.

bribes ... Misusing official expenses and allowances ... Making promises they know they can't keep.' Answers were given on a 0–10 scale. Changes over time were calculated by subtracting the spring 2009 score from the spring 2010 score.

[10] This interpretation is reinforced when we seek to correlate changes in respondents' perceptions of the honesty and integrity of MPs in general with changes in their private morals. Respondents who thought that MPs in general had become less honest were likely to have become less tolerant of avoiding a fare on public transport ($r = -0.08, p < 0.05$) and less tolerant of benefit fraud ($r = -0.12, p < 0.01$). Again, there was no significant association with the changes in attitudes to self-interested lying.

Our final area of inquiry into how integrity perceptions affect citizens' engagement with the outputs of the political system focuses on their attitudes to the law in general. In our third wave of the survey, we asked respondents whether they agreed or not with the statement: 'People should obey the law, even if it goes against what they think is right.' This question has been used in previous studies as a measure of the law's legitimacy, an important normative factor predisposing people to comply with the law (Tyler 1990). The multivariate analysis in Table 7.12 accordingly examines the relationship between integrity perceptions and their support for the norm of compliance. Since the dependent variable, compliance, takes the form of a 1–5 scale, we use ordinal logistic regression. We use the same controls that we employed in other multivariate models reported in this chapter. Some of these factors are already known to affect citizens' beliefs about the importance of the law. Previous research, for example, has shown that older people in Britain are more likely to express support for the law (Pattie *et al.* 2004: 68–70), whereas a strong commitment to law and order is a major feature of the Conservative Party's ideology (Leach 2009). It is also likely, of course, that respondents' personal ethics will reflect and inform their attitude to the law.

The results show a significant and positive relationship between respondents' integrity perceptions and their expressed support for complying with the law, even after controlling for other factors. None of the demographic factors proved to be significant, but Conservative and Labour identifiers were more likely to support the norm of compliance, while individuals who scored more highly on the personal ethical tolerance score were less likely to support it. Interestingly enough, tabloid readers also tended to be more supportive of the norm, a reflection, perhaps, of the hard-line approach taken to law and order in such newspapers, though it is unclear whether such coverage leads or follows opinion.

As with respondents' satisfaction with democracy, sense of external efficacy and commitment to the principle that everyone should vote, there is reasonable uncertainty about the causal direction between integrity perceptions and compliance. It is possible that a person who has a greater tendency to comply with the law judges politicians more harshly because of their prior commitment to the law. However, there are good reasons for thinking that the arrow of causality is more likely to run the other way around, and that perceptions of individual and

Table 7.12 *Modelling compliance with the law*

	Coefficients
Integrity perceptions:	
Overall honesty of politicians	0.26**
	(0.10)
Demographics:	
Gender: male	0.04
	(0.16)
Age: under 35	0.15
	(0.20)
Age: 55+	0.21
	(0.20)
Education: graduate	−0.36
	(0.19)
Income: under £20,000	−0.12
	(0.19)
Income: £40,000+	0.09
	(0.19)
Dispositions:	
Personal ethical tolerance scale	−0.27***
	(0.05)
Attentiveness to public affairs†	−0.07
	(0.09)
Conservative identifier	0.51
	(0.27)
Labour identifier	0.50
	(0.26)
Liberal Democrat identifier	0.29
	(0.27)
Other party identifier	−0.20
	(0.29)
Improvement in personal finances	0.08
	(0.11)
Improvement in national economy	0.01
	(0.09)
Newspaper consumption:	
Tabloid reader	0.46**
	(0.18)
Quality newspaper reader	−0.17
	(0.23)

Table 7.12 (*cont.*)

	Coefficients
Nagelkerke R^2	0.15
N	613

Notes: Ordinal logistic regression; cut points omitted.
** $p < 0.01$, *** $p < 0.001$. Cell entries are coefficients (standard errors).
† Attentiveness to public affairs comes from the May 2009 wave.

institutional integrity are likely to drive individuals' tendency to comply. Previous academic research has shown how satisfaction with political processes and perceptions of procedural justice can shape support for compliance (Tyler 1990; Hibbing and Theiss-Morse 2001, 2002; Allen and Birch forthcoming). In this case, while the micro-causal logic of the relationship is unclear, it may be that the misdemeanours of political elites undermine the moral authority of elected representatives and weaken the sense of civic duty that subtends most people's belief in abiding by legal norms.[11] At any rate, the results do lend clear support to the idea that the state's ability to enforce the law is compromised by a lack of confidence in the integrity of elected politicians.

Conclusion

Much ink has been spilt lamenting the dire consequences of political misconduct for the quality of democracy and the moral fibre of society, yet there have been few attempts to evaluate systematically the way in which integrity perceptions impinge on democratic politics. The analysis presented in this chapter indicates that such perceptions matter; the ethical performance of politicians does impact on citizens' attitudes towards and engagement with public institutions and politics. Taken together, the results suggest that perceived wrong-doing by politicians weakens the sense of political duty held by citizens. This finding is perhaps not surprising. When asked about political conduct, many of our focus group participants spoke of 'double standards' and complained that there appeared to be one law for politicians and another

---

[11] For a more detailed analysis of this relationship, see our account of the 2011 London riots (Birch and Allen 2012).

for themselves. The manifest injustice of this perceived situation, where political elites are viewed as adhering to lower moral standards than the bulk of the population, is bound to rankle. It is just one step from anger at this state of affairs to a degraded understanding of citizenship. It remains for the next chapter to identify some possible means of ameliorating it.

8 | Changing public perceptions: problems and remedies

Y OU CAN'T expect [politicians] to be perfect, but you can expect them to respect the rules. So it's up to the rules to ensure they are adequate.

(Female focus group participant, Hackney)

With the partial exception of Chapter 3, where we surveyed the ethical landscape of British politics up until the 2010 general election, our primary focus throughout this book has been citizens' subjective views of political ethics and politicians' conduct. We have otherwise avoided engaging with debates about actual standards of conduct in British political life and institutional arrangements for ensuring high standards. We have also avoided engaging with the enormously important topic of how such standards and arrangements affect and are affected by subjective evaluations of political ethics, and what has been done and what might be done to improve the moral standing of politicians in the public's eye. In this chapter we turn our attention to such matters.

Our starting point is the failure of recent official attempts to bolster wider public confidence in the integrity of national-level politics. As we saw in Chapter 3, the introduction of various codes of conduct and regulators since the mid-1990s has helped to institutionalise a preoccupation with ethics throughout public life. No generation of British politicians has ever been subject to such extensive and formalised ethics regulation. And yet, politicians are no more trusted than they were before. If anything, public confidence in the integrity of British political institutions and processes has declined.

Some commentators have responded to these trends with an air of resignation. Thus, Peter Riddell in his recent book *In Defence of Politicians* concludes: 'Politicians will never be loved, respected or trusted … The question is, rather, whether we can do anything to make politics work better – for them and for us, the voters' (Riddell

2011: 149). Similar sentiments were expressed by a committee of MPs in a report on the regulation of conduct in British public life. After observing how public opinion had been virtually unmoved by recent ethics reforms, the committee rejected the restoration of trust as a prime objective for regulation: 'we believe that the primary purpose of the ethical regulatory system is to ensure that standards of public conduct remain high' (Public Administration Committee 2007: 16). In adopting such a position, however, politicians risk violating important ethical principles of conduct, including their obligation to pay heed to their standing in the eyes of the public (Thompson 1995). They also expose themselves to accusations of drawing hasty conclusions. As Britain's Committee on Standards in Public Life (2013: 10) concluded in a wide-ranging review of ethical arrangements throughout the public sector: 'It would be wrong to draw the conclusion that there is nothing that can be done ... Visibly high standards of behaviour by public office-holders may not be a sufficient condition for high levels of public trust. But they are a necessary one.'

The remainder of the chapter examines why high standards of behaviour are not always visible and what might be done to make them more visible. The next section describes the perceptions gap that clouds British political ethics, in particular the apparent obliviousness of public opinion to the proliferation of rules, regulations and regulators created to improve standards of conduct. The third section examines why attempts to improve standards have largely failed in terms of their effect on public opinion. It highlights the importance of disappointed expectations and the particular importance of citizens' and politicians' different normative understandings of political ethics. The final section presents our own suggested remedies for bringing together the ethical worlds inhabited by politicians and the public, including more effective elite engagement with political ethics, more effective responses to citizens' ethical concerns, more honest talk in politics, a closer alignment of institutional ethics with public understandings, more effective institutional sanctions for misconduct, more proactive engagement with transparency, and more innovative approaches to public education.

More standards, less trust

As we saw in Chapter 3, an institutionalised preoccupation with standards began in earnest in Britain in the mid-1990s. There are now myriad codes of conduct and a large number of independent ethical 'watchdogs', committees and officials charged with promoting, monitoring and enforcing high ethical standards throughout the British political system. In terms of national-level politics, these watchdogs include the Committee on Standards in Public Life (created in 1994), the Parliamentary Commissioner for Standards (1995), the Electoral Commission (2000), the prime minister's Independent Adviser on Ministers' Interests (2006), the Independent Parliamentary Standards Authority (2009) and the House of Lords Commissioner for Standards (2010). At the regional level, they include bodies such as the Commissioner for Ethical Standards in Public Life in Scotland (2013) and the National Assembly for Wales Commissioner for Standards (2009).[1]

No government has ever mounted an authoritative justification for these changes in their entirety, but politicians have defended individual developments, at least in part, as a way of strengthening public confidence in politics. Thus, John Major, then prime minister, defended his decision to appoint a Committee on Standards in Public Life in October 1994: 'It is important that the public have confidence in our system of public administration ... In the present atmosphere, there is public disquiet about standards of public life and I have concluded that action is imperative' (*HC Debates*, 25 October 1994, vol. 248, col. 758). Thus, Jack Straw, then home secretary, introduced the government's legislation to establish an Electoral Commission in January 2000, and concluded with the challenge: 'The time has come to get down to the business of restoring public confidence in our political institutions' (*HC Debates*, 10 January 2000, vol. 342, col. 45). Thus, Harriet Harman, then leader of the House of Commons, justified the government's hastily drawn-up Parliamentary Standards Bill in 2009: 'The abuse by some Members of our allowance system has caused a high level of public concern. It has required this comprehensive range of actions to ensure that we can say to the public ... "We get it, and we're sorting it"' (*HC Debates*, 23 June 2009, vol. 494, col. 680).

---

[1] Together with a number of older posts or bodies, such as the Comptroller and Auditor General (established in 1866), the Parliamentary Commissioner for Administration (1967) and the Judicial Appointments Commission (2006), which oversee the proper conduct of public business, as opposed to the conduct of politicians and parties, they arguably constitute what has been termed the 'integrity branch' of government (Ackerman 2000; Spigelman 2004).

Unfortunately for their advocates, it is absolutely clear that the introduction of various ethics reforms has not coincided with any discernible improvement in levels of trust in politicians. As we saw in Chapter 6, most people consistently say that elected politicians behave according to low standards of honesty and integrity, that most politicians are motivated by self-interested gain, and that financial and discursive dishonesty in British political life is rife. As we also saw in Chapter 6, most people also seem to think that politicians' standards of honesty and integrity have been declining in recent years.

To appreciate more fully the apparent failure of recent ethics reforms, we must look to other sources for evidence of long-term changes in public sentiment. There are few survey questions that enable us to track trends over time, but the available data all point in the same direction. In the 1981 World Values Survey, some 59 per cent of British respondents tended not to have very much confidence in Parliament or none at all. The proportion rose to 65 per cent in 1999 and, when measured in 2006, came in at 64 per cent. After a twenty-five-year period that embraced a number of major ethics reforms, Parliament was no more trusted than before. A similar picture is painted by available public polling data. In 1985, a Gallup poll found that 79 per cent of respondents said an MP would tell lies if they thought the truth would hurt them politically, 67 per cent said that MPs cared more about special interests than people like them, and 46 per cent claimed that MPs made a lot of money by using public office improperly (see Table 8.1). By contrast, only 42 per cent agreed that most MPs had a personal moral code. The pattern of responses was remarkably similar in 1990, when Gallup again asked the questions, but there was a marked deterioration in attitudes in 1994, and the mood was no better in November 2004 when YouGov posed the same questions. By this time just 17 per cent of respondents agreed that MPs had a personal moral code.

Further evidence that ethics reforms, at least in the House of Commons, have failed to boost public confidence comes from Eurobarometer data. A question included in a number of surveys since 1997 has asked respondents whether they tended to trust the British Parliament. The results, shown in Figure 8.1, show a general downward trend in the intervening years. When the question was first asked, close to half of respondents answered that they tended to trust Parliament. Towards the end of 2010, the proportion had fallen close to a quarter.

Table 8.1 *Percentage agreeing with statements about Members of Parliament*

	1985	1990	1994	2004
Most MPs will tell lies if they feel the truth will hurt them politically	79	78	87	85
Most MPs care more about special interests than they care about people like you	67	67	77	71
Most MPs make a lot of money by using public office improperly	46	51	64	59
Most MPs have a personal moral code	42	43	26	17

Sources: August 1985, October 1990, November 1994 Gallup Political and Economic Indexes; November 2004 YouGov survey for the *Daily Telegraph*.

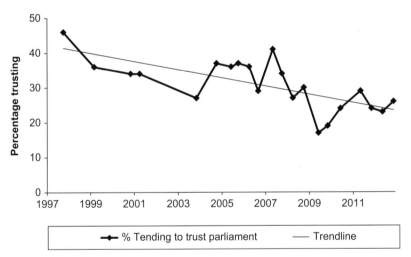

Figure 8.1 Percentage tending to trust the national parliament, 1997–2012
Note: Eurobarometer, available at: http://ec.europa.eu/public_opinion/index_en.htm.

Finally, and shifting the object of ethical evaluation from MPs and Parliament to the government of the day, responses to a question posed by the British Social Attitudes survey show yet another long-term decline in perceptions (see Figure 8.2). When asked whether they tended to trust governments to place the needs of the nation above the interests of their own political parties, only a minority of

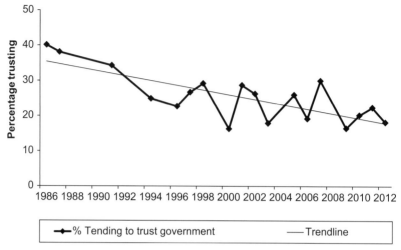

Figure 8.2 Percentage tending to trust governments to place the needs of the nation above the interests of their own political party, 1986–2012
Note: British Social Attitudes, available at: www.britsocat.com.

respondents ever expressed such confidence. The highest levels of confidence were expressed in 1986 and 1987; thereafter, smaller proportions tended to say they trusted the government. To be sure, there have been considerable survey-on-survey fluctuations since the mid-1990s, but the general trend has still been downwards.

Politicians can be forgiven if they feel confused by the absence of any improvement in their standing despite the recent proliferation of ethics regulation. They can also be forgiven if they feel confused by the apparent inconsistencies between the state of subjective political conduct and real political conduct. There is little evidence that British politicians abuse their powers and responsibilities in ways that are all too common in many other parts of the world. Indeed, it would probably be fair to characterise the country's political system and most of its politicians as acting according to comparatively high ethical standards of conduct, albeit with the occasional lapse.

Such a characterisation must come with two immediate health warnings, however. The first, which we return to later, is that it reflects a narrower understanding of ethics than is held by many citizens, one focused on financial integrity. The second caveat is the virtual impossibility of measuring objective standards of conduct. Political integrity cannot be observed directly, and potential proxy indicators, such as press coverage and the number official investigations, must be treated with great caution. For these reasons, attempts to measure real standards of conduct tend ultimately to revert to more or less informed perceptions.

What do these informed perceptions reveal? Previous academic research based on interviews with MPs suggests that new rules and practices introduced at Westminster in the 1990s led to higher standards of conduct in some areas of parliamentary life (Allen 2011). Meanwhile, a series of public inquiries in Britain have generally been upbeat about standards. At the turn of this century, the Committee on Standards in Public Life (2000: 15) noted in its sixth report: 'Many of our witnesses reinforced the view that standards in public life are very high in this country and that the result is a greater freedom from corruption and malpractice than in most other democracies.' Seven years later, a committee of MPs reported how its 'witnesses were convinced that public life in the early twenty-first century was cleaner than it had been before' (Public Administration Committee 2007: 6).

There are areas of concern, to be sure; as a recent report by the Committee on Standards in Public Life (2013: 62) noted: 'Several revelations about historical events have revealed deliberate attempts [by political actors] to get round the rules and cover up the truth.' As we saw in Chapter 3, the expenses scandal showed that many MPs had not fully internalised the 'Seven Principles of Public Life', and there are ongoing concerns about party funding and individuals buying influence with large donations. Yet the same report asserted that 'standards of behaviour have improved significantly in many areas of public life'. The official verdict was thus equivocal, but still more favourable than the public's verdict would appear to be.

Other research also suggests that British politics is cleaner than the public seems to think. A series of reports issued by the Group of States against Corruption, or GRECO, an organisation established in 1999 by the Council of Europe to monitor countries' compliance with anti-corruption standards, have been broadly positive. A report published in the Group's first evaluation round (GRECO 2001: 22–3) concluded that 'corruption is altogether a relatively rare occurrence in the United Kingdom'. It also praised the 'more general campaign to raise standards in public life' that began in 1994. Meanwhile, Britain has always performed well in Transparency International's

Corruption Perception Index (CPI), an annual ranking of countries
determined by expert assessments. Figure 8.3 compares Britain's scores
from 1995 to 2012 with those of four other Western European countries, Denmark, France, Germany and Italy. On the 0–10 scale, where
a lower score indicates a higher level of corruption, Denmark has
consistently been one of the best performing European democracies,
and Italy the worst. Britain has always been far closer to the Danish
benchmark and has usually done better than France and Germany,
the two largest EU members. Assuming that these figures tell us something about the relative probity of British governance, it would again
seem that British politicians are not quite the sinners of their electors'
imaginations.

Four enduring problems

Why have the various ethics reforms of the last two decades failed
to raise public confidence in politicians' honesty and integrity? There
are at least four factors that can help us understand why. None

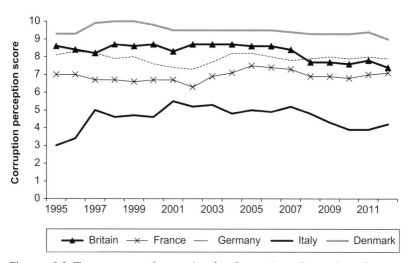

Figure 8.3 Transparency International, Corruption Perception Scores,
1995–2012
Note: The 2012 score was measured on a scale of 0 (highly corrupt) to 100
(very clean). This score was standardised to the 0–10 scale used in previous
surveys.

constitutes a stand-alone explanation. Considering each in turn can also shed light on why there continues to be a gulf between real political conduct and perceived political conduct.

The problem of mediated conduct and misconduct

One feature of British politics that the post-1994 raft of ethics regulation did not change in a way likely to bolster public confidence is press and other media coverage of politicians. Most Britons do not have first-hand experience of political misconduct, and most Britons do not regularly engage directly with politicians. They are, however, exposed to a regular stream of alleged misconduct in the news media, as well as commentary that is often contemptuous in tone. Such exposure will almost inevitably reinforce prevailing levels of distrust towards politicians. Any cases of misconduct will confirm people's negative views; cases of good conduct, which in any event are rarely reported, will be discounted and overlooked.

Far from improving this state of affairs, the spread of ethics regulation, in combination with other developments in British politics, may have exacerbated the potential supply of negative media coverage. The introduction of more rules and investigators means that there are more opportunities for politicians to fall down and to be seen to have fallen down. There are also more opportunities for politicians to play the man rather than the policy. In the House of Commons, for example, the introduction of a code of conduct ushered in a period of complaints about the pettiest infraction of the rules during the late 1990s (Allen 2011). Alleging misconduct is an easy way for politicians to score points, since any allegation of possible misconduct can be publicised and reported in the newspapers. Such consequences were perhaps inevitable. Politicians in the United States soon learned to exploit ethics rules in this way as part of a move to the conduct of 'politics by other means' (Ginsberg and Shefter 1990). British politics has avoided the worst tendencies of American politics in this respect, yet the publication of parliamentary and ministerial codes and the appointment of independent commissioners or advisers to oversee them have undoubtedly institutionalised another avenue of political contestation. Whenever there is any possibility that a rule has been broken, it is all too easy to declare: 'there must be an independent investigation'.

The introduction of ethics rules and regulators has also provided institutional foci for other standards-related activity, and thus potential stories for journalists. Every time a survey is published, or a general inquiry is launched, it is another story of regulators trying to fix problems in political life. Journalists, not that they need reminding, have an opportunity to bash out another story about corrupt or sleazy politicians. A similar consequence arguably followed from moves to increase transparency in politics. Since the advent of the Freedom of Information Act 2000, the evidence for a juicy news story can be obtained by writing one short letter to a public body requesting the potentially incriminating fact. This may be rather lazy investigative reporting, but with the profit margins of newspapers declining, it may be all they can afford. Onora O'Neill (2002) alluded to this point in her 2002 Reith Lectures, where she noted that 'transparency' was neither an adequate means of strengthening trust nor an adequate substitute for it. On the contrary, an obsession with 'transparency', like the public sector obsession with monitoring, auditing and target-setting, can actually weaken trust by breeding suspicion. Rather than a lack of trust, there is actually a culture of suspicion, fuelled by journalism of the type described. Of course, it is not only politicians who suffer from this; it is the entire public sector, but due to their electoral vulnerability, elected representatives are on the sharp edge of this particular precipice.

The problem of citizens' bad judgement

A second feature of British politics that the momentum for more standards has not affected, because it could not affect it, is the presence of bias in citizens' responses to the information presented to them. As we saw in Chapter 6, media coverage and human psychology interact in unfortunate ways, with the former enabling systematic biases inherent in human cognition (Tversky and Kahneman 2000). As a result, people are generally likely to overestimate levels of misconduct in political life and underestimate the integrity of the overwhelming number of politicians. For example, a few moments of thought should be sufficient to make someone realise that the number of serious allegations of misconduct in any given period of time is far less than the number of people holding elected office. During the five years of the 2005–2010 Parliament, only two MPs, George Galloway and Derek Conway, were suspended for breaches of the House of Commons code.

Meanwhile, despite all the allegations made during the expenses scandal, only a handful of former MPs have been convicted of breaking the law, as we saw in Chapter 3. The rules and practices at Westminster may well have fostered unacceptable behaviour, but out of 650-odd MPs, only a tiny minority were actually crooks.

The way people tend to make biased judgements may also be a factor in explaining why people judge politicians in general more negatively than specific politicians with whom they have had some contact (Flinders 2012: 14). For most people, politicians tend to be faraway figures about whom they know little. When surveys ask people about politicians' conduct in general, respondents draw on available information about politicians in general. When surveys ask people about specific politicians, such as their own MP, the same information may be less relevant. Instead, different information may be available, information garnered through local media or word of mouth, and perhaps from direct contact, and such information may well elicit more favourable evaluations.

Our findings suggested a greater tendency to lump all types of politician together than is often supposed, although our respondents still judged local councillors and their own local MP in a more favourable light than MPs and national politicians. It is not clear whether this tendency reflected our survey instruments or the timing of our survey, in particular the impact of the expenses scandal. According to research conducted for the Committee on Standards in Public Life (2011: 17), in 2008, before the expenses scandal, 48 per cent trusted their local MP to tell the truth. In 2010, after the scandal, 40 per cent said the same. Perhaps the quantity of critical media stories about MPs made the notion 'more available' when respondents judged their own MP.

The problem of disappointed expectations

Another way of considering the impact of ethics regulation on public perceptions is to consider the role of citizens' expectations. Academics and policy-makers are increasingly conscious of the role that expectations play in shaping citizens' satisfaction with the delivery of public services (James 2009). A growing body of research confirms that people who tend to have higher expectations concerning the quality of a given service are likely to be less satisfied with the service provided (see, e.g., Curtice and Heath 2012). Politicians, for their part, have always been conscious of the need to manage expectations about what they can deliver, but the logic of political competition encourages them to promise more in order to boost their chances of election. The result is an 'expectations gap', the distance between what citizens come to expect of their politicians and what politicians themselves are actually able to deliver. Such a gap may be closed by improving levels of delivery, by suppressing expectations or by some combination of both.

While much of the literature on expectations has focused on the content and delivery of public policy, Matthew Flinders (2012) has applied the concept of an expectations gap to understand public dissatisfaction with politics more broadly. The same concept may also help to understand the nature of integrity perceptions in Britain today. One clear point that has emerged throughout this book is that most citizens, when asked, tend to say they expect very high standards. As shown in Chapter 4, large proportions of survey respondents consistently expressed the opinion that politicians in the course of their duties should behave according to higher standards than in everyday life. Similarly, very large proportions of respondents made clear that they placed a greater weight on honesty over politicians' ability to deliver, an idea that was also expressed by focus group participants.

Such expectations may be justified on normative grounds, but when members of the public insist on holding to them, they will almost inevitably be disappointed. Politicians are ordinary people, and holding them to extraordinary standards may lead to unrealisable expectations. Most politicians would recognise the additional obligations incumbent upon them as holders of public office, to be sure, but they are ultimately drawn from the society they represent. In the same way that ethics are very much a secondary or tertiary consideration for most people as they go about their business, so ethics are unlikely to be at the forefront of most politicians' minds. Some politicians are likely to stretch ethical principles to the limit in the pursuit of power and/or policy goals. A few are bound to slip. As the Committee on Standards in Public Life (2013: 63) noted:

The behaviour of holders of public office is not independent of that of the society they serve. They come from the same populations on whose behalf they work. So they can be expected to share much the same general standards of morality as the rest of us exhibit in our own lives ... This is not to excuse poor behaviour. But it may help to keep it in perspective.

Expecting citizens to keep things in perspective may not be realistic, however. If people's judgements are anchored to the expectation that no politician should act improperly, the knowledge of even one transgression may lead to more damning judgements about the prevalence of misconduct and its severity.

Recent ethics reforms may have exacerbated the expectations gap surrounding political ethics by increasing the appearance of misconduct. But could such reforms also have affected the size of the gap by altering citizens' expectations? On this point there is no firm evidence. It is possible – we put it no higher – that the spread of codes and regulators has raised expectations in one or both of two ways: by promoting a general sense of aspiration that standards should and will be higher because of new rules and regulations; and by encouraging politicians to attack opponents on ethical grounds, and to promise that their own conduct will be better. Either way, when the inevitable case of misconduct comes to light, public confidence may decline more than it would otherwise have done. Tony Blair frequently, and probably rightly, targeted Conservative 'sleaze' ahead of the 1997 general election and promised to be 'purer than pure' upon his party's election victory that year. Having raised expectations, it must have been all the more galling for many voters that New Labour was soon embroiled in so many sleaze allegations of its own.

The problem of diverse normative understandings

If the push for more ethics regulation since 1994 has done little to lessen the problem of disappointed expectations, it has also done little to lessen another problem: the tendency for representatives and the represented to see the ethical demands of politics in fundamentally different ways. This normative gap is not so widely acknowledged as the expectations gap or the gap between real and perceived political conduct, but it is fundamental to any understanding of contemporary British political ethics. On the one hand, institutional settings and the practice of politics can foster distinctive ethical cultures and beliefs about right and wrong among politicians. On the other hand, the same settings and practices can also shape considerations about the scope for ethics in the first place. When politicians' normative understandings are far removed from those of citizens, they are more likely to behave in ways that the public finds unacceptable, they are likely to find it harder to understand why the public finds their conduct unacceptable, and they are more likely to struggle to respond effectively to the public disapproval.

As we saw in Chapter 4, there are significant differences between citizens' and politicians' evaluations of hypothetical acts, such as a major company making a substantial donation to the government party and the chair of the company being given an honour, an MP being retained by a company to arrange meetings and dinners in the House of Commons, and an MP hiring a spouse or other family member to serve as his or her secretary. Meanwhile, our research suggests that there is a gap between political elites and ordinary members of the public in how political ethics is defined and understood. Whereas elite discourse and regulatory arrangements tend to focus more narrowly on financial conflicts of interest, we have found repeatedly that people often have a broader sense of the appropriate scope of ethical evaluations. Thus, many focus group participants talked of 'spin' and politicians' failure to implement campaign pledges as matters of ethics and integrity. We are certainly not the first to make this point. As Peter Kellner (2004: 838, 840) noted, people are 'repelled by hypocrisy' and want 'authenticity'. Giving straight answers and making promises they can keep are often more important issues than MPs having extra-parliamentary jobs or employing their wives or husbands (Kellner 2004: 839).

Both normative gaps have their origins in the institutionalised nature of political life. Most politicians are members of, or aspire to be members of, institutions that have distinctive cultures and practices. Membership of an institution like Parliament can have the effect of isolating politicians from public opinion, since it exposes them to distinctive institutional norms of conduct and encourages them to mix with like-minded people. It socialises them into behaving in distinctive ways that may jar with citizens' ethical expectations (Rush and Giddings 2011). At the same time, institutional norms almost certainly exacerbate the tendency for politicians to talk about and see ethics in a narrow sense.

On that last point, there is evidence that the advent of more formal ethics regulation in the House of Commons in the mid-1990s changed MPs' behaviour broadly in line with public preferences, but the change related narrowly to their dealings with lobbyists and their mixing of business interests with parliamentary duties (Allen 2008, 2011).

Insofar as more regulation improved standards, it did so in ways that most citizens did not notice or that were not central to citizens' concerns. If anything, the spread of ethics regulation has entrenched a narrow conceptualisation of ethics. Moreover, the reforms did not change, probably because they could not change, the isolated nature of the Westminster village. MPs could not stop being socialised within the Commons any less than barristers or doctors could avoid being exposed to the norms of their professions.

Talk of professions leads to one final feature of contemporary politics that almost certainly limits the scope of ethics in everyday political life. As many commentators have noted, the last fifty years have seen the rise of the career politician (King 1981; Riddell 1993; Cowley 2012). Some commentators go even further and talk about politics as being a profession. Such thinking undoubtedly has a wider resonance, as reflected in the comments of one of our focus group participants:

I'd like to think of politics as of any profession. You don't expect a doctor to do a certain thing that contravenes the medical profession. Or a police officer who is supposed to uphold the law will be punished even more than other persons. It's the same for politicians. (Woman, Egham)

Yet politicians do not, in general, give the appearance of thinking of themselves as members of a unified profession. Tribalism is part and parcel of political life, and there is little enthusiasm among politicians, in comparison with other groups, to guard their collective honour. There is certainly no body to protect politicians' reputations qua politicians.

Partly for these reasons, politicians have given scant thought to the ethics appropriate to their trade. One of the obvious shortcomings with the push for more standards over recent decades is that it has focused on the ethical obligations of particular office holders. It has been surprisingly blind to the fact that those who hold office are also engaged in office-seeking and other political activities. Yet, in the same way that doctors, lawyers, accountants and other professionals need a distinct and functional code of ethics, so too may politicians. Their work may well require an element of moral flexibility that would not be acceptable in other walks of life, and it may also require certain kinds of behaviour that would be inappropriate elsewhere. Such considerations are likely to be alien to many citizens. There has been very little in the way of any public debate about the ethical obligations incumbent upon those seeking to win power, to influence and to lead. In many ways, the recent preoccupation with standards in public life rather than standards of political conduct was probably always going to miss the point.

Possible remedies

When it comes to contemporary British political ethics, a gulf seems to separate politicians from citizens. Citizens think most politicians are a bunch of crooks; politicians generally see themselves as being, in the words of Gordon Brown, 'in politics not for what they can get but for what they can give' (*HC Debates*, 10 June 2009, vol. 493, col. 795). There is also considerable disparity between the way in which political elites and ordinary members of the public understand political ethics. The public as a whole has a far broader view of what is ethical and unethical behaviour in politics than those more actively engaged in political life.

There are a number of potential responses to these issues. One response is to say that there is no real problem with popular antipathy towards politicians. According to this line of thought, people will always be sceptical about politicians' ethics and conduct, perhaps even more so in an age of relatively high levels of education and ready access to mass media. Critical attitudes on the part of the population may actually be functional for democracy (Norris 1999). Another response, as seen in the introduction to this chapter, is to say that there is a problem, but that nothing can be done (Riddell 2011). In answer to the first response, we disagree; there is a problem, and there are undoubted costs when citizens have intensely negative attitudes towards politicians (Hibbing and Theiss-Morse 2002: 209–11). In answer to the second, we also disagree. Clearly, there are no quick fixes for boosting politicians' reputations, but there may be scope for reducing the gulf between citizens and politicians over the long term. Doing nothing is also somewhat contemptuous of popular opinion.

The starting point for our own contribution to this debate is to consider what is practically possible. A radical overhaul of existing ethics structures would be politically untenable in the present climate, and it is far from clear what form any new structures should take. Instead, we suggest experimenting with a number of small changes, both within and outside of existing structures. We leave the recommendation of wider political change and reform to others. It is also important to stress that politicians themselves must take the lead in any effort to effect change. Only they are in a position to do so, and it is they who have the best insights into the demands of their job. The possible remedies we propose are intended to encourage debate rather than constitute prescriptive recommendations. They fall under seven general headings.

More effective elite engagement with political ethics

Our first general suggestion is fairly obvious given the findings of our research. Politicians need to find ways of engaging more closely and effectively with the public's understanding of ethics. This might be done in a number of ways. For a start, there is an ongoing role for an entity like the Committee on Standards in Public Life. After being spared in the Coalition Government's initial cull of non-departmental public bodies in 2010, the Committee was the subject of a 'triennial review', led by Peter Riddell. In his report, Riddell concluded that there was an ongoing need for an ethics monitor or reviewer and went on to make a number of sensible recommendations, not least that 'The Committee should be bolder in picking topics, looking ahead to emerging problems, rather than reacting to controversies' (Riddell 2013: 13). However, the review also concluded that the Committee should 'not regard as one of its objectives as improving public confidence or trust in public bodies and holders of public office' and that its 'biennial research into public attitudes should cease' (Riddell 2013: 13–14). We disagree. The need to save costs is understandable, but there is still a need for an authoritative body, separate from other political institutions, that engages with public attitudes and, on the basis of evidence, informs politicians' and the wider public about popular understandings of political ethics.

There is also arguably a need for a broader public inquiry into standards of conduct in *political* as opposed to public life. The remit of the Committee on Standards in Public Life is rightly focused on the ethics and behaviour of office holders. Yet political conduct is not just about exercising official responsibilities; it is also about the seeking and wielding of power, and politicians' interaction with citizens. Some kind of official inquiry or audit of politicians' and citizens' competing views of political ethics could help focus politicians' minds. It might also help to educate the public. If the Committee on Standards in Public Life is not the appropriate body to undertake such an inquiry, a specially constituted Royal Commission might do the trick, or perhaps a joint committee of Parliament.

In addition to such centrally coordinated research-gathering work, it is also important for politicians at an individual level to engage more directly with citizens' expectations of their conduct, in particular citizens that they might not normally meet. If once per Parliament, for instance, all MPs spent at least a morning or afternoon observing or participating in a focus group on the subject of their conduct, it might help to open their eyes and minds. Many politicians may already have a good understanding of what it is about them that citizens find so distasteful. Many others, however, give the impression through their words and deeds that they do not. There is nothing quite like spending two hours in a room with members of the public as they talk about politics and politicians. We can vouch for that! MPs could take it upon themselves to organise such events, but there would almost certainly be others who could help them, not least academics.

Institutions could also structure politicians' engagement with political ethics more effectively. This could be done through a series of regular debates on the ends and means of political conduct. At present, the House of Commons reviews the MPs' code of conduct at least once every Parliament, and there is then a debate on the revised code. The current debates could, in theory, enable MPs to discuss standards and ethics in political life more widely. In practice, however, these debates have been infrequent, brief and poorly attended, and they have tended to get bogged down in discussions about detailed rule changes rather than the broader ethical contours of political life. For most MPs, ethics is understandably background noise. We think it would help to have that noise occasionally foregrounded. What are the rights and wrongs of political conduct in Britain in the twenty-first century? It is something about which politicians in general have had virtually nothing to say.

Facing up to public unease

Our second general suggestion is also obvious, so obvious in fact that we pause before offering it. However, we feel the point is worth making, if only because we find it so infuriating as politics teachers when we have to tell to our students, again and again, that politicians have failed to address areas of major public concern.

As the lesson of MPs' salaries and allowances show, effectively responding to public unease means taking action in areas where there are known problems. Psychological research points to the ubiquity of cheating among all groups in society, even the most 'honourable', as well as strong human susceptibility to the nefarious influences of conflicts of interest (Ariely 2012), and it is only a matter of time before another party-funding scandal undermines the integrity of British politics, for example, or another MP oversteps the mark in his or her dealings with a lobbyist, or a peer abuses the allowances scheme for members of the House of Lords. To be sure, some of these problems are not easily addressed. The funding of political parties is particularly difficult and raises many competing views about the desirability of state funding (Fisher 2009). However, the problem is not intractable, and today's politicians, by failing to reach agreement, merely bequeath the problem to tomorrow's politicians. If caps on individual donations are not introduced, citizens will always be suspicious that parties are being bought by the rich, and rightly so. Similarly, if MPs are allowed to have financial interests in organisations that frequently seek to lobby ministers or Parliament, citizens will always be suspicious that some MPs are profiting from their position. Paid advocacy is effectively banned in the Commons; paid advice should probably be banned too. It is also easy for informed citizens to be suspicious that many peers claim their daily allowances without contributing to the work of Parliament. The House of Lords authorities might consider restricting paying allowances to those who actively participate in the work of the chamber or a committee, rather than those who merely attend.

Responding effectively to public unease may not always mean acting in accord with immediate demands, of course. There may be cases where politicians need to take decisions that are unpopular in the short term in order to maintain confidence in the system in the longer term. The expenses fiasco is a case in point. Had successive governments had the courage to raise MPs' salaries in line with inflation, rather than engaging in the devious subterfuge of allowing MPs to claim more allowances, their lives would have been simpler and public confidence would not have suffered nearly as much. Now it is very much harder, if not impossible, for MPs to raise their salaries, even when the body charged with setting their pay, the Independent Parliamentary Standards Authority, tells them they should.

Honest talk

Our third suggestion is to encourage politicians to think how they might alter some of the more disliked aspects of general political conduct. There is little doubt that the British style of politics grates with many voters. Some of the most disliked features, however, are the tendencies for politicians to be less than frank, if not evasive, when answering questions, and to make promises that are probably unrealisable. Although such behaviour is well beyond the bounds of current institutional preoccupations with ethics, politicians would be well advised to reflect on how their everyday language is received by the public. It is regarded by many as a feature of political integrity, as the following comment by one of our focus group participants makes clear:

They [politicians] should set out their political stall with a vision of society, and we'd grant them a lot of licence if they stick to that and not shift with the wind. Within that, is a reasonable expectation that they will hold to the belief about the kind of world we should be living [in]. (Man, Egham)

Other commentators have picked up on the need for a style of political rhetoric that inspires without raising hopeless false expectations (Flinders 2012). A former journalist makes the point most succinctly:

Of course, political leaders need to offer a vision and objectives. But they should not raise false, and unrealisable, expectations of what can be achieved in practice ... Ministers, and shadow spokesmen, should be more modest in their aspirations and claims. Oppositions would be wise not to attack, and promise to repeal, everything an incumbent government does. Such instant changes are often themselves reversed before long, damaging both the services affected and the reputation of politicians. (Riddell 2011: 170–1)

It is impossible to change a whole culture of politics overnight, and politicians are unlikely to alter their behaviour without some external pressure or 'nudging'. The same former journalist suggests strengthening the use of public petitions in the House of Commons and obliging politicians occasionally to debate what the public wishes them to. If that means having to contend with populist demands, such as reintroducing the death penalty or expelling asylum seekers, so be it: 'MPs should ... seek to defeat them in argument, not evade them ... A petitions system would force politicians to address such arguments' (Riddell 2011: 163). The idea has much to commend it; but it would also be desirable to force ministers and opposition spokesmen to engage in such debates. Straight talking needs to be practised at the very top of politics.

Another way to nudge politicians into being more honest, at least when making claims in public, might be to introduce some public funding for organisations that monitor the veracity of politicians' and journalists' pronouncements. The broadcaster Channel 4, for instance, has an online 'FactCheck' blog, while an independent organ- isation called 'Full Fact' provides a similar online presence that aims to help citizens to 'see the facts and context behind the claims made by the key players in British political debate'. Increasing the opportunity for citizens to check politicians' claims, as well as the many misleading anti-politician diatribes that appear in newspapers, may just encourage some politicians to think more carefully before opening their mouths.

Aligning institutional ethics with public understandings

If calling for politicians to tone down some of their claims and pledges is vulnerable to claims of wishful thinking, so too may be our fourth suggestion. Institutional rules and norms should as far as possible be aligned with public expectations and understandings. Some MPs, and doubtless many councillors, seemingly take delight in being members of an institution that runs according to closed and distinct rules. Such a mindset is unfortunate. If certain practices are accepted by political elites but not accepted by large proportions of the public, such as MPs paying public money to spouses or other close relatives, then these practices need to be discussed and, unless there are exceptionally good general reasons to the contrary, ended. An argument based on trad- ition is not acceptable. Social norms change, and institutional processes must respond. In the mid-1970s, it would have been inconceivable to most MPs that they needed a code of conduct or an independent figure to investigate alleged misconduct. In the mid-1990s it would have been inconceivable to have had lay members on the House of Commons' Standards Committee. If politicians wish to insist on behaving in ways that run contrary to the weight of public opinion, then they must accept the consequences. The rules and principles governing political conduct in a democracy must be responsive to the social values on which politics rests.

The importance of grounding ethical principles in everyday understandings was noted by the political theorist Mark Philp in advice to the Committee on Standards in Public Life (quoted in 2013: 23):

> Most people are not professional philosophers and while they may have very strong intuitions about certain things, those intuitions are not easily turned into analytically precise principles. But that is one reason why principles in the public domain should be clear, and should depart as little as possible from their ordinary meanings. Too much divergence breeds misunderstanding, and misunderstanding exacerbates mistrust.

In response, the Committee finally acted to revise its own descriptions of the 'Seven Principles of Public Life', which previous research had suggested was unclear to many members of the public. The principles themselves were retained, but definitions were rephrased to make their meaning closer to the ordinary meaning. The reformulated principles, as shown in Table 8.2, are undoubtedly an improvement.

We would go further, however, and suggest that the Seven Principles could also serve as a vehicle for reminding politicians of the public's wider understanding of ethics than the traditional preoccupation with conflicts of interest. More specifically, we would suggest that three additional principles might be developed that apply specifically to holders of office in *political* public institutions such as central government, Parliament and local government. On the basis of our research, we suggest that these might include sincerity, humility and transparency, as set out in Table 8.3. Ultimately, of course, politicians themselves need to debate and determine the details of any additional ethical principles that ought to underpin their 'political' conduct.

More effective sanctions for misconduct

Our fifth suggestion is that politicians find ways of ensuring that colleagues who commit serious misconduct are *visibly* punished. We found that one of the major bugbears expressed by a number of individuals is the sense that politicians who break the rules often seem to get away with it. This feeling is well reflected in a number of spontaneous responses to an open-ended question included in our spring

Table 8.2 *The original and reformulated 'Seven Principles of Public Life'*

	Original	Reformulated
Selflessness	Holders of public office should act solely in terms of the public interest. They should not do so in order to gain financial or other material benefits for themselves, their family or their friends.	Holders of public office should act solely in terms of the public interest.
Integrity	Holders of public office should not place themselves under any financial or other obligation to outside individuals or organisations that might seek to influence them in the performance of their official duties.	Holders of public office must avoid placing themselves under any obligation to people or organisations that might try inappropriately to influence them in their work. They should not act or take decisions in order to gain financial or other material benefits for themselves, their family or their friends. They must declare and resolve any interests and relationships.
Objectivity	In carrying out public business, including making public appointments, awarding contracts, or recommending individuals for rewards and benefits, holders of public office should make choices on merit.	Holders of public office must act and take decisions impartially, fairly and on merit, using the best evidence and without discrimination or bias.
Accountability	Holders of public office are accountable for their decisions and actions to the public and must submit themselves to whatever scrutiny is appropriate to their office.	Holders of public office are accountable to the public for their decisions and actions and must submit themselves to the scrutiny necessary to ensure this.
Openness	Holders of public office should be as open as possible about all the decisions and actions that they take.	Holders of public office should act and take decisions in an open and transparent manner. Information should

Table 8.2 (*cont.*)

	Original	Reformulated
	They should give reasons for their decisions and restrict information only when the wider public interest clearly demands.	not be withheld from the public unless there are clear and lawful reasons for so doing.
Honesty	Holders of public office have a duty to declare any private interests relating to their public duties and to take steps to resolve any conflicts arising in a way that protects the public interest.	Holders of public office should be truthful.
Leadership	Holders of public office should promote and support these principles by leadership and example.	Holders of public office should exhibit these principles in their own behaviour. They should actively promote and robustly support the principles and be willing to challenge poor behaviour wherever it occurs.

Table 8.3 *Proposed additional principles of public life for political institutions*

Sincerity	Holders of public office should be candid and frank at all times when engaging in public political activity.
Humility	Holders of public office should always be attentive to how their behaviour is perceived by members of the public and should conduct themselves, as far as possible, in accordance with public expectations.
Transparency	Holders of public office must ensure that the public has full and complete information about their use of public resources.

2010 survey:[2] 'if any politician is found doing anything dishonest they should be sacked, the same as would happen in any workplace'; 'if I had abused my expenses at work it would have been dealt with in a very harsh way'; 'they lose their jobs if they submit dodgy expenses claims, like any private sector employee would'. Such perceptions may not be accurate, of course, but they are nonetheless a reality that needs to be confronted.

In the wake of the 2009 expenses scandal, all the major parties promised to introduce a system of recall elections for MPs, so that in cases of serious misconduct voters would have an opportunity to eject them immediately rather than waiting until the next election. Recall elections are common in many parts of the United States. They are not part of Britain's democratic landscape. They would, however, appear to be popular. In our spring 2010 survey, we asked respondents whether they supported any number of political reforms that had been proposed by politicians in the wake of the expenses scandal. The results, in Table 8.4, show that 'making it possible for citizens to vote out sitting MPs between general elections' was the most popular of the proposed reforms, supported by nearly 54 per cent of respondents. Those answering may not necessarily have been thinking about

[2] The original question was designed to probe respondents' views on what should be done to improve the ethical behaviour of politicians: 'From what you know, what changes to the political system, if any, do you think might improve the honesty and trustworthiness of politicians?'

Table 8.4 *Support for various reforms to the political system, spring 2010*

Suggested reform	Supporting (%)
Making it possible for citizens to vote out sitting MPs between general elections.	53.8
Having a fully elected House of Lords	37.6
Changing the voting system to the House of Commons	35.7
Changing the law to require people to cast a vote at elections	28.3
Having open primary elections in each constituency to select the parties' candidates before a general election	24.4
Don't know	17.5
None of these	4.2

Note: the responses sum to more than 100 per cent, as respondents were allowed to tick as many boxes as they wished. The question was worded as follows: 'In recent months, various suggestions for reforming the political system have been proposed. Which proposals do you support? Select as many reforms as you like.'

the device as a way of punishing misconduct, but the results do suggest that citizens desire more effective electoral tools to hold their leaders to account.

Instituting a system of recall elections is unlikely to be easy, however. On the one hand, such a device could allow people to unseat MPs on policy or ideological grounds. This type of arrangement may or may not be desirable in a democracy, but such usage certainly broadens the device beyond a means of punishing misconduct. On the other hand, most of the recall proposals offered after 2009 retained a major role for MPs in any event; it would be up to MPs themselves to decide whether misconduct was sufficiently serious to permit a recall election. Perhaps not surprisingly, the Coalition Government has proved rather slow in bringing forward its promised proposals. In many ways, of course, talk of recall elections is missing the point. The House of Commons has long had the power to expel members for misconduct, and it would be far simpler to have a system of automatic disqualification in cases of very serious misconduct. Appropriate procedural safeguards would obviously be needed to ensure that arrangements meet with basic requirements of fairness and due process, but if MPs think that one of their own has acted sufficiently improperly to have their fate decided by voters, why wait for voters to demand a vote?

The House of Commons could also consider introducing a smaller institutional change to improve the visibility of its sanctions. It has long been practice for MPs to apologise to the House for any unparliamentary conduct; in keeping with this spirit, recent practice has seen a number of written apologies published on the Parliament website. MPs could, however, be ordered to publish an apology to their constituents. In the short term, there is the risk that such a practice would undermine integrity perceptions still further. Over the long term, such behaviour might help to focus MPs' minds. It might make them think more of their actions from the point of view of citizens. It might also enable constituents to consider their behaviour on polling day.

Embracing transparency

Our sixth suggestion is for politicians to embrace norms of openness and transparency. An obsession with transparency is potentially harmful to public trust, as seen, yet it is impossible for politicians to escape it in today's world. By no means all citizens are avid followers of politics and wish to know what their MPs, ministers and councillors are up to at all times, but many citizens are. As one focus group participant noted:

[I would like to see] a more concerted effort to be more transparent. Not just expenses, but also what their diaries are, how much time they spend in Westminster or in the constituency. (Man, Egham)

Whether such detailed information would boost confidence in politicians is open to question. Compiling the information could create undesirable financial and other costs. Similarly, we are not convinced of the desirability of requiring MPs and other office holders to publish full details of all their private assets and those of their family, a practice introduced into French politics in 2013 by President Hollande. Such publicity could be construed as an invasion of privacy, it could dissuade many citizens from wishing to stand for elected office, and there is no evidence that it would address a problem.

What is important, however, is that politicians adapt to the new climate of transparency. Attempts to conceal and cover up information rarely work as experience from the expenses scandal and numerous other controversies shows. What this could mean is that all public bodies, including Parliament, should, where practical, strive to make all information that could be requested through a Freedom of Information request available online, if only in its raw form. If it is unreasonable to require public institutions to spend time and money compiling data for every conceivable request, it is not unreasonable to expect the raw data to be made accessible for would-be researchers, whether amateur or professional. In the same way that we suggest greater funding for fact-checking websites, politicians could even consider funding for bodies like the 'They Work for You' website, which collates data on politicians' activities. At a local level, a reasonable embrace of transparency could extend to requiring local authorities to make greater use of recording and webcasting technologies to ensure council meetings are accessible to all. If Parliament can be televised, why not every council plenary and committee meeting?

Public education

Most of our suggestions have so far focused on the 'supply side' of political conduct. But the gulf between political elites and citizens is far from being the fault of politicians alone. Members of the public somehow need to learn that a very great deal of political activity is not motivated by self-serving behaviour and that many politicians are motivated by public-spirited intentions. The public must also accept that there are frequently legitimate reasons why politicians are not able to deliver what they promise or said they would do. It would be helpful if politicians found their confidence and, with a clearer understanding of public disaffection, address it head on.

Formal school citizenship classes could perhaps be rethought with a clearer emphasis on the messy nature of politics, in particular the fact that there are often irreconcilable interests and differences of opinion around most issues, and politicians must respond to and accommodate both (Hibbing and Theiss-Morse 2002). They could also draw more heavily on the wealth of academic research that suggests that politicians keep campaign promises considerably more often than most people believe they do (Rose 1984; Royed 1996; Naurin 2011), and that there is a relatively high degree of government responsiveness to public opinion (Soroka and Wlezien 2010; Bartle *et al.* 2011).

More generally, broadcasters and artists could play a role in providing the public with a more nuanced appreciation of what the job of a politician requires (Stoker 2006). It is perhaps indicative of the British public's attitude towards politics that most popular television series that deal with political issues are satirical comedies, such as ITV's *Spitting Image* and the BBC's *Yes, Minister, The Thick of It, Have I Got News for You* and *Mock the Week*. There is virtually no equivalent in Britain of dramas such as Denmark's *Borgen* or the United States' *The West Wing* that foreground the practical dilemmas and difficult choices involved in government. Those political dramas that have been successful, such as the British *House of Cards* trilogy, Channel 4's *The Politician's Wife* and the BBC's *The Politician's Husband*, have tended to focus on politicians' personal machinations rather than the complexity and difficulty of governing. For any television producers among our readers, a few good dramas on the reality of public life might help to enhance public understanding of the various roles played by politicians and the demands that are placed on them.

Conclusion

In the course of conducting our focus groups, we asked participants to consider what ought to be done to improve public confidence in the integrity of politicians. Some participants desired a simple improvement in politicians' behaviour. As a woman in Bradford put it: 'They should stop fighting amongst themselves and show people that they'll do what they said they would.' Many more participants felt that further institutional reforms were required, with a strong preference for more regulation and oversight, as typified in the following responses:

You can't expect [politicians] to be perfect, but you can expect them to respect the rules. So it's up to the rules to ensure they are adequate. (Woman, Hackney)

I think politicians are not qualified enough to do their jobs. There should be minimum standards to become an MP. (Man, Colchester)

I would want more independent oversight over certain aspects of government. There are aspects of [politicians'] jobs which they should be accountable for to an independent body. That would make me feel better. (Man, Egham)

If past experience is anything to go by, it is not immediately clear that further regulation and oversight by politicians themselves would help. The ethical world of British politicians has never been so heavily scrutinised or regulated, yet there has been no discernible positive effect on public opinion. It is unlikely that any additional regulation in the same mould would greatly improve the situation. Business as usual is not an option if change is to be realised. Instead, politicians need to improve their own understanding of what it is about their behaviour that citizens find so disagreeable. They need to develop a broader view of ethics and accept that it may well encroach upon a realm that they have usually regarded as being exclusively political. Above all, they do need to align their behaviour and practices more closely with what citizens deem to be acceptable. Achieving these goals is obviously easier said than done, but if politicians are serious about avoiding their electors' contempt, they deserve to be taken seriously.

9 | *Concluding remarks*

I THINK THAT people who run for office initially have good intentions, but they somehow change when they get into the system.

(Female focus group participant, Colchester)

Long before he championed passage of the Thirteenth Amendment, long before he delivered his address at Gettysburg, and long before he was elected President of the United States, a young Illinois state legislator, Abraham Lincoln, remarked: 'Politicians are a set of men who have interests aside from the interests of the people and who, to say the most of them, are, taken as a mass, at least one long step removed from honest men' (Basler *et al.* 1953: 65–6).[1] Nine-score and eight years have elapsed since Lincoln made these remarks, but his words, and the sentiment they convey, paint an unnervingly accurate picture of how politics and political conduct is perceived in Britain and most other liberal democracies today. Politicians are generally not trusted. Politicians are generally not liked.

In truth, of course, the moral standing of British politicians in the eyes of the public is not so far removed from the moral standing of politicians in the United States, in France, in Germany or in a host of other established liberal democracies. Politics as a profession always elicits some measure of scepticism, if not cynicism, in the public mind, and it often does so for good and democratically healthy reasons. Yet there also comes a point when the scale of scepticism and cynicism becomes unhealthy for democracy. There is no absolute agreement that this point has been reached in Britain, but there is widespread agreement that public confidence in British political institutions and processes has been eroding in recent years and, moreover, that negative

---

[1] The occasion was Lincoln's 1837 'Speech in the Illinois Legislature Concerning the State Bank'. After making his point, Lincoln immediately added: 'I say this with the greater freedom because, being a politician myself, none can regard it as personal.'

perceptions of politicians' honesty and integrity have been part and parcel of this erosion. Furthermore, there is evidence that this erosion of confidence in Britain has been especially marked in comparison with changes in levels of support in a number of other Western European democracies (Norris 2011). The perceived integrity of politicians is clearly not the only factor that shapes broader levels of support. As large numbers of academic studies have demonstrated, other contextual factors matter, including the policy performance of governments and the extent of party polarisation (Citrin 1974; Weatherford 1992; Ezrow and Xezonakis 2011; Brandenburg and Johns forthcoming). Nevertheless, the perceived integrity of political leaders and elected representatives remains an important factor. This point is no less true in Britain than it is anywhere else.

The reputations of our representatives and representative practices should be of concern to us all. Representation is the core democratic institution in a modern polity. Though some states employ the tools of direct democracy, including initiatives and referendums, these are typically used to decide a minority of policy questions. In Britain, they are barely used at all. Despite a number of recent constitutional changes, representative democracy remains the only model of democracy in town (King 2007). The link between representative actors – whether individual MPs, local councillors, MEPs, MSPs or Welsh, London or Northern Irish assembly members, or 'collectivist' political parties – and citizens remains the principal channel through which most people exercise their democratic rights most of the time. The health of this channel rests in part on the actual and perceived conduct of all those politicians who make it possible.

By most accounts, and by most modern understandings of the term, Britain is not a corrupt country. Though misconduct is difficult to track, the available evidence we have suggests that the level of wrong-doing by British politicians is far lower than in many other countries. Nevertheless, a large proportion of the population are unhappy with the ethical conduct of their leaders. Our own data bear this out. Other survey research tells a similar story. Successive *Audits of Political Engagement* conducted by the Hansard Society reveal that only small minorities of Britons say they trust politicians generally. Meanwhile, periodic surveys commissioned by the Committee on Standards in Life suggest that, whilst most citizens have a neutral or marginally positive view of overall standards of conduct in public life in general, such views do not extend to the 'political' part of public life. Thus, only 23 per cent of respondents in the Committee's 2010 survey said that standards in public life in general were 'quite low' or 'very low', but only 26 per cent of respondents trusted MPs or government ministers to tell the truth (Committee on Standards in Public Life 2011: 12, 17). It is the apparent discrepancy between the state of actual political conduct in Britain and the state of perceived or subjective conduct which motivates our research and which we have set ourselves to explore in this volume.

Our basic argument, which we first outlined in Chapter 1 and which unfolded over subsequent chapters, is easily stated. For a start, there is a considerable disparity between the way in which most members of the public understand political ethics and the way in which it is construed in institutional codes of conduct and in elite practices. As we saw in Chapter 4, citizens tend to have a far broader and more all-encompassing view of what is ethical and unethical behaviour in politics than those more actively engaged in political life. To be sure, as shown in Chapter 5, a common set of ethical norms, derived from collectively held understandings of political roles, the importance of abiding by the law and politicians' duty to enhance the public good, do appear to resonate with most sectors of society. Nevertheless, the boundaries of citizens' broader conception of 'the ethical' embrace the words that politicians use, the promises they make (and sometimes break), how politicians relate to and engage with them, and the consistency of politicians' words and deeds. Citizens also tend to hold their elected leaders to very high, perhaps unrealistically high, standards.

A second feature of our argument, related to the first, is the almost inevitable gap between citizens' aspirations as to how their politicians should behave and their perceptions of how politicians actually behave. Partly because of the disparity in ethical understandings, partly because of the structures of modern democratic practice and partly because of human psychology, there is a widespread sense that politicians frequently deviate from ethical norms. Not only do such perceptions generate widespread popular dissatisfaction with politicians and their behaviour, as shown in Chapter 6, but they also lead many members of the public to view the British political system as being wracked by corruption and misconduct.

This viewpoint in turn has impacts that ripple out over political and social life. Critical attitudes towards politicians' ethics and integrity are associated with a diminished willingness to obey the law and a lower probability of following political leadership. As shown in Chapter 7, popular disillusionment with the behaviour of elected representatives also makes it less likely that an individual will engage with politics and participate in key aspects of democratic life. The public's generally jaundiced view of political elites does indeed matter in a variety of important ways.

An obvious question that arises from our analysis is: what is to be done? Alternatively, what practical measures can be taken to improve people's view of politics and politicians? No amount of hand-wringing and exhortations for politicians to increase opportunities for popular participation will help to address damning perceptions of politicians' conduct as long as the fundamental discrepancy between elite and mass expectations remains. We are also sceptical that grand gestures and large-scale 'ethics reforms' are the answer. Too many times in the past these have been tried and they have largely failed, as discussed in Chapter 8. Instead, we suggest seven modest, but potentially far-reaching, changes that might help to remedy the problem of popular disaffection with political elites: more effective elite engagement with political ethics; more effective responses to public opinion; more honest talk; a closer alignment between institutional ethics and public understandings; more effective sanctions for misconduct; targeted transparency; and more innovative approaches to public education. Though no remedy is ever likely to close the gap completely between popular and elite perceptions of how elected representatives ought and do behave, the measures we suggest are each designed to lead to incremental steps in this direction. Taken together as a package, they can be expected to go some way towards synchronising standards in public life with popular expectations.

It only remains for us to point out that, while we hope our findings improve wider understandings of and contribute to the debate about contemporary political disaffection, the present volume leaves much important work unfinished. One area where more research is needed is in our understanding of the very long-term trajectory of popular perceptions. If today's citizens are indeed more sceptical of politicians' motives and ethics than those in the past, it would help to know whether those earlier more positive views were the 'norm' or were themselves an aberration, and, if the latter, why. The paucity of relevant survey data stretching back into the past is a major handicap, but scholars with a more historical disposition could well contribute to our broader understanding of public opinion in this area.

More research is also needed to deepen our understanding of contemporary British popular attitudes. In addition to exploring in greater detail the short-term dynamics that shape ethical beliefs and integrity perceptions, future work could usefully address such questions as popular perceptions of elected representatives at the regional level, the impact of social media on popular engagement with the political process and perceptions of political elites, and the ways in which the different representative styles of MPs and other politicians affect the views their constituents hold. Another obvious next step would be to widen the scope of analysis and to examine the extent to which the findings reported here hold also in other established democracies.

One final area where more research is needed is in the political consequences of citizens' perceptions of politicians. Research in the United States suggests that the well-documented decline in trust in government has played into the hands of those who favour a less activist state (Hetherington 2005). To what extent, if any, has the climate of public opinion in Britain had any macro-level consequences for British public policy? Has the same climate had any impact on parties' strategies, whether over the 'long campaign' between elections or over the 'short campaign' in the run-up to polling day? Are politicians and party strategists even conscious of the current public mood or does it play no part in their calculations? Such questions take us far from our own project's initial starting point, but they are important and potentially fruitful future avenues of inquiry nonetheless. Perhaps the answers, as well as the significance of such questions, will become clearer in future.

We conclude, however, with one final thought. The topic of political conduct is one that is bound to bubble beneath the surface of any democracy, but concerns about the integrity of elected leaders have shot to the surface of British political life all too frequently in recent decades. It is perhaps time to re-think how representatives and the represented relate to each other. Though this volume has only begun to sketch out a few of the changes that might be needed, we hope to have gone some way towards mapping the relevant terrain and identifying the salient issues. Above all, it is now the turn of the politicians themselves to re-examine the role they play in public life and the fitness for purpose of contemporary political conduct.

Appendix: data and variable construction

As set out in Chapter 1, the vast majority of the survey data that we analyse in this book come from questions included in waves 2, 3, 5 and 6 of the British Cooperative Campaign Analysis Project (B/CCAP). B/CCAP was a panel study based on a sample of approximately 10,000 respondents; individual teams of researchers could 'hire' sections of this sample and ask them questions at various points in time. Our participation in B/CCAP was funded by the British Academy (grant No. SG-52322) and the Economic and Social Research Council (grant No. RES-000-22-3459). All the B/CCAP surveys were conducted online by the YouGov opinion polling organisation. Wave 2, 'spring 2009', was completed between 21 April and 6 May; wave 3, 'autumn 2009', was completed between 23 and 28 September; wave 5, 'spring 2010', was completed between 23 April and 4 May; and wave 6, the post-election survey, was completed between 15 and 30 June 2010. Our initial panel comprised 1,388 adult respondents from across Britain; this represented a response rate of 70.17 per cent of YouGov's pre-selected sample. YouGov provided weighting variables for each wave reflecting the demographic characteristics of the entire adult population. Data concerning candidates' and MPs' attitudes, which we describe in Chapter 4, come from the 2005 British Representation Study. See Nicholas Allen and Sarah Birch (2012) for further details.

The variables that appear below appear in at least one of our figures or tables. Other questions to which we refer in prose only are described in full in the text or in footnotes.

Gender: 0 = female, 1 = male.

Age: We constructed two dummy variables based on reported age, one designating those aged under 35 years, and one designating those aged 55 years and over. Our reference category was thus those aged between 35 and 54 years.

Education: We constructed a dummy variable based on responses to the following question: 'What is the highest educational or work-related qualification you have?' Coded 1 if respondent answered 'University or CNAA first degree (e.g., BA, BSc, BEd)' or 'University or CNAA higher degree (e.g., MSc, PhD)'. All other responses were coded 0.

Income: We constructed two dummy variables based on responses to the question: 'What is your gross household income?' One variable included all those respondents whose reported household income was less than £20,000 per annum, and the other included all those whose reported household income was greater than £40,000 per annum. Our reference category was those respondents whose reported household income was between £20,000 and £40,000 per annum. We generally use relevant data from wave 2 of the B/CCAP survey, but we use data from wave 5 in our analyses in Chapter 7, as noted.

Attentiveness to public affairs: 'Some people seem to follow what's going on in government and public affairs most of the time whether there's an election going on or not. Others aren't interested. Would you say you follow what's going on in government and public affairs.' Coded 1 = hardly at all, 2 = only now and then, 3 = some of the time, 4 = most of the time. We use relevant data from wave 2 of the B/CCAP survey.

Personal ethical tolerance scale: This variable was created by summing responses to the following three items: 'For each of the following actions, please say whether you think it can always be justified, never be justified, or something in between. Please use the 0–10 scale, where 10 means it can always be justified and 0 means it can never be justified ... (i) Avoiding a fare on public transport ... (ii) Telling a lie if it is in your interest ... (iii) Claiming government benefits to which you are not entitled.' The resulting 0–30 sale, which we interpreted as tolerance of dubious behaviour, had a Cronbach's alpha of 0.71. We use relevant data from wave 2 of the B/CCAP survey.

Party identification: Our party identification dummy variables were created on the basis of responses to the following question: 'Do you generally think of yourself as a little closer to one of the parties than the others? If yes please indicate which party.' The resulting variables were: Conservative identifier; Labour identifier; Liberal Democrat identifier; other party identifier; and no sense of party identification.

Our reference category was usually the last of these. We generally use relevant data from wave 2 of the B/CCAP survey, but we use data from wave 5 in our analyses in Chapter 7, as noted.

Improvement in personal finances: 'We are interested in how people are getting along financially these days. Would you say that you (and your family living here) are much better off, better off, worse off, or much worse off than you were a year ago?' A five-point ordinal scale where 1 = much worse off, and 5 = much better. We use relevant data from waves 2, 3 and 5 of the B/CCAP survey.

Improvement in national economy: 'Would you say that over the past year the nation's economy has ... got much better, got better, stayed about the same, got worse, or got much worse?' A five-point ordinal scale where 1 = got much worse, and 5 = got much better. We use relevant data from waves 2, 3 and 5 of the B/CCAP survey.

Newspaper readership: We constructed two dummy variables on the basis of responses to the following question: 'Which daily morning newspaper do you read most often?' An individual who reported reading the *Financial Times, Daily Telegraph, The Guardian, The Independent, The Times, The Scotsman* or the *Glasgow Herald* was coded as 'quality newspaper reader'. An individual who reported reading the *Daily Express, Daily Mail, Daily Mirror/Record, Daily Star* or the *Sun* was coded as 'tabloid reader'. We generally use relevant data from wave 2 of the B/CCAP survey, but we use data from wave 5 in our analyses in Chapter 7, as noted.

Expectations of higher standards: 'Some people say that elected politicians (such as MPs and local councillors [MPs, MSPs and local councillors in Scotland; MPs, local councillors and Assembly Members in Wales and London]) should only be held to the same standards of honesty and integrity as the average person. Others say that elected politicians should be held to much higher standards of honesty and integrity than the average person. Using the following scale – where 1 means that politicians should be held to the same standards as the average person and 5 means that politicians should be held to much higher standards – where would you place yourself?' A five-point scale where 1 = politicians should be held to the same standards and 5 = politicians should be held to much higher standards. We use relevant data from waves 2, 3 and 5 of the B/CCAP survey.

Successful and hard-working or honest politicians?: 'Some people say that it is more important to have elected politicians who are honest, even if they are not always successful and hard-working. Others say that it is more important to have politicians who are successful and hard-working, even if they are not always honest. Using the scale below – where 1 means it is more important to have honest politicians and 4 means it is more important to have successful and hardworking politicians – where would you place yourself?' A four-point scale where 1 = more important for elected politicians to be honest and 4 = more important for elected politicians to be successful and hard-working. We use relevant data from wave 2 of the B/CCAP survey.

Deliver the goods or honesty and trustworthy?: 'People want competent and honest politicians, but they disagree over which trait is more important. Some people say that it is more important to have politicians who can deliver the goods for people, even if they aren't always very honest and trustworthy. Other people say that it is more important to have politicians who are very honest and trustworthy, even if they can't always deliver the goods. What do you think? Using the 0–10 scale below, where 0 means it is more important to have politicians who can deliver the goods and 10 means it is more important to have very honest and trustworthy politicians, where would you place yourself?' An eleven-point scale where 0 = more important to have politicians who can deliver the goods and 10 = more important to have very honest and trustworthy politicians. We use relevant data from wave 3 of the B/CCAP survey.

'Grey' conduct: This variable was created by calculating the arithmetic mean of *inverted* responses to the following four items: 'Below is a list of hypothetical situations involving elected politicians. Please indicate on a scale of 1–7 whether you feel that the actions in each situation are corrupt (1) or not corrupt (7) . . . (i) An MP is retained by a major company to arrange meetings and dinners in the House of Commons at which its executives can meet parliamentarians . . . (ii) An MP hires a spouse or other family member to serve as his or her secretary . . . (iii) A Cabinet Minister uses his or her influence to obtain a contract for a firm in his/her constituency . . . (iv) At Christmas, an MP accepts a crate of wine from an influential constituent.' The resulting 1–7 sale, where a higher score now meant behaviour was judged to be more corrupt, had a Cronbach's alpha of 0.62. We use relevant data from wave 2 of the B/CCAP survey.

'*Black*' *conduct*: This variable was created by calculating the arithmetic mean of *inverted* responses to the following five items: 'Below is a list of hypothetical situations involving elected politicians. Please indicate on a scale of 1–7 whether you feel that the actions in each situation are corrupt (1) or not corrupt (7) ... (i) A Cabinet Minister promises an appointed position in exchange for campaign contributions ... (ii) A major company makes a substantial donation to the government party. Later, the chair of the company is given an honour ... (iii) A local councillor, while chair of the planning committee, authorises planning permission for property owned by him or her ... (iv) An MP uses his/her position to get a friend or relative admitted to Oxford or Cambridge, or some other prestigious institution ... (v) An MP is issued a first-class airline ticket as part of a parliamentary delegation. He or she exchanges the ticket for an economy fare and pockets the difference.' The resulting 1–7 scale, where a higher score now meant behaviour was judged to be more corrupt, had a Cronbach's alpha of 0.73. We use relevant data from wave 2 of the B/CCAP survey.

Overall honesty and integrity perceptions: 'Overall, how would you rate the standards of honesty and integrity of elected politicians in Britain today?' Coded 1 = very low, 2 = somewhat low, 3 = neither high nor low, 4 = somewhat high, 5 = very high. We use relevant data from waves 2, 3 and 5 of the B/CCAP survey.

Perceived improvement or decline in politicians' standards: 'Do you think that the standards of honesty and integrity of elected politicians in Britain have been improving in recent years, have been declining, or have they stayed about the same?' Coded 1 = improving, 2 = declining, 3 = stayed about the same, 4 = don't know. We use relevant data from waves 2, 3 and 5 of the B/CCAP survey.

Evaluations of different politicians and other actors' integrity, including honesty of local MP: 'For each of the following groups, please say whether you think they are completely honest and trustworthy, or not at all honest and trustworthy. Please use the 0–10 scale where 10 means completely honest and trustworthy and 0 means not at all honest and trustworthy ... government ministers ... MPs in general ... journalists ... judges ... local councillors ... your local MP.' Coded 0 = not at all honest and trustworthy, 10 = completely honest and trustworthy. We use relevant data from waves 2 and 5 of the B/CCAP survey.

Straight answers/bribes/expenses/empty promises: 'In your opinion, how much of a problem is the following behaviour by elected politicians in Britain today? Please use the 0–10 scale, where 10 means it is a very big problem and 0 means it is not a problem at all ... Not giving straight answers to questions ... Accepting bribes ... Misusing official expenses and allowances ... Making promises they know they can't keep.' Coded 0 = not a problem at all, 10 = a very big problem. We use relevant data from waves 2, 3 and 5 of the B/CCAP survey.

'Only the tip of the iceberg': 'How strongly do you agree or disagree with the following statement ...? The scandals involving elected politicians that are reported in the newspapers and on television are only the tip of the iceberg in terms of the misconduct that actually goes on.' Coded 1 = strongly disagree, 2 = tend to disagree, 3 = neither agree nor disagree, 4 = tend to agree, 5 = strongly agree, 6 = don't know. We use relevant data from wave 2 of the B/CCAP survey.

'In it just for themselves': 'How much do you agree or disagree with the statement that politicians are in it just for themselves?' Coded 1 = strongly disagree, 2 = tend to disagree, 3 = neither agree nor disagree, 4 = tend to agree, 5 = strongly agree, 6 = don't know. We use relevant data from wave 3 of the B/CCAP survey.

Perceptions of different parties' MPs: 'Thinking about differences between the political parties, which party's MPs are more honest or are there no differences between them?' Coded 1 = Conservatives, 2 = Labour, 3 = Liberal Democrats, 4 = other, 5 = no difference between them, 6 = don't know. We use relevant data from wave 3 of the B/CCAP survey.

Satisfaction with democracy: 'On the whole are you very satisfied, fairly satisfied, a little dissatisfied or very dissatisfied with the way that democracy works in this country?' Coded 1 = very dissatisfied, 2 = a little dissatisfied, 3 = fairly satisfied, 4 = very satisfied. We use relevant data from wave 5 of the B/CCAP survey.

Efficacy: 'Some people say it makes a difference which party is in government. Others say that it does not make a difference which party is in government. Using the following scale – where 1 means it makes a difference which party is in government and 5 means that it does not make a difference which party is in government – where would you place yourself?' The five-point scale was recoded so that 1 = lowest sense of efficacy, 5 = highest sense of efficacy. We use relevant data from wave 5 of the B/CCAP survey.

Duty to vote: 'To what extent do you agree or disagree with the following statements? ... It is every citizen's duty to vote in an election.' Coded 1 = strongly disagree, 2 = tend to disagree, 3 = neither agree nor disagree, 4 = tend to agree, 5 = strongly agree. We use relevant data from wave 5 of the B/CCAP survey.

Engagement with the 2010 general election campaign: We constructed a dummy variable, coded 0 = did not engage, 1 = did engage, if respondents said they had done at least one of the following during the election campaign: 'Worn a badge or sticker for a candidate', 'Discussed a candidate with someone', 'Went to hear a candidate speak', 'Visited a political party website', 'Visited a candidate website' or 'Watched a video of a candidate on the internet'. We use relevant data from wave 5 of the B/CCAP survey

Turnout: We constructed a dummy variable, coded 0 = did not vote, 1 = did vote, if respondents said they had voted in the 2010 general election. We use relevant data from wave 6 of the B/CCAP survey.

Reported vote choice: We constructed a dummy variable, coded 0 = voted for a major party, if respondent said they had voted for Labour, the Conservatives or the Liberal Democrats in the 2010 general election, and 1 = voted for a minor party, if respondents said they voted for any one of several other political parties. Those who said they had not voted were excluded from the analysis. We use relevant data from wave 6 of the B/CCAP survey.

Compliance with the law: 'To what extent do you agree or disagree with the following statements? ... People should obey the law, even if it goes against what they think is right.' Coded 1 = strongly disagree, 2 = tend to disagree, 3 = neither agree nor disagree, 4 = tend to agree, 5 = strongly agree. We use relevant data from wave 5 of the B/CCAP survey.

References

Ackerman, Bruce. 2000. 'The new separation of powers', *Harvard Law Review* 13(3): 633–729.

Adonis, Andrew. 1997. 'The UK: civic virtue put to the test', in Donatella della Porta and Yves Mény (eds), *Democracy and Corruption in Europe*. London: Pinter, pp. 103–17.

Alatas, Syed Hussein. 1990. *Corruption: Its Nature, Causes and Functions*. Aldershot: Avebury.

Allen, Nicholas. 2008. 'A new ethical world of MPs?' *Journal of Legislative Studies* 14(3): 297–314.

2011. 'Dishonourable members? Exploring patterns of misconduct in the contemporary House of Commons', *British Politics* 6(2): 210–40.

Allen, Nicholas and Sarah Birch. 2011. 'Political conduct and misconduct: probing public opinion', *Parliamentary Affairs* 64(1): 61–81.

2012. 'On either side of a moat? Elite and mass attitudes towards right and wrong', *European Journal of Political Research* 51(1): 89–116.

Forthcoming. 'After the 2009 expenses scandal: British process evaluations in context', *Political Studies*.

Almond, Gabriel A. and Sidney Verba. 1963. *The Civic Culture: Political Attitudes and Democracy in Five Nations*. Princeton University Press.

Alvarez, R. Michael and John Brehm. 2002. *Hard Choices, Easy Answers: Values, Information, and American Public Opinion*. Princeton University Press.

Anderson, Christopher. 1995. *Blaming the Government: Citizens and the Economy in Five European Democracies*. Armonk, NY: M. E. Sharpe.

Anderson, Christopher J. and Yuliya V. Tverdova. 2003. 'Corruption, political allegiances, and attitudes toward government in contemporary democracies', *American Journal of Political Science* 47(1): 91–109.

Anechiarico, Frank and James B. Jacobs. 1996. *The Pursuit of Absolute Integrity: How Corruption Control Makes Government Ineffective*. University of Chicago Press.

Ariely, Dan. 2012. *The (Honest) Truth about Dishonesty: How We Lie to Everyone – Especially Ourselves*. London: HarperCollins.

Atkinson, Michael M. and Gerald Bierling. 2005. 'Politicians, the public and political ethics: worlds apart', *Canadian Journal of Political Science* 38(4): 1003–28.

Atkinson, Michael M. and Maureen Mancuso. 1992. 'Edicts and etiquette: regulating conflict of interest in Congress and the House of Commons', *Corruption and Reform* 7(1): 1–18.

Baker, Amy. 2000. *Prime Ministers and the Rule Book*. London: Politicos.

Barnett, Steven. 2002. 'Will a crisis in journalism provoke a crisis in democracy?' *Political Quarterly* 73(4): 400–8.

Bartle, John, Sebastian Dellepiane-Avellaneda and James Stimson. 2011. 'The moving centre: preferences for government activity in Britain, 1950–2005', *British Journal of Political Science* 41(2): 259–85.

Basler, Roy P., Marion Dolores Pratt and Lloyd A. Dunlap (eds). 1953. *The Collected Works of Abraham Lincoln*, 9 vols. New Brunswick, NJ: Rutgers University Press, vol. I.

Beard, Edmund and Stephen Horn. 1975. *Congressional Ethics: The View from the House*. Washington, DC: Brookings Institution.

Beer, Samuel H. 1965. *Modern British Politics: A Study of Parties and Pressure Groups*. London: Faber.

Behnke, Nathalie. 2002. 'A Nolan Committee for the German ethics infrastructure?' *European Journal of Political Research* 41(5): 675–708.

Bennett, W. Lance and Shanto Iyengar. 2008. 'A new era of minimal effects? The changing foundations of political communication', *Journal of Communication* 58(4): 707–31.

Birch, A. H. 1964. *Representative and Responsible Government: An Essay on the British Constitution*. London, Allen & Unwin.

Birch, Sarah. 2010. 'Perceptions of electoral fairness and voter turnout', *Comparative Political Studies* 43(12): 1601–22.

Birch, Sarah and Nicholas Allen. 2012. '"There will be burning and a-looting tonight": the social and political correlates of law-breaking', *Political Quarterly* 83(1): 33–43.

Blair, Tony. 2007. 'Tony Blair's "Media" speech: the prime minister's Reuters speech on public life', *Political Quarterly* 78(4): 476–87.

Blais, André, Joanna Everitt, Patrick Fournier, Elisabeth Gidengil and Neil Nevitte. 2005. 'The political psychology of voters' reactions to a corruption scandal', paper presented at the Annual Meeting of the American Political Science Association, Washington, DC.

Bowler, Shaun and Jeffrey A. Karp. 2004. 'Politicians, scandals, and trust in government', *Political Behavior* 26(3): 271–87.

Brandenburg, Heinz and Robert Johns. Forthcoming. 'The declining representativeness of the British party system, and why it matters', *Political Studies*.

Butt, Sarah and John Curtice. 2010. 'Duty in decline? Trends in attitudes to voting', in Alison Park, John Curtice, Katarina Thomson, Miranda Phillips, Elizabeth Clery and Sarah Butt (eds), *British Social Attitudes: The 26th Report*. London: Sage, pp. 1–18.

Calvert, Jonathan, Claire Newell and Michael Gillard. 2009. 'Revealed: Labour lords change laws for cash', *Sunday Times*, 25 January.

Campbell, Angus, Philip E. Converse, Warren E. Miller and Donald E. Stokes. 1960. *The American Voter*. New York: Wiley.

Chang, Eric C. C. and Yun-han Chu. 2006. 'Corruption and trust: exceptionalism in Asian democracies?' *Journal of Politics* 68(2): 259–71.

Chibnall, Steven and Peter Saunders. 1977. 'Worlds apart: notes on the social reality of corruption', *British Journal of Sociology* 28(2): 138–54.

Citrin, Jack. 1974. 'The political relevance of trust in government', *American Political Science Review* 68(3): 973–88.

Clarke, Harold D. and Alan C. Alcock. 1989. 'National elections and political attitudes: the case of political efficacy', *British Journal of Political Science* 19(4): 551–62.

Clarke, Harold D., David Sanders, Marianne Stewart and Paul Whiteley. 2009. *Performance Politics and the British Voter*. Cambridge University Press.

2011. 'Valence politics and electoral choice in Britain, 2010', *Journal of Elections, Public Opinion and Parties* 21(2): 237–53.

Committee on Standards in Public Life. 1995. *First Report of the Committee on Standards in Public Life*, Cm 2850-I. London: Stationery Office.

1998. *Fifth Report of the Committee on Standards in Public Life: The Funding of Political Parties in the United Kingdom*, Cm 4057-I. London: Stationery Office.

2000. *Sixth Report of the Committee on Standards in Public Life: Reinforcing Standards*, Cm 4557-I. London: Stationery Office.

2004. *Survey of Public Attitudes towards Conduct in Public Life*. London: BMRB Social Research.

2008. *Survey of Public Attitudes towards Conduct in Public Life 2008*. London: BMRB Social Research.

2011. *Survey of Public Attitudes towards Conduct in Public Life 2010*. London: Committee on Standards in Public Life.

2013. *Fourteenth Report of the Committee on Standards in Public Life: Standards Matter: A Review of Best Practice in Promoting Good Behaviour in Public Life*, Cm 8519. London: Stationery Office.

Converse, Philip E. 1995. 'Foreword', in Richard E. Petty and Jon A. Krosnick (eds), *Attitude Strength: Antecedents and Consequences*. Mahwah, NJ: Lawrence Erlbaum, pp. xi–xvi.

Cowley, Philip. 2012. 'Arise, novice leader! The continuing rise of the career politician in Britain', *Politics* 32(1): 31–8.

Curtice, John, Stephen Fisher and Robert Ford. 2010. 'Appendix II: Analysis of the results', in Dennis Kavanagh and Philip Cowley (eds), *The British General Election of 2010*. Basingstoke: Palgrave Macmillan, pp. 385–426.

Curtice, John and Oliver Heath. 2012. 'Does choice deliver? Public satisfaction with the health service', *Political Studies* 60(3): 484–503.

Dahl, Robert A. 1998. *On Democracy*. New Haven, CT: Yale University Press.

Dalton, Russell J. 2004. *Democratic Challenges, Democratic Choices: The Erosion of Political Support in Advanced Industrial Democracies*. Oxford University Press.

Davis, Charles L., Roderic Ai Camp and Kenneth M. Coleman. 2004. 'The influence of party systems on citizens' perceptions of corruption and electoral response in Latin America', *Comparative Political Studies* 37(6): 677–703.

della Porta, Donatella. 2000. 'Social capital, beliefs in government, and political corruption', in Susan J. Pharr and Robert D. Putnam (eds), *Disaffected Democracies: What's Troubling the Trilateral Countries?* Princeton University Press, pp. 202–28.

Drewry, Gavin and Dawn Oliver. 2004. 'Parliament and the law relating to parliamentary standards', in Oonagh Gay and Patricia Leopold (eds), *Conduct Unbecoming: The Regulation of Parliamentary Behaviour*. London: Politicos, pp. 181–212.

Doig, Alan. 1984. *Corruption and Misconduct in Contemporary British Politics*. Harmondsworth: Penguin.

  1996. 'From Lynskey to Nolan: the corruption of British politics and public service?' *Journal of Law and Society* 23(1): 35–56.

  2005. 'Sleaze and trust: Labour trades mistrust for sleaze', *Parliamentary Affairs* 58(2): 394–407.

  2006. 'Regional variations: organisational and procedural dimensions of public ethics delivery ten years after Nolan', *Parliamentary Affairs* 59(3): 458–73.

Dolan, Kathleen, Bruce McKeown and James M. Carlson. 1988. 'Popular conceptions of political corruption: implications for the empirical study of political ethics', *Corruption and Reform* 3(1): 3–24.

Easton, David. 1965. *A Systems Analysis of Political Life*. New York: John Wiley.

  1975. 'A re-assessment of the concept of political support', *British Journal of Political Science* 5(4): 437–57.

Eggers, Andrew C. and Alexander Fisher. 2011. 'Electoral accountability and the UK parliamentary expenses scandal: did voters punish corrupt

MPs?' Political Science and Political Economy Working Paper, No. 8/ 2011, Department of Government, London School of Economics.

Eggers, Andrew C. and Jens Hainmueller. 2009. 'MPs for sale? Returns to office in postwar British politics', *American Political Science Review* 103(4): 513–33.

Erikson, Robert S., Michael B. MacKuen and James A. Stimson. 2002. *The Macro Polity*. Cambridge University Press.

Ezrow, Lawrence and Georgios Xezonakis. 2011. 'Citizen satisfaction with democracy and parties' policy offerings', *Comparative Political Studies* 44(9): 1152–78.

Fackler, Tim and Tse-min Lin. 1995. 'Political corruption and presidential elections, 1929–1992', *Journal of Politics* 57(4): 971–93.

Finkel, Steven E. 1985. 'Reciprocal effects of participation and political efficacy: a panel analysis', *American Journal of Political Science* 29(4): 891–913.

Fiorina, Morris P. 1981. *Retrospective Voting in American National Elections*. New Haven, CT: Yale University Press.

Fisher, Justin. 2009. 'Hayden Phillips and Jack Straw: The continuation of British exceptionalism in party finance?' *Parliamentary Affairs* 62(2): 298–317.

Fisher, Justin, Jennifer Van Heerde and Andrew Tucker. 2010. 'Does one trust judgement fit all? Linking theory and empirics', *British Journal of Politics and International Relations* 12(2): 161–88.

Flinders, Matthew. 2012. *Defending Politics: Why Democracy Matters in the Twenty-First Century*. Oxford University Press.

Flinders, Matthew and Alexandra Kelso. 2011. 'Mind the gap: political analysis, public expectations and the parliamentary decline thesis', *British Journal of Politics and International Relations* 13(2): 249–68.

Franklin, Bob. 1997. *Newszak and News Media*. London: Arnold.

Frohlich, Norman and Joe Oppenheimer. 2000. 'How people reason about ethics', in Arthur Lupia, Mathew D. McCubbins and Samuel L. Popkin (eds), *Elements of Reason: Cognition, Choice, and the Bounds of Rationality*. Cambridge University Press, pp. 85–107.

Gamson, William A. and Andre Modigliani. 1989. 'Media discourse and public opinion on nuclear power: a constructionist approach', *American Journal of Sociology* 95(1): 1–37.

Gay, Oonagh and Patricia Leopold (eds). 2004. *Conduct Unbecoming: The Regulation of Parliamentary Behaviour*. London: Politicos.

Getz, Robert S. 1966. *Congressional Ethics: The Conflict of Interest Issue*. Princeton, NJ: Van Nostrand.

Gibbs, John C. and Steven V. Schnell. 1985. 'Moral development "versus" socialization: a critique', *American Psychologist* 40(10): 1071–80.

Ginsberg, Benjamin and Martin Shefter. 1990. *Politics by Other Means: The Declining Importance of Elections in America*. New York: Basic Books.

GRECO. 2001. *First Evaluation Round: Evaluation Report on the United Kingdom*. Strasbourg: Council of Europe.

Greene, Joshua D. and Jonathan Haidt. 2002. 'How (and where) does moral judgment work?' *Trends in Cognitive Sciences* 6(12): 517–23.

Greene, Joshua D., R. Brian Sommerville, Leigh E. Nystrom, John M. Darley and Jonathan D. Cohen. 2001. 'An fMRI investigation of emotional engagement in moral judgment', *Science* 293: 2105–8.

Grødeland, Åse B., William L. Miller and Tatyana Y. Koshechkina. 2000. 'The ethnic dimension to bureaucratic encounters in postcommunist Europe: perceptions and experience', *Nations and Nationalism* 6(1): 43–66.

Haidt, Jonathan. 2012. *The Righteous Mind: Why Good People are Divided by Politics and Religion*. London: Allen Lane.

Hampshire, Stuart (ed.). 1978. *Public and Private Morality*. Cambridge University Press.

Hay, Colin. 2007. *Why We Hate Politics*. Cambridge: Polity.

Heath, Oliver. 2011. 'The great divide: voters, parties, MPs and expenses', in Nicholas Allen and John Bartle (eds), *Britain at the Polls 2010*. London: Sage, pp. 120–46.

Heidenheimer, Arnold J. (ed.) 1970. 'The context of analysis: introduction', *Political Corruption: Readings in Comparative Analysis*. New York: Holt, Rinehart & Winston, pp. 3–28.

Herrick, Rebekah. 2003. *Fashioning the More Ethical Representative: The Impact of Ethics Reforms in the US House of Representatives*. Westport, CT: Praeger.

Hetherington, Marc J. 2005. *Why Trust Matters: Declining Political Trust and the Demise of American Liberalism*. Princeton University Press.

Hibbing, John R. and Elizabeth Theiss-Morse. 2001. 'Process preferences and American politics: what the people want government to be', *American Political Science Review* 95(1): 145–53.

  2002. *Stealth Democracy: Americans' Beliefs about How Government Should Work*. Cambridge University Press.

Hirschman, Albert O. 1970. *Exit, Voice, and Loyalty: Responses to Decline in Firms, Organizations, and States*. Cambridge, MA: Harvard University Press.

Irving, Clive, Ron Hall and Jeremy Wallington. 1963. *Scandal '63: A Study of the Profumo Affair*. London: Heinemann.

Jackson, Michael and Rodney Smith. 1996. 'Inside moves and outside views: an Australian case study of elite and public perceptions of political corruption', *Governance: An International Journal of Policy and Administration* 9(1): 23–41.

James, Oliver. 2009. 'Evaluating the expectations disconfirmation and expectations anchoring approaches to citizen satisfaction with local public services', *Journal of Public Administration Research and Theory* 19(1): 107–23.

Jennings, Bruce. 1985. 'Legislative ethics and moral minimalism', in Bruce Jennings and Daniel Callahan (eds), *Representation and Responsibility: Exploring Legislative Ethics.* New York: Plenum Press, pp. 149–65.

John, Peter, Graham Smith and Gerry Stoker. 2009. 'Nudge nudge, think think: two strategies for changing civic behaviour', *Political Quarterly* 80(3): 361–70.

Johnston, Michael. 1986. 'Right and wrong in American politics: popular conceptions of corruption', *Polity* 18(3): 367–91.

1991. 'Right and wrong in British politics: "fits of morality" in comparative perspective', *Polity* 24(1): 1–25.

Jones, Philip and John Hudson. 2000. 'Civic duty and expressive voting: is virtue its own reward?' *Kyklos* 53(1): 3–16.

Karp, Jeffrey A. and Susan A. Banducci. 2008. 'Political efficacy and participation in twenty-seven democracies: how electoral systems shape political behaviour', *British Journal of Political Science* 38(2): 311–34.

Kahneman, Daniel. 2011. *Thinking, Fast and Slow.* London: Penguin.

Kaye, Robert P. 2005. 'Reluctant innovators: regulating conflict of interest within Washington and Westminster', in Julia Black, Martin Lodge and Mark Thatcher (eds), *Regulatory Innovation: A Comparative Analysis.* Cheltenham: Edward Elgar, pp. 45–65.

Kellner, Peter. 2004. 'Britain's culture of detachment', *Parliamentary Affairs* 57(4): 830–43.

Kelso, Alexandra. 2007. 'Parliament and political disengagement: neither waving nor drowning', *Political Quarterly* 78(3): 364–73.

Kenny, Michael. 2009. 'Taking the temperature of the British political elite 3: when grubby is the order of the day …', *Parliamentary Affairs* 62(3): 503–13.

King, Anthony. 1981. 'The rise of the career politician in Britain – and its consequences', *British Journal of Political Science* 11(3): 249–85.

1986. 'Sex, money, and power', in Richard Hodder-Williams and James Caeser (eds), *Politics in Britain and the United States: Comparative Perspectives.* Durham, NC: Duke University Press, pp. 173–222.

(ed.). 2002. 'Tony Blair's first term', *Britain at the Polls 2001.* New York: Chatham House, pp. 1–44.

2007. *The British Constitution.* Oxford University Press.

2009. 'MPs' expenses: where do they go from here?' *Daily Telegraph*, 11 May.

Kohlberg, Lawrence. 1984. *The Psychology of Moral Development, vol. II: Essays on Moral Development.* San Francisco, CA: Harper & Row.

Koutsoukis, Kleomenis S. 2006. 'Political scandals and crisis management in Greece, 1821–2001', in John Garrad and James L. Newell (eds), *Scandals in Past and Contemporary Politics.* Manchester University Press, pp. 123–36.

Krebs, Dennis L. and Kathy Denton. 2005. 'Toward a more pragmatic approach to morality: a critical evaluation of Kohlberg's model', *Psychological Review* 112(3): 629–49.

Kuklinski, James H. and Paul J. Quirk. 1998. 'Reconsidering the rational public: cognition, heuristics, and mass opinion', in A. Lupia, M. D. McCubbins, and S. L. Popkin (eds), *Elements of Reason: Cognition, Choice, and the Bounds of Rationality.* Cambridge University Press, pp. 153–82.

2000. 'Reconsidering the rational public: cognition, heuristics, and mass opinion', in Arthur Lupia, Mathew D. McCubbins and Samuel L. Popkin (eds), *Elements of Reason: Cognition, Choice, and the Bounds of Rationality.* Cambridge University Press, pp. 153–82.

Kumlin, Staffan and Peter Esaiasson. 2012. 'Scandal fatigue? Scandal elections and satisfaction with democracy in Western Europe, 1977–2007', *British Journal of Political Science* 42(2): 263–82.

Kunda, Ziva. 1990. 'The case for motivated reasoning', *Psychological Bulletin* 108(3): 480–98.

Lascoumes, Pierre (ed.). 2010. *Favoritisme et corruption à la française. Petits arrangements avec la probité.* Paris: Presses Sciences Po.

Laswell, Harold. 1936. *Politics: Who Gets What, When, and How?* New York: McGraw-Hill.

Leach, Robert. 2009. *Political Ideology in Britain,* 2nd edn. Basingstoke: Palgrave Macmillan.

Levi, Margaret and Laura Stoker. 2000. 'Political trust and trustworthiness', *Annual Review of Political Science* 3: 475–507.

Lieberman, Matthew D., Darren Schneider and Kevin N. Oschner. 2003. 'Is political cognition like riding a bicycle? How cognitive neuroscience can inform research on political thinking', *Political Psychology* 24(4): 681–704.

Lijphart, Arend. 1999. *Patterns of Democracy: Government Forms and Performance in Thirty-Six Countries.* New Haven, CT: Yale University Press.

Linde, Jonas and Joakim Ekman. 2003. 'Satisfaction with democracy: a note on a frequently used indicator in comparative politics', *European Journal of Political Research* 42(3): 391–408.

Listhaug, Ola. 1995. 'The dynamics of trust in politicians', in Hans-Dieter Klingemann and Dieter Fuchs (eds), *Citizens and the State*. Oxford University Press, pp. 261–97.

Little, Richard and Mark Wickham-Jones (eds). 2000. *New Labour's Foreign Policy: A New Moral Crusade?* Manchester University Press.

Lloyd, John. 2004. *What the Media are Doing to Our Politics*. London: Constable & Robinson.

Lodge, Milton and Charles S. Taber. 2000. 'Three steps toward a theory of motivated political reasoning', in Arthur Lupia, Mathew D. McCubbins and Samuel L. Popkin (eds), *Elements of Reason: Cognition, Choice, and the Bounds of Rationality*. Cambridge University Press, pp. 183–213.

2013. *The Rationalizing Voter*. Cambridge University Press.

Lowell, A. Lawrence. 1908. *The Government of England*, 2 vols. New York: Macmillan, vol. II.

Mackenzie, G. Calvin, with Michael Hafken. 2002. *Scandal Proof: Do Ethics Laws make Government Ethical?* Washington, DC: Brookings Institution.

Mancuso, Maureen. 1995. *The Ethical World of British MPs*. Montreal: McGill-Queen's University Press.

Mancuso, Maureen, Michael M. Atkinson, André Blais, Ian Greene and Neil Nevitte. 1998. *A Question of Ethics: Canadians Speak Out*. Toronto: Oxford University Press.

Marcus, George E., W. Russell Neuman and Michael Mackuen. 2000. *Affective Intelligence and Political Judgment*, Chicago and London: University of Chicago Press.

Margetts, Helen and Gerry Stoker. 2010. 'The experimental method: prospects for laboratory and field experiments', David Marsh and Gerry Stoker (eds), *Theory and Methods in Political Science*, 3rd edn. Basingstoke: Palgrave Macmillan, pp. 308–24.

Marquand, David. 2008. *Britain since 1918: The Strange Career of British Democracy*. London: Weidenfeld & Nicolson.

McAllister, Ian. 2000. 'Keeping them honest: public and elite perceptions of ethical conduct among Australian legislators', *Political Studies* 48(1): 22–37.

McCann, James A. and David P. Redlawsk. 2006. 'Political corruption and ethical judgements of American citizens: are government officials held to a higher standard?' paper presented at the Annual Meeting of the Southern Political Science Association, Atlanta, GA.

McDonald, Michael D., Silvia M. Mendes and Ian Budge. 2004. 'What are elections for? Conferring the median mandate', *British Journal of Political Science* 34(1): 1–26

McManus-Czubińska, Clare, William L. Miller, Radosław Markowski and Jacek Wasilewski. 2004. 'Why is corruption in Poland "a serious cause for concern"?' *Crime, Law and Social Change* 41(2): 107–32.

Miller, Arthur H. 1974. 'Political issues and trust in government', *American Political Science Review* 68(3): 951–72.

Miller, William L., Åse B. Grødeland and Tatyana Y. Koshechkina. 2001. *A Culture of Corruption? Coping with Government in Post-Communist Europe.* Budapest: CEU Press.

Naurin, Elin. 2011. *Promising Democracy: Parties, Citizens and Election Promises.* Basingstoke: Palgrave Macmillan.

Nelson, Thomas E. and Donald R. Kinder. 1996. 'Issue frames and group-centrism in American public opinion', *Journal of Politics* 58(4): 1055–78.

Newell, James L. 2008. 'Ethical conduct and perceptions of public probity in Britain: the story so far', *Perspectives on European Politics and Society* 9(1): 39–52.

Newton, Kenneth. 1999. 'Mass media effects: mobilization or media malaise?' *British Journal of Political Science* 29(4): 577–99.

2006. 'May the weak force be with you: the power of the mass media in modern politics', *European Journal of Political Research* 45(2): 209–34.

Norris, Pippa (ed.). 1999. *Critical Citizens: Global Support for Democratic Government.* Oxford University Press.

2002. *Democratic Phoenix: Reinventing Political Participation.* Cambridge University Press.

2004. *Electoral Engineering: Voting Rules and Political Behavior.* Cambridge University Press.

2011. *Democratic Deficit: Critical Citizens Revisited.* Cambridge University Press.

Norton, Philip. 1998. 'The Conservative Party: "in office but not in power"', in Anthony King (ed.), *New Labour Triumphs: Britain at the Polls.* Chatham, NJ: Chatham House, pp. 75–112.

Norton, Philip and David M. Wood. 1993. *Back from Westminster: British Members of Parliament and their Constituents.* Lexington, KT: University Press of Kentucky.

O'Leary, Cornelius. 1962. *The Elimination of Corrupt Practices in British Elections 1868–1911.* Oxford: Clarendon Press.

O'Neill, Onora. 2002. *A Question of Trust: The BBC Reith Lectures 2002.* Cambridge University Press.

Oborne, Peter. 2005. *The Rise of Political Lying.* London: Free Press.

2007. *The Triumph of the Political Class.* London: Simon & Schuster.

Oliver, Dawn. 1997. 'Regulating the conduct of MPs: the British experience of combating corruption', *Political Studies* 45(3): 539–58.

Paldam, Martin. 1986. 'The distribution of election results and the two explanations of the cost of ruling', *European Journal of Political Economy* 2(1): 5–24.

Parker, Suzanne L. and Glenn R. Parker. 1993. 'Why do we trust our congressman?' *Journal of Politics* 55(2): 442–53.

Pattie, Charles and Ron Johnston. 2012. 'The electoral impact of the UK 2009 MPs' expenses scandal', *Political Studies* 60(4): 730–50.

Pattie, Charles, Patrick Seyd and Paul Whiteley. 2004. *Citizenship in Britain: Values, Participation, and Democracy.* Cambridge University Press.

Peele, Gillian and Robert Kaye. 2008. 'Conflict of interest in British public life', in Christine Trost and Alison L. Gash (eds), *Conflict of Interest in Public Life: Cross National Perspectives.* Cambridge University Press, pp. 155–87.

Perkins, Roswell B. 1963. 'The new federal conflict of interest law', *Harvard Law Review* 76(6): 1113–69.

Peters, John G. and Susan Welch. 1978. 'Political corruption in America: a search for definitions and a theory, or if political corruption is in the mainstream of American politics why is it not in the mainstream of American politics research?' *American Political Science Review* 72(3): 974–84.

1980. 'Effects of charges of corruption on voting behavior in congressional elections', *American Political Science Review* 74(3): 697–708.

Pharr, Susan J. 2000. 'Officials' misconduct and public distrust: Japan and the trilateral democracies', in Susan J. Pharr and Robert D. Putnam (eds), *Disaffected Democracies: What's Troubling the Trilateral Countries?* Princeton University Press, pp. 173–201.

Pharr, Susan J. and Robert D. Putnam (eds). 2000. *Disaffected Democracies: What's Troubling the Trilateral Countries?* Princeton University Press.

Philp, Mark. 2007. *Political Conduct.* Cambridge, MA: Harvard University Press.

Platt, D. C. M. 1961. 'The commercial and industrial interests of Ministers of the Crown', *Political Studies* 9(3): 267–90.

Popkin, Samuel L. 1991. *The Reasoning Voter: Communication and Persuasion in Presidential Campaigns.* Chicago University Press.

Powell, Jr., G. Bingham. 1986. 'American voter turnout in comparative perspective', *American Political Science Review* 80(1): 17–43.

2000. *Elections as Instruments of Democracy: Majoritarian and Proportional Visions.* New Haven, CT: Yale University Press.

Powell, Jr., G. Bingham and Georg S. Vanberg. 2000. 'Election laws, disproportionality and median correspondence: implications for two visions of democracy', *British Journal of Political Science* 30(3): 383–411.

Prince, Rosa. 2009. 'MP Nigel Griffiths faces sleaze inquiry over sex shame', *Daily Telegraph*, 23 March.

Prior, Markus.2010. 'You've either got it or you don't? The stability of political interest over the life cycle', *Journal of Politics* 72(3): 747–66.

Public Administration Committee. 2007. *Fourth Report: Ethics and Standards: The Regulation of Conduct in Public Life*, HC 121-I, 2006–07. London: Stationery Office.

Redlawsk, David P. and James A. McCann. 2005. 'Popular interpretations of "corruption" and their partisan consequences', *Political Behavior* 27(3): 261–83.

Riddell, Peter. 1993. *Honest Opportunism: The Rise of the Career Politician*. London: Hamilton.

2011. *In Defence of Politicians: In Spite of Themselves*. London: Biteback.

2013. *The Report of the Triennial Review of the Committee on Standards in Public Life*. London: Cabinet Office.

Ridley, F. F. and Alan Doig (eds). 1995. *Sleaze: Politicians, Private Interests and Public Reaction*. Oxford University Press.

Roberts, Bob. 2009. 'Jacqui Smith's fury at her husband's porn viewing on expenses', *Daily Mirror*, 30 March.

Robinton, Madeline R. 1970. 'The British method of dealing with political corruption', Arnold J. Heidenheimer (ed.), *Political Corruption: Readings in Comparative Analysis*. New York: Holt, Rinehart & Winston, pp. 249–58.

Roodhouse, Mark. 2002. 'The 1948 Belcher Affair and Lynskey Tribunal', *Twentieth Century British History* 13(4): 384–411.

Rose, Richard. 1984. *Do Parties Make a Difference?* London: Macmillan.

Rose, Richard and William Mishler. 2010. 'Experience versus perception of corruption: Russia as a test case', *Global Crime* 11(2): 145–63.

Rose, Richard, William Mishler and Christian Haerpfer. 1998. *Democracy and its Alternatives: Understanding Post-Communist Societies*. Baltimore, MD: Johns Hopkins University Press.

Rosenthal, Alan. 1996. *Drawing the Line: Legislative Ethics in the States*. Lincoln, NE: University of Nebraska Press.

Rothstein, Bo and Eric M. Uslaner. 2005. 'All for all: equality, corruption, and social trust', *World Politics* 58(4): 41–72.

Royed, Terry J. 1996. 'Testing the mandate model in Britain and the United States: evidence from the Reagan and Thatcher eras', *British Journal of Political Science* 26(1): 45–80.

Rundquist, Barry S., Gerald S. Strom and John G. Peters. 1977. 'Corrupt politicians and their electoral support: some experimental observations', *American Political Science Review* 71(3): 954–63.

Rush, Michael and Philip Giddings. 2011. *Parliamentary Socialisation: Learning the Ropes or Determining Behaviour?* Basingstoke: Palgrave Macmillan.

Sabato, Larry. 1991. *Feeding Frenzy: How Attack Journalism has Transformed American Politics.* New York: Free Press.

Saint-Martin, Denis. 2006. 'Path dependence and self-reinforcing processes', in Denis Saint-Martin and Fred Thompson (eds), *Public Ethics and Governance: Standards and Practices in Comparative Perspective.* Oxford: JAI Press, pp. 5–28.

Sanders, David, Harold D. Clarke, Mariane C. Stewart and Paul Whiteley. 2007. 'Does mode matter for modeling political choice? Evidence from the 2005 British Election Study', *Political Analysis* 15(3): 257–85.

Schumpeter, Joseph A. 1954. *Capitalism, Socialism and Democracy*, 2nd edn. New York: Harper.

Searing, Donald D. 1982. 'Rules of the game in Britain: can the politicians be trusted?' *American Political Science Review* 76(2): 239–58.

1994. *Westminster's World: Understanding Political Roles.* Cambridge, MA: Harvard University Press.

Searle, G. R. 1987. *Corruption in British Politics 1895–1930.* Oxford: Clarendon Press.

Sears, David O. 2001. 'The role of affect in symbolic politics', in James H. Kuklinski (ed.), *Citizens and Politics: Perspectives from Political Psychology.* Cambridge University Press, pp. 14–40.

Seligson, Mitchell A. 2002. 'The impact of corruption on regime legitimacy: a comparative study of four Latin American countries', *Journal of Politics* 64(2): 408–33.

Shaw, Malcolm. 1990. 'Members of Parliament', in Michael Rush (ed.), *Parliament and Pressure Politics.* Oxford: Clarendon Press, pp. 85–116.

Singer, Peter (ed.). 1994. *Ethics.* Oxford University Press.

Soroka, Stuart N. and Christopher Wlezien. 2010. *Degrees of Democracy: Politics, Public Opinion, and Policy.* Cambridge University Press.

Spigelman, James J. 2004. 'The integrity branch of government', *Australian Law Journal* 78(11): 724–37.

Stanlis, Peter J. (ed.). 1963. *Edmund Burke: Selected Writings and Speeches.* Garden City, NY: Anchor Books.

Stark, Andrew. 2000. *Conflict of Interest in American Public Life.* Cambridge, MA: Harvard University Press.

Stoker, Gerry. 2006. *Why Politics Matters: Making Democracy Work.* Basingstoke: Palgrave Macmillan.

2011. 'Anti-politics in Britain', in Richard Heffernan, Philip Cowley and Colin Hay (eds), *Developments in British Politics 9.* Basingstoke: Palgrave Macmillan, pp. 152–73.

Stokes, Donald. 1963. 'Spatial models of party competition', *American Political Science Review* 57(2): 368–77.

Thaler, Richard H. and Cass R. Sunstein. 2008. *Nudge: Improving Decisions About Health, Wealth, and Happiness.* New Haven, CT: Yale University Press.

Thompson, Dennis F. 1987. *Political Ethics and Public Office.* Cambridge, MA: Harvard University Press.

  1995. *Ethics in Congress: From Individual to Institutional Corruption.* Washington, DC: Brookings Institution.

Thompson, John B. 2000. *Political Scandal: Power and Visibility in the Media Age.* Cambridge: Polity Press.

Tversky, Amos and Daniel Kahnemann (eds). 2000. *Choices, Values, and Frames.* Cambridge University Press.

Twyman, Joe. 2008. 'Getting it right: YouGov and online survey research in Britain', *Journal of Elections, Public Opinion and Parties* 18(4): 343–54.

Tyler, Tom R. 1990. *Why People Obey the Law.* New Haven, CT: Yale University Press.

Vavreck, Lynn and Douglas Rivers. 2008. 'The 2006 Cooperative Congressional Election Study', *Journal of Elections, Public Opinion and Parties* 18(4): 355–66.

Wallace, R. Jay. 2007. 'Moral psychology', in Frank Jackson and Michael Smith (eds), *The Oxford Handbook of Contemporary Philosophy.* Oxford University Press, pp. 89–113.

Walzer, Michael. 1973. 'Political action: the problem of dirty hands', *Philosophy and Public Affairs* 2(2): 160–80.

Warren, Mark E. (ed.). 1999. *Democracy and Trust.* Cambridge University Press.

  2004. 'What does corruption mean in a democracy?' *American Journal of Political Science* 48(2): 328–43.

  2006. 'Democracy and deceit: regulating appearances of corruption', *American Journal of Political Science* 50(1): 164–74.

Watt, Nicholas. 2009. 'Employment minister faces inquiry call over £60,000 second-home allowance', *The Guardian*, 23 March.

Weatherford, M. Stephen. 1992. 'Measuring political legitimacy', *American Political Science Review* 86(1): 149–66.

Welch, Susan and John G. Peters. 1977. 'Attitudes of US state legislators toward political corruption: some preliminary findings', *Legislative Studies Quarterly* 2(4): 445–63.

Whiteley, Paul, Harold D. Clarke, David Sanders and Marianne Stewart. 2013. 'Why do voters lose trust in governments? Public perceptions of government honesty and trustworthiness 1997–2013', paper presented at a special one-day conference on 'Citizens and Politics in Britain Today: Still a Civic Culture?', London School of Economics, London, 26 September.

Williams, Sandra. 1985. *Conflict of Interest: The Ethical Dilemma in Politics*. Aldershot: Gower.

Winnett, Robert and Gordon Raynor. 2009. *No Expenses Spared*. London: Bantam.

Wroe, Andrew, Nicholas Allen and Sarah Birch. 2013. 'The role of political trust in conditioning perceptions of corruption', *European Political Science Review* 5(2): 175–95.

You, Jong-sung and Sanjeev Khagram. 2005. 'A comparative study of inequality and corruption', *American Sociological Review* 70(1): 136–57.

Zaller, John R. 1992. *The Nature and Origins of Mass Opinion*. Cambridge University Press.

1998. 'Monica Lewinsky's contribution to political science', *PS: Political Science and Politics* 31(2): 182–9.

Index